THE COLONIAL RISE OF THE NOVEL

The Colonial Rise of the Novel provides the first feminist and anti-imperialist account of the development of the novel. Far from describing the universality of the novel – as emphasized in previous studies – Azim makes clear how the novel as a genre silenced and excluded both woman and people of colour. In what is both a provocative and important contribution to post-colonial and feminist criticism, Azim examines closely texts by writers such as Aphra Behn and Charlotte Brontë. Her conclusions force a radical rethink of Western literature's most enduring form. A major intervention into a rapidly evolving debate.

Firdous Azim is Associate Professor of English at Dhaka University, Bangladesh.

THE COLONIAL RISE
OF THE NOVEL

Firdous Azim

London and New York

First published 1993
by Routledge
11 New Fetter Lane, London EC4P 4EE

Simultaneously published in the USA and Canada
by Routledge
29 West 35th Street, New York, NY 10001

Typeset in 10 on 12 point Bembo by
Intype, London
Printed in Great Britain by
T. J. Press (Padstow) Ltd, Padstow, Cornwall

British Library Cataloguing in Publication Data
Azim, Firdous
The Colonial Rise of the
Novel
I. Title
809.3
Library of Congress Cataloging in Publication Data
Azim, Firdous
The colonial rise of the novel / Firdous Azim.
p.   cm.
Includes bibliographical references and index.
1. Brontë, Charlotte, 1816–1855—Political and social views.
2. English fiction—History and criticism—Theory, etc.   3. Feminism
and literature—Great Britain—History.   4. Literature and society—Great
Britain—History.   5. Women and literature—Great Britain—
History.   6. Social problems in literature.   7. Imperialism in
literature. 8 Colonies in literature.   9. Sex role in literature.
10. First person narrative.   I. Title.
PR4169.A98 1993
823′.8–dc20 92–40810

ISBN 0–415–07024–4 ISBN 0–415–09569–7 (pbk)

for my father and mother

CONTENTS

ACKNOWLEDGEMENTS

I would like to acknowledge the many people who have made it possible for me to write this book, which was originally written as a thesis for the University of Sussex. I would like to thank Jacqueline Rose and Geoffrey Hemstedt, who had helped me immensely during that period. My stay at Sussex helped to formulate ideas about the politics of culture. I remember Sue Dare with fondness for the friendship she gave me during my stay in Brighton.

Friends and family are remembered with gratitude for their cooperation and encouragement during the writing. My friends at Naripokkho are thanked for the sisterly warmth and affection, and for providing a forum where the politics of culture can continue to be discussed. I especially thank Shireen Huq and Nausheen Rahman, for their warmth, friendship and a sharing of adventures. I also thank Ijaz Hossain for his wonderful support during the writing of the thesis.

Finally, to my husband, Bashir, I owe an immense gratitude, for cooperation, understanding, encouragement and affection. My children, René and Partha, have suffered the strain of having a mother who is stuck to the computer, and I thank them for bearing with me.

LIST OF ABBREVIATIONS

Standard English editions have been used for all the novels referred to. I have referred to the Penguin editions for Charlotte Brontë's novels. For the juvenilia, different collections and editions have been used, all of which are noted in the bibliography.

Abbreviations

BM	*Blackwood's Edinburgh Magazine*
BPM	Brontë Parsonage Museum
CH	*The Brontës: The Critical Heritage* (1974, ed. M. Allott).
JE	*Jane Eyre*
Leaf	*Leaf from an Unopened Volume* (1986, ed. C. Lemon).
MF	*Moll Flanders*
O	*Oroonoko*
OLR	*Oxford Literary Review*
P	*The Professor*
Poems	*The Poems of Charlotte Brontë* (1984, ed. T. Winnifreth).
R	*Roxana*
RC	*Robinson Crusoe*
S	*Shirley*
SHCBM	*The Miscellaneous and Unpublished Works of Charlotte and Patrick Branwell Brontë* (1936, ed. Wise and Symington).
SHLL	*The Brontës: Their Lives, Friendships, and Correspondence in Four Volumes* (1933, ed. Wise and Symington).
V	*Villette*

I have tried to refer to each of the Brontës by their full name. However, when the name Brontë occurs by itself, it refers to Charlotte Brontë.

INTRODUCTION

To speak a language is to take on a world, a culture.
(Franz Fanon, 1967, *Black Skin, White Masks*, p. 38)

This book tries to grapple with some of the issues that face a teacher of English in a post-colonial nation. A teacher of English in Bangladesh has to consider not only its status as a language of colonisation and imperialism, but also the somewhat anomalous position that English occupies in a state based on a notion of linguistic nationalism. The relationship between language and identity, in such a historical conjuncture and context, is mediated and refracted by many elements.

The importance of English is felt at many levels in Bangladesh, and can, in no way, be seen as confined to the English departments at universities and institutes of higher education. The status of English is a topic of debate in the popular media, in newspapers and on television and radio. Private English language schools proliferate as the formal state educational system seeks to fulfil its promise of establishing Bengali as the *only* language of state.

The definition of Bengali national identity is based on a notion of Bengali culture determined by the use of the Bengali language. National identity and language had merged in the struggle for political independence, as the erstwhile East Pakistan had sought to differentiate itself from the Western wing of that nation. The establishment of Bengali for Bangladesh as the only language of state is therefore crucial: it is its *raison d'être*, its mark of national identity.

Despite this, English, studied as language and literature, remains an important part of the educational curriculum. My university at Dhaka offers 120 places every year for its

1

undergraduate course, and more than a thousand applications are received for this largely Leavisite programme. A teacher of English in this context is forced to question the status of that language, and the relevance of its propagation.

The linguistic contradictions at the national level translate themselves into crises felt within the university departments of English. For instance, attempts to move away from the Leavisite course are constantly balked, at one level, by completely practical and mundane, but very real, constraints of the availability of books, critical material and so on. Juggling about with the syllabus and designing fresh courses are simply not possible within such resource constraints. Beyond these largely practical difficulties, the task of syllabus design and modification has to take into account the question of the aim and purpose of teaching English literature. There is a very conservative effort to keep up the old 'classical' syllabus, and the teaching of English is justified on the basis of introducing young minds to the glories of a language enriched by the genius of Shakespeare or Milton. Within this tendency, there is an unwillingness to question the relevance of these texts, or of looking at their history in our subcontinent, and the way that these texts are received, even within the limited context of the classroom, is never brought to analysis. A conservative teaching practice takes refuge in the text, hiding behind it.

Proposed syllabus modifications and changes refuse to ask directly the obvious question: why and to whom are we teaching English literature? Nonetheless, the question surfaces, and has to be tackled. Faced with the language difficulties of the students, for example, a language-teaching component has been introduced. The 'purity' of literature teaching has thus been adulterated, as language and literature teaching do not require the same skills of either the student or the teacher. The question of relevance has also emerged, and the proposed addition of a course on Third World literatures written in English can be seen as a manifestation of this. Whereas such courses, including writings by V. S. Naipaul, Wole Soyinka, Chinua Achebe, Salman Rushdie and Nirad Chaudhuri, are an undisputed part of the syllabus in many English departments round the world, the resistance that the introduction of this course met with in Dhaka is worth mentioning. The significance of such writing was questioned, and the inclusion of literature in the colonial tongue by Third World

2

writers rejected. Third World writing in English was seen as a manifestation of our colonial shame, as a vestige of our colonial heritage which is better forgotten. It was argued that if we are to look for the genuine expression of Third World peoples – our own selves – we can look to no better site than to literature in the mother tongue – Bengali, in our case.

The status of English, then, is constantly weighed against that of Bengali. The political commitment to the establishment of Bengali is undisputed. The definition of national identity along lines of a national language also presupposes a link between the language and the people. Thus the study of Bengali literature remains, to a large extent, unproblematised – it is easily studied as the genuine, authentic site of expression of the Bengali nation.

However, the study of the literature of our own country, while not being problematised, is problematic. Bengali literature has been designed along lines similar to those of English, and the way that both subjects are defined in the academic departments – the way that they are taught – is similar. In that sense, the history of Bengali literature cannot ignore colonial influences. For example, genre study within Bengali literature divides the field into poetry, prose and drama, which then is further subdivided into lyrics, sonnets or novels, essays and so on. These divisions are imitative of the way in which English literature has been periodised and marked off into different genres, and draw the same connections between history and the formal properties of writing. The teaching of Bengali remains conservative, as canon-questioning is as strongly resisted as within English. The connections between the growth of Bengali language and literature and colonisation, the influence of Western thought and modes of writing on Bengali, when commented on, are praised from a humanist angle – the best of the West is seen to have seeped into our culture and literary forms. The imperial underpinnings of the Bengali language, formed as it was within the parameters of colonial rule and within the historical project of framing a system of education for a colonised nation, are ignored. Bengali is seen as unified and homogeneous, and is attributed the status of the language of the people. Linguistic divisions and usages within the Bengali nation are overlooked, as the politics that defines a 'standard' Bengali is not brought to light.

The nation's commitment to Bengali manifests itself as a search for authenticity, for the motherland created by the mother

3

tongue. The class aspect of access to language is not considered, and given that a large number of the people of the country are illiterate, the notion of a *literary* heritage acquires a quite different dimension. The divisions between folk and formal literature remain sharp, and issues of national division and difference more stark. A good example of how these divisions translate into literary writing can be seen in Gayatri Spivak's readings of Mahasweta Devi. Spivak (1987) translates two short stories, 'Draupadi' and 'The Breast-Giver', by the well-known Bengali woman writer, Mahasweta Devi, to show the class-differentiated position of women within native elite discursive systems. 'Draupadi' tells the story of a *santal* tribal woman, a *naxal* collaborator and her relations with her male, middle-class, Calcutta-born, urban, revolutionary colleagues, as well as with the state representatives of power: the police. The echoes of the mythical Draupadi in the tribal revolutionary, Dopdi, do not function to bring the woman centre-stage, but keep her hidden within Draupadi's mythical sari or Dopdi's near-nakedness. Similarly, 'The Breast-Giver' tells the story of Jashoda, a professional wet-nurse, whose body is (literally) used for the upbringing of the scions of the affluent Haldar household. Jashoda's final suffering from breast cancer is ironical, and emblematic of woman's effacement from the dominant systems. The native culture itself is divided by class, and the celebration of things Bengali does not address the question of oppression and domination within native society.

★

This book, *about* the novels of Charlotte Brontë, is obviously based on traditional literary criticism. Despite its Leavisite basis, it aims to problematise the concepts that that school of criticism takes for granted. The novel, seen as a narrative spun by and around a notion of a coherent and unified subject, posed by the European Enlightenment, is examined to show how the notion of unity is broken and fragmented, both in the terrain that the narrative spans and also in the concept of a unity of subjectivity.

Feminist literary criticism, inaugurated through an examination of the nineteenth-century women's novel, in its initial phase based itself completely on the notion of this unified subject within the narrative. However, as the stress moved from an examination of the social realism of the novels, feminist criticism began to recognise that the narrative voice spinning the tale is neither homogeneous nor unified, and that the narrative terrain it creates is split between a sense of social reality and the creation of fantasies, dreams and desire. Also, even as theme, or social positioning, a feminine voice does not speak to all women in the same manner, as class and ethnic divisions amongst women have to be taken into consideration. This recognition of a split terrain, as well as of a split voice, has resulted in the re-examination of the women's voice and its special address.

The novels of Charlotte Brontë have played a central role in this feminist tradition. Her writings were marginalised within the Leavisite canon, and not given the status occupied by the writings of women novelists like Jane Austen or George Eliot. This neglect has been righted by feminist literary criticism, which, both in its early and later phases, has given a central position to the novels of Charlotte Brontë, as witnessed in Kate Millett's celebration of *Villette* (*Sexual Politics*, 1969) or by the fact that Elaine Showalter begins her history of women's writing with the work of Charlotte Brontë (*A Literature of their Own*, 1977). The *shift* in feminism's critical position can also be traced through responses to Charlotte Brontë's writings, as later feminists (Cora Kaplan, 1986, Judith Newton, 1981 or Mary Jacobus, 1986) re-examine the voice of the central female narrator in her novels.

The differences of class and race that feminism has been faced with, the complex and divided terrain of narration that feminist criticism has been uncovering, tie in with the concerns and critiques of colonial discourse and history, which, in the process of unearthing the colonial terrain, have stressed the *cultural* ramifications of Western imperialism. Such an examination, perhaps inaugurated in Edward Said's *Orientalism* (1978), shows the collusion between the literary text and the process of Western political domination, and the creation of images of the 'Orient' that separate the worlds of the coloniser and the colonised, always imaging the latter as passive and backward – fixed in time. Subsequently, Homi Bhabha has built on this thesis to show how the worlds of the coloniser and the colonised are bound in a Lacanian mirror-image, and the identities of both subjects constructed within that colonial moment.

The colonising enterprise was accompanied by the creation of a Westernised native bourgeoisie, on whom had devolved the task of defining a national identity, and who had, in many instances, carried on the task of national liberation. The focus in this book is on the place of the English literary text in colonial and post-colonial pedagogical practices, and the connections between the subject/s of literature and the formation of colonial subjectivities. The effects of Western education have often been seen as 'liberating' – there is a widely held view that the teachings of the Western Enlightenment had helped to 'liberate' the Eastern, Black or Oriental nations from obscurantist, medieval and feudal ways of life. While my study in no way subscribes to that view, at the same time it does not position itself along with the rhetoric of a 'decolonising' mission, which dismisses the English text as that of the colonial master.

This book attempts to answer that original question: why are we studying English at all? This question has to be approached in today's context, and the status of English is tied up with notions of the need and relevance of English worldwide. Bangladesh, as part of the Indian subcontinent, cannot afford to dwell in isolation, and the ties it builds with its immediate neighbours testify to a common history – that of British rule. The system of education is part of our colonial heritage, and it is indeed surprising how much of that heritage is still visible in our pedagogical practice.

I will begin by looking at the presence of the English literary pedagogical text in the Indian classroom in terms of a colonial encounter. The first chapter will examine both terms in the encounter, laying the field for the textual examinations that follow. The book can be seen as divided into two parts: the first dealing with a *history* of the novel and reframing that history from a colonial perspective; and the second rereading the novels of Charlotte Brontë from within this historical perspective, to highlight the imperialism in these genres in order to critique, as well as extend, the concerns of feminist literary criticism.

The novels of Charlotte Brontë have been chosen as the theme of this book as these provide a rich field in which to review and re-examine the status of the novel as woman's text, to see how the imperialist venture/theme remains a part of the novel, and to devise ways of approaching the text from a post-colonial perspective. Also, it is a critical effort, extending and textualising the ongoing project of examining women's status in the dissemination and production of literature and culture. This process is even more fraught when undertaken from a Bangladeshi or South Asian pedagogical practice which is concerned with furthering a colonial task. As we have seen, the teaching of English reception of English texts, allied to colonial history, ar cannot be, simply dismissed as colonial hangover. It and the recent 'flowering' of English writing from the maan subcontinent is witness to the fact that English studies do not occupy a moribund position, but are dynamic and provide a rich arena for writing.

I have tried to trace an imperialist background for the novel, and to show how the world of the novel is tied to the historical task of colonial, commercial and cultural expansion.

The book begins with a discussion of two novels: Aphra Behn's *Oroonoko* (1688) and Daniel Defoe's *Roxana* (1724). These texts are used, not merely to trace a trajectory along which the history of the novel can be placed, but to ally the search for the origins of the novel to the search for origins that lies at the heart of the eighteenth-century discourse on human subjectivity: a search that takes the narrative terrain to sites from which the human subject has either travelled or been forcibly ejected. The figure of the child in Locke's *Essay on Human Understanding* is echoed in the figure of the savage in his *Essay on Government*. *Oroonoko*, looking at the establishment of colonial government in Surinam, uses the figure of the savage to highlight the division between civilisation and savagery.

The feminist enterprise of novel criticism repeatedly identifies the novel as a woman's genre, in which female authors write about women's lives. Aphra Behn, author of *Oroonoko* (the first English woman novelist, if not the first English novelist), writes about a Black man and the settlement of a colonial society. Daniel Defoe's *Roxana*, on the other hand, is about a woman. This male-authored text (and Defoe is still taught as the first English novelist in many a novel course) uses a female first-person voice to create a narrative where the identity of the narrator is kept in doubt. The search for the narrator's identity is carried on in conjunction and opposition to other female characters, who, kept outside the centre of the discourse, construct and enrich the position of the central narrator. Female identities and subjects are differentiated along lines of race and class. The triumphant female who emerges at the end of the novel – 'Roxana' – is then seen as herself divided between her identity as a rich and prosperous Countess and a person haunted by a secret grief and loss. Female identity remains problematic, and evasive of stable definitions.

The second part of this book, which deals with the novels of Charlotte Brontë, uses the terrain and motifs established in the first section to reread these novels. The feminist interest is extended to include the colonial motif, a constant feature in these writings.

Chapter 4 uses a history of Brontë criticism to show how the literary concerns established in the previous novels are visible, albeit in a transformed manner, in the contemporary critical reception of Charlotte Brontë's novels. The individualist spirit of the eighteenth-century novel lives on in these critical writings, and the motifs of colonial and sexual adventure are transformed into a notion of sexual transgression. This chapter also tries to trace a feminist history of Brontë criticism, a history which, in its initial phases, reproduced the presuppositions of the nineteenth-century contemporary response, and obfuscated the imperialist underpinnings of this writing. The writings of Cora Kaplan and Gayatri Spivak are used as a springboard for departure. By bringing in the image of Other women, they point to the necessity of recognising class and ethnic divisions in the textual terrain covered by the Brontë novels.

The rest of the book is divided into various readings of Charlotte Brontë's prose writings. Chapter 5, on the juvenile work, written in collaboration with her brother Branwell, seeks to highlight the colonial enterprise that lies at the heart and forms the central theme of the juvenilia. This chapter also establishes the motifs and images of the Black/Other woman that surface within Charlotte Brontë's writings, and the ways in which these images originate from, and propagate an Orientalist colonial discourse.

The male narrative voice of the juvenilia persists in *The Professor*, the first 'mature' novel. Chapter 6 looks at *The Professor* to show how a male subject (who, after all, is placed at the centre of the concept of the unified subject) is riddled with problems as well. Chapter 7 looks at two novels with female protagonists – one, *Jane Eyre*, the most popular and well-known example of a female *Bildungsroman* in the genre of the English novel – to show how the triumph of the central female narrating subject is effected at the cost of the obliteration of other female subjects, differentiated by culture and class from the central narrator, Jane Eyre. *Shirley*, the other novel under examination, is a third-person narrative. This novel, about industrial strife and class divisions, presents gender and class differences within English society. This juxtaposition does not work to bring the two subordinated categories together, but to highlight the problems of femininity in middle-class Victorian society. Charlotte Brontë's last novel, *Villette*, is not given a separate reading, as many of the concerns expressed and presented in the other chapters would merely be repeated in another textual analysis. However, comparisons with *Villette* are constantly made.

This book revaluates the writings of Charlotte Brontë in the light of the difficulties posed by the tenacious holding on to the notion of a unified subject, both in novel criticism and in feminist literary criticism. A consideration of the significance of class and ethnic division in an examination of the account of female subjectivity is essential. By bringing in these elements, I hope to effect a new reading of Charlotte Brontë's works, which will see its struggle for the voicing of a feminist and female position as problematic as well as riddled with other categories of subjective and social division.

1

THE SUBJECT/S OF THE NOVEL

This chapter will map out the main features in the encounter between the English text and the Third World post-colonial subject. Both positions in this encounter are problematic and complex – be it that of the Third World subject as s/he tries to decipher meaning through the master('s) text, or that of the text, and the ways in which it is formulated as a central term in this meeting. The reason I have used the novel as the example of the master's text is to highlight the complexities of this encounter. The novel, as a genre, has a difficult existence – at one level it has been given very reluctant status as literature, and was not even included in the Oxbridge literature syllabus until the 1930s (Lovell, 1987, *Consuming Fiction*, p. 12). The history of the novel traces the moment of its birth to the seventeenth and eighteenth centuries, and identifies the central narrating subject as its main formal property. The status of this central narrating subject acquires significance when allied to the contemporary linguistic and philosophical task that was an attempt to define the subject as homogeneous and consistent, and to delineate the constituents of the citizen-subjects brought into being by the Western Enlightenment discourse. Moreover, the novel has historically been linked to women, and feminist literary criticism has used this preponderance of women within the genre to bring into focus the status of other marginalised subjectivities in literary discourse. The novel, as the discourse of the master, occupies a somewhat anomalous position – its history is one of struggle with and against that master, while it also seeks to be recognised by it and to emerge with full status into the field of English, as both literary and pedagogical text. The history of the novel can either be read as a narrative of growth, or the focus can be kept on the dichotomies and contradictions within the genre, and the tensions of its positioning within literature. A juxtaposition of the novel with the Other subject/student of literature demonstrates the many layers that pertain to cultural encounters, and to the recounting of those encounters. So let us spend this first chapter looking at the postcolonial subject facing the English text, and, while completely eschewing the notion of a binary opposition, analyse the ways in which both terms in this encounter are structured.

THE COLONIAL SUBJECT

Examination of the post-colonial subject is best approached by way of Homi Bhabha's introduction to Fanon's *Black Skin, White Masks* (1986). What is most valuable about this analysis is the recognition of the split in the colonial world and the way that this split is seen to apply to both the coloniser and the colonised. Positions of dominance and domination are not easily compartmentalised, and echo each other. The fear/desire oscillation draws both subjects into a mirror-image. The notion of mimicry is manifested in the covert positioning of the colonised subject, who, while seeking to reproduce, subverts imperial power. Bhabha's reading of Fanon highlights the intervention of colonialism in the formation of the subject. Psychoanalysis sees the human subject as formed in a dialectical relationship to the site of an imaginary Other (the Lacanian mirror-image). This site is now seen to be provided by the Other subject of colonialism – the Black or the native. However, the image of the Black man refracts and interrupts, rather than providing easily identifiable positions:

> The Black presence ruins the representative narrative presence of Western personhood: its past tethered to treacherous stereotypes of primitivism and degeneracy . . .
> (Bhabha, 1986, Foreword to Fanon, *Black Skin, White Masks,*
> p. xii)

The white man encounters his image as Other in confrontation with his Black double, to which he would like to ascribe a notion of primitiveness, origin or savagery. This easy identification is belied, as the Black man reflects not the Other but the ambivalence of the mirror-image: 'The image is at once a metaphoric substitution, an illusion of presence and by that same token a metonymy, a sign of its absence and loss' (Bhabha, 1986a,

11

p. xviii). The image in the colonial mirror recreates the Black man as a twinning, a mimic or a double, and it is within this process of reflection that the identities of both coloniser and colonised are formed. Bhabha insists that colonial mimicry does not perform the task of a faithful reconstruction; instead it works as a refraction, and transforms the colonial situation, throwing back an unfamiliar, and even unrecognisable image into the colonial mirror.

The birth of the nations of the post-colonial world and the subsequent task of the building of the Third World nation – the struggle for liberation and the growth of nationalism within once-colonised countries – has to take into cognisance the relation between these movements and the colonial power. The struggle for national independence is often read – too easily – as a struggle for liberation from the colonial yoke, ignoring the links and continuities with the colonial power. Similarly, the search for national identity often seeks expression in pre-colonial forms, ignoring the way that colonial identities and history have been irrevocably affected by the colonial experience. Romilla Thapar has said regarding our knowledge of Indian history that

> A major contradiction in our understanding of the entire Indian past is that this understanding is derived from the interpretation of Indian history made in the last two hundred years.
>
> (Thapar, 1966, *A History of India, vol. 1*, p. 3)

That is, during and after the period of British rule. Knowledge of our past has been filtered through the imperialist prism, and any historical re-creation has to keep this process in mind.

The subject of English in the Indian subcontinent has a special historical significance, as it was first introduced as an academic subject for the education of Indians. This history is traced in detail in Gauri Viswanathan's pioneering work *Masks of Conquest* (1990). The *significance* of this historical fact needs to be reiterated. English as an academic discipline arose out of a need for the colonial power to define its own identity, and this definition was guided by and kept the colonial subject/terrain/task constantly in view. Bhabha's mimetic relationship – the mirror-image – is in operation here: it is in confrontation/encounter with its colonised subject that the colonising power defines the terrain against which it would like to be identified. Macaulay, advocating the importance of English to the task of colonial governance, emphasised that it represented 'the best part of the English nation'. English, according to Macaulay's famous 1835 minute, was to serve a twofold purpose: British civil servants in India, schooled in the 'best part of the English nation', would successfully *impress* the natives with the glories of their colonial masters, and, at the same time, the introduction of English as a subject for Indians would create colonial subjects able to carry on some of the administrative and governing tasks of the British Empire. The Western-educated native was to act as a 'conduit' for the British.

Gauri Viswanathan's very important study highlights the split in the colonial situation:

> The split between the material and discursive practices of colonialism is nowhere sharper than in the progressive rarefaction of the rapacious, exploitative, and ruthless actor of history into the reflexive subject of literature.
>
> (Viswanathan, 1987, 'The Beginnings of English Literary Study in British India', *OLR*, p. 23)

This split divides the coloniser into dichotomous roles – as a carrier of culture and as a rapacious governor of colonial territory. The debates around colonial education agreed on one point: English education was to function as a buttress, filling in the gaps in the edifice of British power. The educational project, in all its aspects – in its Anglicist or Orientalist phase, in the debates between a secular and missionary/religious education – was concerned with the building of this buttress. English literature as a subject for academia was born in this context.

The imperial purpose that English served has been seen in other studies of the history of English as well. Baldick (1983) stresses the role of English as a 'civilising subject', both within England and in the colonies. Literary criticism had always performed an ideological task. The 'rise of English' is traced from the latter half of the nineteenth century by Terry Eagleton (1983). English literature (within England) was introduced to bring hitherto socially marginalised sections into the fold of tertiary education, and was first institutionalised as a subject in Working Men's and Women's Colleges, i.e., it had been relegated in the higher education system to that section of the population who were deprived of Latin and Greek (a classical) education. Arnold's proposal to establish poetry/literature as a substitute for religion is a sufficient indication of the ideological task English was meant to serve.

English, both for the colonisers and the colonised, was designed to give an impression of English cultural superiority. The designing of English *as a subject* in the curriculum always had to keep the colonial mirror image in direct view. The history of the introduction of English into the curriculum points significantly towards the place of culture in the process of political and economic domination.

In the Indian context, despite the inbuilt power hierarchies within the encounter, the situation can also be seen as a meeting of cultures, a *cultural* encounter within the colonial terrain. In the Indian subcontinent the establishment of English education had to take account of existing indigenous educational systems. The debate between the amalgamation or rejection of existing Indian pedagogy and culture divides the history of British rule into Orientalist and Anglicist camps or phases. English education was introduced as a secularised pedagogical practice, the government being opposed to the task of religious conversion favoured by the missionaries (the debate between the missionaries and the government educational institutions is recorded in detail by Viswanathan). The secular nature of British education in India split the colonial terrain further along lines of secular (colonial) or religious (native) education. Religion remained part of the indigenous terrain, whereas the public modern colonised world was to be faced armed with the intellectual tools imparted by the colonial masters.

Indian acceptance of British education was guided by the attractions of the job market. Significantly, a religious education was kept out of the official educational curriculum, and the Western address to the Indian subject was through the discourse of the eighteenth-century Enlightenment. A separation of religion from official education and the relegation of Indian thought to the religious sphere served as an ideal means to bring to the forefront concepts of rationalism, equality and humanism, which were then equated solely with the Western Enlightenment tradition. In this context, the teachings of Tom Paine became more potent than the Bible could have been, and the glories of the West shone with greater brilliance when compared with the atavism and darkness that was seen to accrue to indigenous forms of learning.

★

The experimentation with English in India as a pedagogical subject provides an example of the status of culture in the establishment of political and economic domination. It is a colonial encounter of a different kind, where the position of both subject and student is in the process of construction. British pedagogical practice was not introduced into virgin soil, but had to consider existing cultural and educational practices. The native response to this was to devise ways through which the benefit of Western learning and science could be made commensurate to native/ Indian beliefs and systems of learning. Gauri Viswanathan's book has traced in great detail the coloniser's strategies, designed to keep political power intact. The other side of the story (which is yet to be told) is how the native educated elite devised ways in which it could benefit from Western learning and science, while keeping native/Indian identities intact. The best illustration of this can perhaps be found within the histories of the two famous Calcutta colleges – the Hindu college and the Sanskrit college – and the ways that both Bengali and English were emerging in the early part of the nineteenth century in Bengal to further and spread the 'light' of Western education in the region.[1]

THE TEXT: ORIGINS OF THE NOVEL

Examinations of the origins of the English novel take us back to the eighteenth century and can be linked to the philosophical and ideological debates around the status of the human individual and its relationship with language. The notion of a beginning echoes the search for origins that lies at the heart of the eighteenth-century discourse on human subjectivity and the rise of human civilisation. My examination of the 'origins' of the English novel will be linked in with the European colonial project, and the ideological and political implications of the dissemination of the novel as literature and its function in the creation of the colonial terrain.

Novel criticism, which can be seen to have originated with Watt's influential *The Rise of the Novel* (1957), squarely traces the origins of the form to the rise in capitalist practices. Watt's largely sociological and economic analysis concentrates on factors such as the growing rate of literacy, the shift in the writing profession from the institution of patronage to that of publishing houses, the proliferation of bookshops and circulating libraries. Watt's note on the growing leisure of women, and their entry into the market as consumers of fiction, has a significance for the feminist reader. Watt's thesis is interesting in that it draws in the contemporary philosophical discourse on human subjectivity and its relation to language in the delineation of the development of the novel. One of the hallmarks of the novel – the creation of individual characters, marked off by a name, or the narrative of the 'life' or 'adventures' of this character – is part of the discourse around the creation of the individual human subject undertaken within contemporary philosophical disquisitions. John Locke's *Essay Concerning Human Understanding* (1690), describing the growth and development of a coherent human subject and the relationship between that subject and language, is the most well-known contemporary piece of philosophical writing.

Let us look briefly at Locke's essay, as the notion of subjectivity developed within that treatise has important links with other subjectivities or other states of subjectivity that need to be annihilated in order to reach the position of unity that was envisaged as the ideal. Locke sees the child as gathering a use of language in its progress towards human subjectivity. Through memory, association and consent, human societies and the individuals placed within them, assign significance to words. The child, placed within this signifying system, learns a use of language, and finds its place within the system. While this consistent brick-by-brick building process is described, the *Essay* nonetheless is forced to encounter gaps and failures in the process. Locke feels constrained to include a chapter entitled the 'Abuse of Words', where the properties of wit and eloquence are discussed. The deceptive properties of language are highlighted, where the user deliberately manipulates words so that their meaning is no longer easily decipherable, and the perfect correspondence between language and meaning belied. Significantly, the deceptive properties of wit and eloquence are equated in Locke's Essay with the 'fair sex'. Similarly, Locke's image of a consistent growth of subjectivity is marred as the human consciousness under production itself records lapses in this process of growth, exemplified in states such as madness or drunkenness. Locke's philosophical search is aimed towards the creation of a system of ideal correspondence, but is constantly balked by gaps and fissures which it is forced to encounter, both in the concept of a consistent subjectivity and in the linguistic system in which this subject is seen to be placed.

Locke has emphasised psychological processes, such as memory and reflection, in the gradual building up of the storehouse of knowledge in the human mind:

> The Senses at first let in particular *Ideas*, and furnish the yet empty Cabinet: and the Mind by degrees growing familiar with some of them they are lodged in the Memory . . .
>
> (Locke, 1961, vol. 1, pp. 15–16)

This stress on the function of memory brings into focus the concept of representation. Other philosophers, for example Diderot in *D'Alembert's Dream* (1769), link the subject together by memory. Memory functions as a trace or the representation of the object, rather than the object itself. Diderot's treatise takes the human subject away from a purely sensational existence to a consideration of human consciousness, which operates by recreating or representing images of sensory data. A simple equation between sensory perception and data and human perception is broken down, and the question of the relation between the subject and representational and signifying systems begins to be debated.

Fiction, theatre, representation – these are the words used to describe the human subject (in the works of Locke, Diderot, Hume and Hobbes, to name the most prominent thinkers of the period). Language, in eighteenth-century linguistic speculation, was seen as a perfect system of representation, issuing from the coherent and unified subject, which this system presupposed. But, when we look at the progress of linguistics in that era, we see that gaps emerged within this conception, and that representational form, 'objective' reality and subjectivity could never come together as an ideal whole.

The political ramifications of this project are visible when the concept of development of language is used as a measure of human civilisation. Again, the search for the origins of human civilisation is based on a notion of development from animal or pre-linguistic states, where the development of language becomes the measure of the development of human civilisation. The acquisition of language, as seen in Monboddo's concept of the orangutan or Condillac's image of the speechless statue, gestures towards an originating moment, where the human subject (both individually *and* in society) acquires language as a means of communication and representation.[2] In this context, Rousseau's *Second*

17

Discourse (1753) is an important document envisaging the savage instinctual state from which civilised man must have emerged. The Condillacan framework is maintained, and the acquisition of language becomes one of the factors marking man's progress from the state of savagery to domestic and then to more elaborate forms of social and political organisation. Based on the hierarchisation of civilisations and its correspondence to linguistic situations, and on the tenuousness of the object/word correspondence scheme, a notion of language and linguistic ability was used to designate and categorise human societies, which are seen to be held together by consent.

However, as Locke has argued, because there are no innate ideas in human minds, the concept of universal consent, or universal signification, becomes an impossibility. The processes through which this 'consent' is achieved are camouflaged in these treatises. Locke, in his *Treatise on Government*, argues that the meanings of words are fixed by consent, but that there is nothing binding in this system of signification. The consent that binds linguistic communities is vulnerable to change. Rousseau traces the coherence or even origins of signifying systems to the natural inequalities between men, highlighting the hierarchised nature of the signifying systems that bind society.

The concept of the origin of language, therefore, has overt implications for the way contemporary social division was conceived. Language becomes a hegemonic structure, unifying but also formalising and creating divisions between human individuals and societies. Eighteenth-century linguistic speculation is characterised by a desire to make a perfect correspondence between language and subjectivity. The futility of the project can be seen in the fragmenting process that these concepts are forced to encounter, both in the theory of language and in the social functions it was required to perform.

Those linguistic considerations that had decided social and cultural division were translated into social and pedagogical practices in contemporary England, specifically in the fields of language and English study. English and its study can be seen to serve the same purpose within England as in the colonies. While language was posited as a unifying factor, social divisions in England followed a pattern of linguistic stratification. To quote John Barrell:

the language of Britain was seen and used as a means of

impressing on the inhabitants of the country the idea of their unity, while at the same time it could be used (as it still is, of course) as a means of confirming, also, the divisions it pretended to heal.

(Barrell, 1983, *English Literature in History 1730–80: An Equal, Wide Survey*, p. 111)

Barrell uses the example of the writings of Thomas Sheridan to reveal how the language of the 'four distinct nations' of England was being brought to one level. Class divisions in England followed this linguistic stratification. Similarly, the eighteenth-century English linguist J. Butler's *Proposals* (1772) divides society into seven classes, according to occupation, and emphasises the role of literature and language teaching in the bridging of these divisions.[3]

Language teaching in the eighteenth century took up Locke's notion of a brick-by-brick building scheme, and proceeded, step by step, from spelling, reading and dictation to composition. Grammar, says Olivia Smith, reinforces existent class assumptions.

> The basic vocabulary of language study – such terms as 'elegant', 'refined', 'pure', 'proper' and 'vulgar' – conveyed the assumption that correct usage belonged to the upper classes and that a developed sensibility and an understanding of moral virtue accompanied it. Grammar, virtue, and class were so interconnected that rules were justified or explained not in terms of how language was used but in terms of reflecting a desired type of behaviour, thought process, or social status.
>
> (Smith, 1984, *The Politics of Language: 1791–1819*, p. 9)

The hierarchisation of civilisations according to language usage did not refer to other lands and peoples only, but had domestic political dimensions in the creation of a hierarchised society within the mother countries. A politics of language was deployed to stratify people according to language usage, and systems of education and government constructed to ratify and maintain this.

★

The 'emergence', 'appearance' or 'rise' of the novel took place within an area of speculation and debate about language and subjectivity. Gaps in the word/object formula tended to be over-looked in this scheme. The subject of the novel (both in the sense of theme and narrating subject) reproduced this oversight, and by ignoring the social and political divisions in which such a notion had originated, recreated them in fictional representations.

So the early emphasis on realism in novel criticism, based on a notion of an objective representation of social reality, makes the same presuppositions as the eighteenth-century linguistic project. Realism puts subject and object of representation into dichot-omous positions, and sees 'reality' as something *external* to the narrating subject. The 'world' of the novel is then built around the relationship between the narrator and 'objective' reality, and the value of a novel adjudged on its closeness to reality.

The notion of realism in novel criticism has been severely questioned by the poststructuralist and postmodernist schools. Barthes's reading of Balzac's *Sarrasine*, (*S/Z*, 1974), is a seminal text in this connection. I have used two critiques – one by Lennard Davis, *Factual Fictions* (1983), and the other by Marthe Robert, *Origins of the Novel* (1980) – to trace the effects of the breakdown of the concept of realism in the reading of the novel. Davis approaches the genre in the light of discourse analysis, largely influenced by a Foucauldian methodology. Robert, on the other hand, uses psychoanalysis to centre her history of the develop-ment of the novel on a Freudian pattern of subjectivity and growth. These critiques, by approaching the genre from two aspects, discursive and subjective, show the fluctuations and detract from the hitherto-established grounding in realism.

Factual Fictions: The Origins of the English Novel (1983) takes up the notion of the fact/fiction, or reality/fantasy divide, and while disagreeing with the view that the novel arose out of the romance, establishes the close connection between the novel and journalistic modes of writing, such as newspapers and ballads. Because the nature and content of 'news' had not been defined during the seventeenth and early eighteenth centuries, the demarcating limits between fact and fiction were not clear, and journalism itself remained a heterogeneous blend of 'factual' and 'fictional' rep-resentation. The novel exists within and shares this heterogeneity. Novels are described as 'prose narratives in print' which examine closely the lives of whores, pimps, rogues, adventurers and such like. Davis associates the 'underworld' concerns of the novel with its 'subversive' nature:

the whole project of the novel, its very theoretical and structural assumptions, were in some sense criminal in nature, and that part of the nature of this criminality was specifically associated with the threat of violence and social unrest from the lower classes.

(Davis, 1983, pp. 123–4)

The subversive nature manifests itself at two levels: at the linguistic, fact and fiction blending with ease, and in the creation of a terrain which is neither one nor the other; and in the more social aspect which, by turning the focus on the elements which the social cannot account for, acts as a comment on all that the massive task of classification and definition cannot incorporate into itself. In this formulation, theft and sex are juxtaposed, pointing to the disturbing nature of both. The novel becomes a form dealing with adventures in far-off lands, Oroonoko and Robinson Crusoe on the one hand, and the sexual adventures of bold and courageous women at home – Zara, Rivella, Moll Flanders and Roxana, on the other. It is interesting that the voice of adventure and sexuality has been predominantly attributed to the female, highlighting the precise nature of this voice, its status as either marginal or potentially subversive, and its identification with sexuality and fantasy.

Marthe Robert's approach in *Origins of the Novel* (1980) looks for the 'origins' of the novel in fantasy, and views the genre as a discourse in which the writing subject, by creating a scenario and defining a territory, exposes, and sometimes works out, the elements of its psychic life. The Lockean subject had been seen to be held together by a notion of consistency and constancy of growth. Psychoanalysis is another discourse concerned with the construction of the subject, and with the function of language in the structuring of that subject. Marthe Robert's history of the origins of the novel is ensconced within a psychoanalytical tradition, and views the novel (in both its individual and particular instances) and the genre (its history and development), as following the pattern of development in Freud's essay, 'Family Romances'. Instead of ascribing the heterogeneity of the novel to the discursive terrain from which it originated, this reading concentrates on the various positions that psychoanalysis ascribes to the subject. The novel as narrative is bound together by this subject, and the heterogeneity of novelistic modes and forms (its history) is traced to the fluctuating positions in which the subject is placed.

Robert's analysis also ascribes to the novel a twofold reference to 'truth' or 'reality'. The novel relates an imaginary tale, told by the author/hero. The claim to reality that is made by the novel/ist has to be accounted for. The novel is profoundly duplicitous, protesting sincerity and truthfulness while spinning dreams and fables. The 'truth' of the novel rests on the success of the 'delusion' it can pass off as 'reality' – it 'masquerades as reality' (Robert, 1980, p. 15). The novel embodies different parts of the Family Romance, and puts into motion the various tableaux that form the narrative, and is therefore bound to, and bound within, a terrain of fantasy where 'truth' ('facts' of life) and delusion (desire) intermingle.

This critique also draws on the notion of unitary subjectivity lying behind and constructing these texts – whether as author (Defoe, Cervantes, Stendhal or Flaubert) or character (Robinson Crusoe, Don Quixote, etc.). Robert divides the Family Romance into three sections, each section representing a story that the child tells her or himself, which is then read as the history of the development of the genre. However, while tracing the variegated progress of the novel from fairy story to maturer forms, Robert's analysis keeps intact the concept of a unified narrative voice as the spinner of the tale.

Robert identifies the distinguishing feature of the novel, which sets it apart from other forms of literature (tragedy, opera, farce, comedy, etc.) as the idea that the novel is not bound by any rules but has a predetermined content, based on the principles of the Family Romance. It has 'a *compulsory content* and an *optional form*, admitting of as many variations as the imagination can invent' (Robert, 1980, p. 32; italics in the original). This complete doing away with representational means again brings back the question of reality: the novel is, as it were, *there*, without any props or tools to set it up:

> Unlike all other representational genres the novel is never content to *represent but aims rather at giving a complete and genuine account of everything, as if, owing to some special dispensation or magic power, it had an unmediated contact with reality.*
>
> (Robert, 1980, p. 32, my emphasis)

The novel, as a literary representational form, is seen to draw on *no* other structures besides the psychic structures governing and constructing human subjectivity. Its lack of stylistic control brings it closer to the subject it emanates from and represents, so that it constructs that subject in a more authentic manner than other literary forms. The notion of a word/object equivalence that had guided many eighteenth-century thinkers is transferred here: a coherent, unified representation is not what is posited or sought, but nevertheless, a notion of a 'genuine', 'complete', even *authentic* form of representation is seen to exist in the novel, mirroring and holding the subject in its attempt to construct a narrative for itself.

However, while concentrating on the narrative of the growth of the novel, Robert's analysis ignores the vicissitudes of the journey to subjectivity that marks Freud's account of the development of the human subject. The recognition of self, in Freudian psychoanalysis, is made possible only through a recognition of the Other, and the child's differentiation from that Other. In *Beyond the Pleasure Principle*, for example, Freud interprets his grandson's game as an effort (on the part of the human child) to master an unpleasurable situation (the necessary absences of its mother). The game becomes, at this level, a recreation of the mother's coming and going – *fort-da*. However, as has been pointed out, (by Moustapha Safouan, 1983), the game is a game of *fort*, as it was purely by chance that the child discovered a stringed toy which could be made to come back. To the child, the mother's absences had constituted a 'hole in the perceptual field', and what the game was doing

> was to isolate and abstract this hole as the 'place' that could engulf everything, including itself, a place in which the thing, or the specular image of the thing, has sufficient permanence to break free of accidents of appearance and disappearance.
> (Safouan, 1983, *Pleasure and Being: Hedonism, from a Psycho-analytical Point of View*, p. 56)

Safouan's reading of Freud's description of his grandson's game radically alters the notion of any kind of mastery. The child is trying to discover a field of permanence and to break free of the game of appearance and disappearance. However, the only way that this repetition can be arrested is not in the fact of appearance, but in disappearance: if the toy could not have been pulled back, the game would have ended. In 'Creative Writers and Day-Dreaming', Freud compares the writer to the daydreamer. In this light, his comments could be read not as emphasising a continuity between writing and daydreaming, but as a pointer to the radical dislocation involved in both acts.

Lacan uses the image of the child looking at itself in the mirror to describe this play of absence and presence. The child recognises itself in the mirror and this recognition is, of necessity, split. The child becomes the subject and the object: gazing (the subject) at its image (the object), and the identity it acquires is split into the recognition of 'je/moi'. The mirror becomes the Other site which affirms the child's identity, while alienating it (by projecting it elsewhere) from its own self. The process of recognition affirms a presence that is spectral and is no presence at all.

Psychoanalysis concentrates on the gaps in the construction of human subjectivity. Freud's recounting of the *fort-da* game gives the child's play a narrative pattern – a fictional and playful reproduction of the necessary absences of his mother. Lacan's formulation of the mirror-image as the site in which the child recognises its human status also presupposes a misrecognition, by which the hollow image – the representation – presents the human subject with images around which the notion of its self is created. A false, fictional representation is presented as the place from where a notion of human subjectivity emerges and to which it is inextricably bound.

Robert's use of Freud's Family Romance concentrates on the development of subjectivity as a progression and ignores the notion of lack and separation that lies at its heart. One could argue that such a concept is potentially present in Davis's account. The notion of disjuncture and dislocation that Davis's discursive history brings to light splits the fictional ground of the novel between factual and fictional forms of representation. The novel should be read as situated in this split domain, and the splits acquire greater significance when read as the narrative of a split subject. Realism had read the novel as a representation of social reality tied to the perception of the author. The author and the subject of the novel need, however, to be set at a distance, at the same time as we need to stress the split nature of the subject, as both the narrator and the narrative discursive terrain covered by the novel. These two analyses represent very different ways of looking at the emergence and development of the novelistic form in the eighteenth century. Yet both critiques point to the hetero-geneity of the form, in terms of the central subject around which its narrative is woven and with reference to the discursive field it creates and represents.

WOMEN AND THE NOVEL

Ian Watt's sociological analysis pointed out the changes in the position of women under the new bourgeois and capitalist order, and drew a link between the growing 'leisure' of women and the habit of novel-reading. Of course, what Watt's thesis overlooked was that women were appearing not just as novel-readers, but as writers. Locke's discussion of the deceptive properties of wit and eloquence linked these with the 'fair sex'. In Davis's discussion of the origins of the novel, the constant oscillation between fact and fiction and the mingling of the factual and fictional terrain are seen as the hallmarks of the emerging genre. The history of English (as a subject in the curriculum) also illustrates the manner in which women were incorporated into the formal higher edu-cational sphere. Somehow, all these factors are made to cohere to point to the predominance of women in the production, con-sumption and dissemination of the novel.

Novel criticism has been a favourite feminist endeavour, and feminist literary criticism was, in fact, inaugurated with a stress on the novel. While it is no longer possible to hold on to that early celebration of the female first-person narrative, or to Showalter's notion of a 'gynocritical' reading, the relationship of women to the novel, both as producers and consumers, neverthe-less continues to be examined. Terry Lovell's book *Consuming Fiction* (1987), looks at the predominance of women as novel-writers from the inception of the novel, and links the problematic positioning of the novel to the ambivalent position that women occupy within capitalist systems of production. Novel-writing is placed within the sphere of commodity production. Lovell avow-edly fills the gap in Watt's thesis, emphasising the preponderance of women in the novel-producing market. The difficulties of incorporating the genre of the novel as 'literature' (i.e. as part of our intellectual heritage), may be traced to the difficulties of placing women within that heritage.

The novel is a bourgeois capitalist form, in the manner of its production as well as in the themes that it contains. The stress

25

94-525

on the individual subject – the novel is a narrative that traces the growth of an individual subject – adds to its bourgeois dimensions. Women, as producers of this genre, or as subjects, reproduce many of the assumptions and ideals of capitalism. At the same time, the heterogeneous forms of the novel question and subvert these assumptions (especially in the Gothic mode. Watt's emphasis on realism led to the neglect of the Gothic form.). Ignoring women as novel-*writers*, Watt fails to show the variations in the genre. Women, positioned ambivalently within capitalist bourgeois ideology, dominate the novelistic form, thus making the genre itself a carrier of the ambivalences of capitalist ideology.

Consuming Fiction, as a history of the novel, is invaluable for the ways in which it links women's position within capitalist bourgeois ideology and the status of the novel as a petty bourgeois commodity, both in the manner of its production and as a carrier of bourgeois ideology. The status of women within the novel (as writers, theme and consumer), remains problematic. As writers, women within literary production are relegated to a secondary position, so that the novel is not easily given 'literary' status. Women's ideological status as writer is always in jeopardy. At one level, women, as bearers of bourgeois ideology, reproduce capitalist bourgeois messages. But, given the contradictions in the economic basis of capitalism itself (the dichotomy between production and consumption) this message is not so clear-cut. Novel-reading is a spare-time activity, and so is placed outside the parameters of necessary economic activity. As a leisure-time activity, it appeals to the other side of the split subject of capitalism:

> The novel is deeply implicated in this fracture within capitalism's imaginary selves. The nineteenth-century realist novel had its face turned towards both poles. It produced, as it had to under conditions of commodity capitalism, narratives which entertained, and which in entertaining, opened up attractive and even frightening prospects outside of the ordered regularity of a mundane bourgeois world. But it framed these narratives within a plot and an authorial voice which reaffirmed the moral values of that world.
>
> (Terry Lovell, 1987, *Consuming Fiction*, p. 16)

Realism, and the novel's appeal to realism, is seen as a strategy designed to acquire for the novel status as 'useful' capitalist production. But, given that it is a leisure-time activity (and this is true even for the way in which its production was envisaged – the novel was often portrayed as being 'dashed off' by any lady [Lovell, 1987, p. 9]), it is to capitalism's other self that it appealed. The novel remains a blend – of fact and fiction, of unity and rupture – and the Gothic mode subverts and challenges the presuppositions of the realistic school, disturbing the easy narrative of growth that capitalist ideology would have liked to provide for its subjects. The dangers of novel-reading inhere in these fantasy elements. Mary Wollstonecraft castigates novel-reading for its creation of a 'romantic twist of mind', to which women readers are more susceptible. The novel dwells in those pleasurable and deceptive areas that Locke had ascribed to wit and eloquence, where the coherence of the signification attributed to language breaks down.

Feminist literary criticism extended the initial feminist belief in the personal as the political to novels, and read the voice of the central narrator in the same manner as it did the narratives of female lives gleaned from its consciousness-raising sessions: as 'true' delineations of female realities. Feminism has taken for granted that the dominance of women as producers, as objects and as consumers of this literary genre meant that a kind of 'authentic' female voice could be heard within it, that the novel provided a way into women's realities, both social and psychic. However, with the questioning of the status of that voice, both politically and within academia, it is very difficult to maintain the voice in its position of centrality. First, there is a difficulty in translating personal experience into political theory. Second, academic disciplines, such as history and anthropology, have become suspicious of the process by which 'genuine' accounts are related over a distance of time and space. The breakdown of the notion of the subject within the realist school of criticism has its echoes in the questioning of the homogeneity and authenticity of the subject that early feminism took for granted. Feminism has had to take into account differences (specifically of race and class) within its own ranks, and has been constantly balked in the task of defining the category of woman. The strategy evolved has been to recognise the differences *between* women, and to constantly (re)define its categories in the process of analysis. Feminism, both academically and politically, remains a fraught field, but it is from within these very tensions that it draws its dynamism and excitement.

*

The task of defining a coherent and unified female subject that feminist literary criticism set for itself has therefore come to a pause. Now is the moment for reflection and reconsideration, and to retrace the constituents of this female subject. Divisions between women are now highlighted, especially by Black women who insist that their realities are different, and formed within other differentiating moments and processes.[4]

Let us look, in some detail, at Cora Kaplan's essay 'Pandora's Box: Subjectivity, Class and Sexuality in Socialist Feminist Criticism' (in Kaplan, 1986), which tries to trace the tensions manifested within the modern feminist movement to the eighteenth-century discourse on human subjectivity. The concept of the unified human subject came into being in a sexually differentiated arena, and feminism has reproduced many of its assumptions, based as it is on similar notions. Both romantic and Enlightenment theories were gender differentiated, and positioned women and men differently. Feminine sexuality was given a prominent place in that formulation, and discussions of femininity and female subjectivity centred around this concept. The best example of this can be seen in the difference in the educational scheme chalked out for Emile and Sophie in Rousseau's *Emile*. *The Vindication of the Rights of Woman*, in so far as it is a response to Rousseau, recreates the ambivalences about the status of female sexuality, and while granting women civic status, continues to see female sexuality as dangerous and demeaning for the female subject.

This initial discomfort with the status of female sexuality and femininity is part of feminism's heritage, in its formulation of a political position and in its cultural and literary analyses. At the same time, feminist literary criticism tends to celebrate woman's marginalisation, and to see her position as one of potential revolt, devising a canon of women-authored texts while ignoring class and cultural differences in women's writings. Kaplan reviews this canon – Wollstonecraft, Radcliffe, Brontë and Woolf (the latter largely in response to Brontë) – not for a celebration of femininity, but to see how feminist readers ignore other divisive factors within these texts. A simple 'gynocritical' reading is rendered impossible, and attention drawn to a critical revaluation of women's texts.

Feminism thus has had to face the problems inherent in the notion of a unified subjectivity and a unified field of representation. It has also recognised the impossibility of providing for itself a history of writing through which a feminine or feminist identity can be delineated. It has seen how the dominance of women in the sphere of novel-writing and reading does not lead to the creation of a 'nation' of women, but has begun to recognise the fact that even women's writings partake of the differences, and are placed within the processes of domination, oppression, etc., within which the novel had come into being.

THE NOVEL AND IMPERIALISM

The imperialist heritage of the novel can be traced to the moment of its birth, and is visible in its themes, as well as in the problematic nature of its status as 'literature'. The novel is placed in a position of difficulty – it oscillates between a factual and fictional world, it reproduces, while subverting, the tenets of capitalism, it has a long history which places it somewhere on the fringes of respectable writing. Its uneasy positioning is echoed in the history of its reception and criticism.

Feminism's stress on the novel initially took the notion of unified subjectivity unquestioningly. That moment had been prompted by a desire to formulate a history of women's writing, through which a community of women could be defined. The impossibility of that notion is brought into focus when the historical and social processes guiding and controlling novel production and the access of women to this sphere of writing are analysed. The formation of a list of texts leading to the formation of a nation/community is belied, as the differentiated arena in which texts are produced and disseminated is analysed.

Feminism's journey through the annals of the English novel is especially interesting and significant as it records an effort to find an *other* voice in this genre of writing. This voice had been identified as women's voice, which had been marginalised and dominated within a system of patriarchal bourgeois ideology. But differences in the positioning of women (earliest brought out in Françoise Basch's *Relative Creatures*, 1974) made it impossible to hold on to this voice as central and as centrally determining of all women's realities. In this early feminist historicising of the novel, Charlotte Brontë's writings occupied a central position. In that work (Showalter, Moers, Millett, Gubar and Gilbert) the writing of the Brontës provided a popular point of departure, and the lives and works of the Brontë sisters were read as representing many of the problems associated with women. Charlotte Brontë wrote 'about' women: her books are seen to be female-centred, to embody a protest against and to present a critique of the feminine situation. The first break with this was the recognition of the Gothic as part of the tradition of women's writing, resulting in a diversion from realism to concentrate on the fantasy elements in the text. Even within this, Charlotte Brontë's works remain central, representing, as they do, a blend of, or oscillation between, realist and fantasy forms.

However, this easy celebration of women's voices in the novel overlooked crucial factors in the history of the origins of the novel. Gayatri Spivak, commenting on *Jane Eyre*, writes that nineteenth-century British literature cannot be read 'without remembering that imperialism, understood as England's social mission, was a crucial part of the cultural representation of England to the English' (Spivak, 1985, p. 243). The birth of the novel coincided with the European colonial project; it partook of and was part of a discursive field concerned with the construction of a universal and homogeneous subject. This subject was held together by the annihilation of other subject-positions. The novel is an imperial genre, not in theme merely, not only by virtue of the historical moment of its birth, but in its formal structure – in the construction of that narrative voice which holds the narrative structure together. Charlotte Brontë's novels have to be read against this background, and I hope to further the task of unpacking the constituents of the woman's voice in fictional representations.

Histories of the novel generally treat colonialism as a theme, reflected within the narrative terrain. The theme of colonialism is looked at from different perspectives. For example, Martin Green's *Dreams of Adventure, Deeds of Empire* (1979), is celebratory, and appreciates novels such as *Robinson Crusoe* for the spirit of adventure, leading to the establishment of colonial rule and trade. The subject of the novel is outward-reaching, exploring and victorious. On the other hand, Patrick Brantlinger's *Rule of Darkness: Imperialism and British Literature* (1988) traces the development of the British novel from the early part of the nineteenth century to the twentieth century as reflective of the fluctuations of Britain's imperial history, which, from the initial adventurousness of Marryat's seafaring novels, progresses to the dark visions presented in Joseph Conrad's writings. I propose to carry this argument further, and to show that the translation of imperialism into the novelistic genre is not limited to its thematic concerns, but refers to the formation of the subjective positions of the coloniser and the colonised within the colonial terrain. The narration in the novel is also dependent on the centrality of the narrating subject. The notion of the centrality of this subject and of the homogeneity of its narration had also come into being within the colonising enterprise, as has the necessity of constructing a pedagogical subject out of the texts of English literature. The relationship between the novel and the imperialist project is many-faceted, and can be viewed from at least three vantage-points: of theme, of the formation of subject-positions, and of the formation of a pedagogical subject.

Feminism's entry into literary criticism had been marked by a concentration on the novel. However, critiques of English as a colonial subject have not homed in on the novel in a similar manner. They have looked at the *politics* of the literary text: how it has forwarded the task of imperial domination, in the way that subjectivities so formed have taken on many of the assumptions of the colonising project itself. While African writings (by Franz Fanon, Chinua Achebe, Ngugi, to name only a few) show the relation between the linguistic and psychological/psychic modes of colonisation, a more recent Indian enterprise bases itself on a direct focus on the English literary text within the Indian classroom. Here, again, the text is not necessarily represented by the novel, as seen in Ania Loomba's *Gender, Race, Renaissance Drama* (1989), where the texts of the Renaissance and Jacobean stage are analysed to produce meaning within the Indian classroom. Similarly, *Woman, Image, Text* (ed. Lola Chatterjee, 1986), looks at a whole range of literary texts, including the novel, and examines their relevance in the Indian educational system. This enterprise keeps the category of gender central in its analyses, and uses the large numbers of Indian women studying English literature to draw the links between the literary text and women's position.

'The Prisonhouse of Orientalism' (Z. Pathak *et al.*, 1991) is an article based on an examination of three separate novels taught in the first-year M.Phil. course at the University of Delhi.[5] It is an effort to make the English text speak to, and within, an Indian classroom. The links it makes between the text and its students range from the thematic to the subjective, especially as regards the feminine subjectivities portrayed in the novels.[6] Most interestingly, and significantly, the stress is not on creating binary oppositions between Western texts and Eastern realities, but to show how, and to what extent, these texts echo Eastern realities, and how our realities can be comprehended through these texts.

Despite the brutality and the violence that accompanied colonialism, the subjects on either side cannot be separated into easily discernible and decipherable positions. These positions, while opposed, merge at points into the mirror-image described by Bhabha. This merging, historically and ideologically, is perhaps most clearly visible in the pedagogical task of the formulation of English as an academic discipline and subject. An examination of this historical and pedagogic phenomenon is being undertaken primarily by women. Of course, the large numbers of women engaged in teaching/studying English (cf. L. Chatterjee, 1986 and Loomba, 1989) may be responsible for this. This new dimension highlights, yet again, the feminine presence in literary study.

A significant result of this feminine presence has been that the position of women within the literary text is being put through another review, and the colonial confrontation/encounter is now the meeting between literature, the text and woman as theme and subject. Woman's problematic positioning within capitalism, as shown by Terry Lovell, is now extended into her problematic positioning within nationalist discourses, and the subject of English itself is shown to occupy a very difficult and fragmented position within a post-colonial pedagogical terrain. While an easy dismissal of the English text as colonial is not recommended, the meanings wrested out of the English text have a fraught existence within the classroom. While Pathak *et al.* disclaim the aim of forming yet another canon (of novels that echo colonialism or have an Indian reference/relevance) they nonetheless choose texts that deal directly with the colonial/imperial experience. Another set of texts seems to be in construction, and though a celebratory tendency is definitely eschewed, certain texts are shown to be *more* relevant than others.

I would like to come back to Spivak's contention that *all*

nineteenth-century British literature contains and conveys imperial messages, and to ally this contention with the fact that a notion of English literature as a subject – as a set of texts conveying English cultural superiority – came into being in nineteenth-century British India. The nineteenth-century British Indian reform movement was concerned not only with education but also with social reforms, centring on women.[7] I would like to juxtapose all these elements to look at nineteenth-century woman's novels, and to show how the motifs of colonial encounters are replayed within them.

2

SLAVERY AND SEXUALITY IN *OROONOKO*

The search for origins and originating moments which characterised most eighteenth-century philosophical speculation on the
relation between language and subjectivity led to an examination
of childhood, either of the individual, as in Locke, or of civilisation, as in the works of Lord Monboddo, Condillac and Rousseau. Locke's negation of the concept of innateness fails to explain
the faculty of reflection. Mankind's 'progress' towards a civilised
state is marked by the creation and maintenance of signifying
systems, primary amongst which is language. However, the difference between men and the higher primates (Monboddo's
orang-utan, for example) is difficult to distinguish, as speech
organs are present amongst the latter as well.[1] Other writers,
such as Condillac (1974 [1746]) build on Locke's theories, and
show how the primary *cris de nature* were gradually differentiated,
so that by convention sounds became associated with feelings,
thoughts and concepts. The birth of language may be accidental,
but the significatory system that it builds is subsequently held
together by agreement and convention.

In the history of the English novel, the search for origins
usually leads to *Robinson Crusoe* as a starting-point for the genre.
Though Watt explains this by his usual appeal to realism as its
distinguishing feature, other historians of the novel, including
Lennard Davis, consider this story of a marooned individual on
a desert island as the supremely wrong place to begin this history.
The opening passage from Marx's *Grundrisse* explains how this
contradictory image – a man alone on a remote island – comes
to be the point of origin for a representative form which is based
on the examination of the relations between the individual and
society. The eighteenth-century individual, formed *within* social

and political structures, is given an opportunity to examine the status of these structures and his/her own individuality in these remote islands:

> But the epoch which produces this standpoint, that of the isolated individual, is also precisely that of the hitherto most developed social (from this standpoint, general) relations. The human being is in the most literal sense a political animal, not merely a gregarious animal, but an animal which can individuate itself only in the midst of society – a rare exception which may well occur when a civilised person in whom the social forces are already dynamically present is cast by accident into a wilderness – is as much of an absurdity as is the development of language without individuals living together and talking to each other.
>
> (Marx, 1977, *Grundrisse*, p. 84)

A Robinsonnade is an impossibility as the individual, created within social systems, can never be separated from them. Such a subject, cast away by shipwreck (the typical Robinsonnade dream) into a luxuriant, but barren, wilderness, carries with him/her the social and signifying structures in which s/he had been constructed as an individual. Seen in this light, the first-person narratives describing far-off places remain rooted within the bounds of their own society, while desiring to flee and free themselves of social constraints. The oscillation between society, the unknown, and the subject who is traversing between two worlds, is the dominant theme in these novels.

This chapter, which looks at Aphra Behn's *Oroonoko*, will make the case for it as the first English novel. I do not intend to analyse the distinguishing features of the genre, or to explain why this prose narrative should separate itself from others to emerge as the first novel. However, there is a serious motive behind making the claim, as, by taking the date of the birth of the novel further back in time to a text that again deals with settlers on a distant land, the theme and terrain of the novel continue to concentrate on these remote lands. Colonial conquest and settlement remain the constant feature. What is different, most interestingly, in *Oroonoko*, is the narrative position. No longer does the novel originate from a first-person recounting of the self, but from a first-person account of someone else's life. Subject and object of narrative are sharply separated, and a white female narrator tells the story of a Black slave in the British colony of Surinam.

In this chapter I will look at the ambivalent attitudes towards other lands and peoples in the general discursive field in the eighteenth century. The reading of *Oroonoko* that follows concentrates on the subject/object dichotomy in the narrative, the status of the Black man and the manner of his entry into the field of representation, and finally the significance of *Oroonoko* as the originating English novel.

ADVENTURE, EXPLORATION AND THE OTHER

We saw in Chapter 1 the ways in which the eighteenth century constructed the concept of the sovereignty of the human individual in opposition to other subject-positions, which it had either dominated or annihilated in the process. We have also seen that this process of definition (of the individual, or of the systems in which s/he is placed) was brought into existence along with colonial encounters, as a result of a meeting between people of different cultures. However, the confrontration with the Other subject did not easily, or naturally, result in these opposing positions – it was always disturbed and hovered on the edge of identification, or of a recognition of self. The separation between the Other and self is forced, as self and Other are bound in a dialectical relationship.

The novel, when looked at as the discourse of this homogeneous subject, must also take into consideration the history of the genre, as novels of colonial adventure are part of its originating moment. The novel of colonial adventure has been given, in *Robinson Crusoe,* a significant role as the progenitor of the novel in general, and a similar genealogy is traced when *Oroonoko* is read as the first novel. The creation of a self in relation and opposition to an Other does not merely serve to place the narrating subject in positions of dominance and security, it also highlights the fissures and points of danger to which such a concept is vulnerable. Thus, while Martin Green (1979) celebrates this adventurous spirit, Brantlinger's more detailed study (1988) reveals the shifts in the position of the narrating subject as the colonial enterprise moves in time from its initial discoveries and conquests to the more complicated aspects of colonial trade and establishment. The preponderance of the theme of voyage and discovery in the novel must be reiterated, and the significance of this theme as part of the origins of a genre re-examined.[2]

It is not surprising that many histories of the novel have alighted on *Robinson Crusoe* as the starting-point for the genre, or that the recent feminist enterprise has discovered *Oroonoko* as a more apt point of beginning. It is because the discourse of the novel is based on the notion of a sovereign subject, and the position of that subject is determined within a confrontation with its Other, that the novel of adventure occupies such a significant place in the annals of the English novel. However, even when the novel 'domesticates' itself, comes home to roost, as it were, many of its concerns are worked out through a reference to that Other. The notion of that Other, in turn, is brought into and held in place within an area of tension, oscillating between celebration and condemnation.

The notion of a sovereign, transcendent, unified homogeneous subject rests on the obliteration or neglect of factors that disturb such a concept. Both social ('real') and psychic elements are involved in this. The novel as the discursive form that accompanies this notion rests on a similar process. The central subject who weaves the narrative is also based on the forceful negation of other elements, deliberately ignoring other subject-positions. This purpose is served by an invocation of the Other and its subsequent dismissal. Thus the novel is an imperialist project, based on the forceful eradication and obliteration of the Other.

SEXUALISATION OF THE LAND

Explorations and discoveries of new lands involved a meeting – a coming into contact – with unknown peoples and cultures. The European attitude towards these new lands and their inhabitants was ambiguous. Todorov (1984, *The Conquest of America: The Question of the Other*) describes how the discovery of the land was welcomed with unmitigated glee and triumph, whereas its inhabitants had a strange appearance – they had to be *understood*, known and controlled. He divides his book into four portions: Discovery, Conquest, Love and Knowledge. Discovery and conquest are of the land, whereas their inhabitants are to be brought under control through various discursive methods. Knowledge of the Other precedes an emotional relationship with that Other, and discovery and conquest were facilitated and completed through these processes. But attitudes towards the new lands and peoples cannot be so systematically differentiated, and the oscillation between fear and fascination evoked by the Other relates to the strangeness of both the land and the people.

Walter Raleigh's fulminations on the discovery of Guiana celebrate the land for its virginity – 'Guiana is a country that hath yet her maidenhood, never sacked, turned, or wrought' – envisaging it as a passive maiden waiting to be raped and exploited, full of untapped riches and resources. The value of the discovery was measured in terms of this virginity. Active verbs, such as 'conquer' and 'possess' are reserved for the 'Christian princes': 'It hath never been entered by any army of strength, and never conquered or possessed by any Christian prince' (Raleigh, 1981, *Discovery of Guiana, 1595*, p. 507).

When transformed into novelistic discourse, this joyous, buoyant, confident sexuality is tinged with a fearful hesitation. A good example of this can be found in the short novel *The Isle of Pines* (Henry Neville, 1668) which is presented as a

> True Relation of certain English persons, who in Queen Elizabeth's time, making a *Voyage to the East Indies were cast away* . . .
>
> (*Isle of Pines*, in *Shorter Novels: Seventeenth Century*, p. 225)

and images the island as a fantasy of fecundity, where everything 'bred exceedingly', be they the chicken brought from the shipwreck, or the four women and one man who survived the storm. The novel exemplifies the expectations aroused by such discoveries: to be shipwrecked on a beautiful island, to be free from material and financial concerns as natural fertility makes life easy and comfortable, and to be free of the sexual and class constraints of European society (note that the male protagonist sleeps with and impregnates all the four women, one of whom is his 'master's daughter' and another a Black slave). The idea is of a new civilisation over which the white man has total control.

The initial fear evoked by the island must be kept in mind while looking at the picture of uninterrupted fecundity and prosperity that the *Isle of Pines* paints.

> We were at first afraid that the wild people of the country might find us out, . . . We also stood in fear of wild

beasts . . . But above all, that we had greatest reason to fear, was to be starved to death for want of food.

(Isle of Pines, pp. 229–30)

The fear is of the inhabitants as also of the conditions in the island. The island is, fortunately enough, 'wholly uninhabited by any people' (p. 231) and natural conditions favour prosperity and growth.

These remote (is)lands uphold a promise of plenitude and abundance at the same time as, because of their strangeness, remoteness and novelty, they embody fear and danger. The (is)land therefore becomes an ambivalent and ambiguous symbol, signalling both fear and desire. Their unexplored nature provides the arena of the unknowable and unknown (in Raymond Williams's sense) while, by displacing subjects from known and familiar structures and surroundings, they represent unlimited and fantastic possibilities.

The other fantasy associated with the (is)land is of the breakdown of all sexual barriers. This apparent breakdown in the fantasised sexual paradise nevertheless keeps the man in a position of supremacy, and the women are imagined as passive recipients of his lust. Moreover, the dominant triumphant male does not shed any of the social factors that contribute towards the creation of notions of sexuality, race and class. His preference is always for his master's daughter – 'by whom I had most children, being the youngest and the handsomest, [she] was most fond of me, and I of her' (*Isle of Pines*, pp. 233–4). The Negro is lascivious, seducing him in the dark of the night, and was the 'first that left bearing, so I never meddled with her more' (*Isle of Pines*, p. 233). Easily dispensed with, even the children that the Black woman bears are white, so that the island is subsequently settled by a totally white population.

The fantasy of the remote (is)land, while providing a site for the study of origins, of other cultures, for anthropological journeys, is ultimately brought to the service of a reiteration of social and sexual divisions wrought within the mother countries.

THE NOBLE SAVAGE

Sir Walter Raleigh's detailed classification of the peoples and civilisations that he meets in the virginal land of Guiana proves that these lands were not uninhabited. The fear and desire evoked by these remote (is)lands were exacerbated by the strangeness of the inhabitants, who in the first place, were associated with a search for origins. The cult and notion of the 'noble savage' arose out of a romantic disillusion with European civilisation and a search for innocence and authenticity. Travelogues presented a mixture of fact and fiction, which found in the novel a suitable discursive terrain for this mixture. The inhabitants of these lands were considered undesirable from the commercial and colonial point of view, so strategies to deal with natives had to be devised. These ranged from complete annihilation and systematic genocide to devising educational programmes to incorporate the Other into European systems.

The ambiguity of the response to these new peoples – the mixture of fear and wonder – finds expression in contemporary writings. Montaigne's essay 'On the Canniballes' (first translated by John Florio into English in 1603) is perhaps the most famous of these. First the new-found lands are celebrated and compared to the lost Atlantis. This idea is soon dismissed, as these strange lands (situated outside the pale of European civilisation) could not be considered its fount. The comfort and ease of savage life is ascribed, not to superior social organisation, but to the fecundity and fertility of the places in which savages lived. Admiration is tinged with envy.

The title of Montaigne's essay – 'On the Canniballes' – also bears a special significance, as of all the 'horrors' that colonial encounters presented, cannibalism aroused the most fear, and was the practice that separated most starkly the 'savage' from the 'civilised' subject. Montaigne's essay does not dwell on the horrors of cannibalism, but spends time in describing the land, with its comforts and luxuries. Cannibalism becomes a symbol of the strange and the horrible, disturbing the peace of these Edenic places. However, while cannibalism is used to represent this stark differentiation, colonial encounters contain stories of equally horrible European practices.[3]

Locke again provides a good place to centre the examination of the 'growth' from a state of savagery to civilisation, and for looking at savagery as representing the childhood of man. His essay *Concerning Civil Government* (1690) contrasts men living in a state of nature with those living in an organised society, and considers the formation of civil government:

When any number of men have so consented to make one community or government, they are thereby presently incorporated, and make one body politic; wherein the majority have a right to act and conclude the rest.

(Locke, *An Essay Concerning Civil Government*, 1952, p. 46)

The search in the *Essay* is for the 'origins' of civilisation – a time *before* government, which, in its very conception, is futile, since in that ideal state of Nature (if it ever existed) there was no need for records or words. Locke's *Essay* reiterates the significance of words and language (in this case, the written word) as these give to human civilisation, as to the human child, the faculty of memory and a signifying system that provides a means of linking past and future. The failure of connecting words with objects coherently and consistently led to the breakdown of the mind/object/word schema on which the Lockean notion of the human subject was based. In a similar manner, when Locke tries to see the movement from a state of nature to civil government as progress, he is forced to recognise that factors such as external violence make the exercise of government necessary. Like the growth of a child, this development is ambiguous and is marked by breaks, gaps, lack and violence. A return to a state of nature is an ambiguous movement, which cannot be viewed as a regression or celebrated simply as a romantic return to roots or origins. This same uncertainty and ambivalence is attributed to the status of the savage in eighteenth-century European thought.

The concept of the noble savage is therefore held in tension and is riddled with all the contradictions that accompanied encounters with other cultures.[4] Expanding trade and commerce formed an inextricable part of the excitement and adventure of geographical exploration and discovery.[5] The questioning of the status of the savage (the Negro and the American Indian) denied these people complete human status, easing the plunder of their lands and allowing human bodies to be treated as commodities and the perpetration of mass genocide. David Dabydeen, for example, shows how by attributing a sub-human status to the slave, the slave trade could be allowed to flourish:

Lord Grosvenor could argue in Parliament that the slave trade was an 'unamiable trade' but could add, with no recognition of the callousness of his comparison, that so also

41

'were many others: the trade of a butcher was an unamiable trade, but it was a very necessary one, not withstanding'.
(Dabydeen, *Hogarth's Blacks*, 1985a, p. 30)

Despite putting primitive peoples on an earlier and lower rung of humanity, European settlers and thinkers could not ignore the question that the 'innocence' and 'purity' of these earlier states of civilisation evoked – that of the 'origins' of civilisation. The image of the savage (like the image of the child) carried with it an image of one's own past, while, at the same time, commercial interests dictated a need to obliterate points of resemblance or correspondence. Contradictory feelings were aroused by the figure of the savage, and he was, like the land he inhabited, viewed with fascination and desire, and invested in as a site of untold possibilities – a site where a picture of one's own infancy could be unearthed, and the bounds of civilisation could be transgressed. However, as a matter of historical fact, the colonial enterprise saw a reworking and remodelling of European and capitalist systems. To go back to Locke's essay, *Concerning Civil Government*: European presence manifested itself as an act of external violence, European traders created needs (lack) which could not be met directly by nature, and so the eighteenth-century concept of civil government was established in these other lands.

OROONOKO: A FEMINIST DISCOVERY

Aphra Behn's *Oroonoko* provides an apposite point at which to start a feminist history of the novel. However, early feminist accounts of the novel (Showalter, Moers) were more concerned with nineteenth-century and 'realist' novels. This concentration on realism could not remain unadulterated, and notions of fantasy soon began to permeate the discourse. The terrain that the voice in the novel was concerned to unravel was seen, in fact, like the voice itself, to be formulated and held together as fantasy. The way sexuality is understood in relation to writing has been crucially affected by this shift. As the concentration moves away from realism, so sexuality in the novels is regarded not as mere content – a delineation of the limitations (or otherwise) of socially sanctioned sexual positions for women – but crucially in terms of the form of the novel itself, as a working out of the ways in which the personal, psychic or emotional interject into the social, how they are formed by the social, and how they, in turn, modulate and influence society. Added to which there has been an effort to define and describe gender categories, no longer seen as inhering in a simple notion of woman, but as arising out of different and variegated social formations, which are, in turn, divided into other categories. A notion of difference *between* women has therefore acquired significance, and the study of the female voice, within literature, has been affected by these new developments. It is in this light that *Oroonoko* becomes of interest to the feminist reader.

The writings of Aphra Behn have recently been 'discovered' by women writers and critics. Jane Spencer's *Rise of the Woman Novelist* (1986) starts with Behn, putting the history of the women's novel into better and further perspective. More recently, Virago republished Aphra Behn's *Love Letters Between a Nobleman and His Sister* (1987), and Maureen Duffy (who introduces the *Love Letters* to the readers) has published a biography of Behn, entitled *The Passionate Shepherdess: Aphra Behn 1640–89* (1977). The emphasis in both Spencer's and Duffy's writing is on the fact that Behn was a woman writer, that she wrote for a living and that her writings have generally been either maligned or neglected by the male literary establishment. The rehabilitation of Behn and her works is being conducted more or less along the old lines: she is celebrated as yet another woman novelist who speaks boldly (especially as regards sexual matters) across the centuries. The publication of *Love Letters* serves to bring to light a lesser known text than *Oroonoko* and also shows Behn's 'mastery' of the epistolary form prior to Richardson (Duffy, 1987, p. 224). *Oroonoko* is celebrated in similar terms. It is read not only as the first novel to be written by a woman, but also as the first 'emancipation' novel, dealing in detail with the misery and plight of Black slaves. While Duffy rightly points out the limitations of *Oroonoko* as an emancipation novel (as indeed of the genre as a whole), she obliterates, rather than plays on, the difference in colour between the white narrator and the Black protagonist. What she admires in Oroonoko is the rational, European man (Buckingham, for instance) who has perspicacity enough to point out the shortcomings and flaws in Christianity as it is practised. He, she reiterates, is not a 'noble savage' but 'a civilised, both in his native and European terms, and educated prince' (Duffy, 1977, p. 268). Duffy upholds the 'individual' celebration of Oroonoko

– he is great because he embodies, despite belonging to another race, the qualities of European rationalism. Oroonoko is wonderful precisely because he is not a typical Negro. However, while he is not a Negro, it is very difficult to see him as a white person, and the text, despite all its efforts to incorporate him into the white social framework, fails to do so. Neither Negro nor European, Oroonoko is made to take his abode with the white women, who regard him with affection and amusement. There is a sexualisation of the Black man, at the same time as his sexuality is effaced, leaving him free to wander and commune openly with the women. It is as if the slave, as slave, is castrated and therefore not a danger.

Duffy refuses to comment on the danger that is heralded by the slave's assertion of individuality and independence. Instead she has recourse to a notion of 'symbolic realism', and reads the text as an allegory of the Stuart tragedy. Oroonoko, Imoinda and their unborn child are seen to be James, Mary and the yet unborn prince. 'Even Oroonoko's "blackness" was a characteristic of the Stuarts' (Duffy, 1977, p. 267).

By glossing over the fact that *Oroonoko* is a text where questions of race, sexuality and power are most powerfully portrayed, Duffy renders an incomplete and unsatisfactory reading of the novel. The crux of the interest in *Oroonoko* lies in the fact that it is a text where white woman meets Black man, that it delineates and concerns itself with an area (Surinam), where the subjects under scrutiny are displaced, and where three ethnic groups live together (and far apart) within a system of white colonial domination. Written by a white female author and using a white female narrative voice, it sets itself up as a celebration of a particular Black slave. The characteristics that this voice picks out and selects as worthy of admiration bring the object of study within familiar parameters. However, its inability to draw in the Black subject altogether soon comes across, and it is at this point that the narrator and the object under scrutiny part ways, and Oroonoko breaks out in rebellion. Aphra Behn, or the authorial voice, is unable to follow Oroonoko in his rebellion, and the text can only portray the disintegration and dismemberment of the Black subject, instead of examining the causes of his rebellion. What, then, is at stake is not the 'sympathy' of this voice (questions of whether *Oroonoko* is an 'emancipation' novel or not therefore become irrelevant), but its limitations. Questions of power, sexual and racial difference dominate in *Oroonoko*, and it is unfortunate that the recent critical interest in Aphra Behn does not examine these issues in more detail.[6]

I am reading *Oroonoko* to focus on its sexual and racial dimensions, and to show how it fits into the imperialism that is part and parcel of the novelistic genre. While doing so, I would like the reader to keep in mind that *Oroonoko* is being read as a site of origin (fantasised, no doubt) and in this light *instead* of *Robinson Crusoe* as the first English novel. This insistence on origins helps to reformulate the history of the novel. The feminist perspective from which this is done foregrounds, beyond the usual liberal feminist concerns (unearthing writings by women), the dilemmas that confront modern-day feminism in the definition of its politics. Written by a (white) woman, recreating a colonial situation, delineating a Black man, recalling a love story between a Black man and woman, telling the story of a Black prince – the text is fractured and fissured at many points. Questions of class, race and sexuality raise their heads, and are resolved, within the pages of the text, by a complete and violent annihilation of the Black slave rebellion. *Oroonoko* stands witness to and is part of the imperial project, as its initial admiration for its Black subject proves to be flirtatious and frivolous.

The novel begins by insisting on its reality and veracity:

> I do not pretend, in giving you the history of this royal slave, to entertain my reader with adventures of a feign'd hero, . . . And it shall come simply into this world, recommended by its own proper merits, and natural intrigues, there being enough of reality to support it, and to render it diverting, without the addition of invention.
>
> (*O*, p. 147)

Familiar novelistic devices are visible here. There is an insistence on veracity, and a sense of a readership is expressed as the author/narrator addresses an audience/the readers. The 'reality' to be presented is set at two levels: part of the narrative relates directly to the experiences of the author/narrator, and the other part is heard by and therefore is related to the narrator. In *Oroonoko*, the narrative consciously points to its fluctuating positions. Thus: 'I was myself an eye-witness to a great part of what you will find here set down; and what I cou'd not be witness of, I receiv'd from the mouth of the chief actor in this history . . . ' (*O*, p. 144).

The narrator is inscribed directly into the story, while at other points remaining outside it. *Oroonoko* is, moreover, not divided into preface and chapters, but is presented as a continuous narrative. By merging the autobiographical details of her life into the text, the author links the narrative to her own identity. Her life is veiled in mystery – her name, her birth, her marriage, her travels, even the real identity of the person interred in Westminster Abbey[7] – being impossible to decipher. This is echoed in the difficulty of separating the factual and fictional elements in *Oroonoko*.

The text is set in two continents: first in Africa, where Oroonoko is seen in his 'natural' habitat – this is the part of the hero's life of which the author has no first-hand experience, and which is narrated to her – and the second in Surinam, which appears as a recounting of the author's 'real' experiences. In this way, the 'life' of the main protagonist is seen to have originated in a distant land, whence he is brought into another, where Western European (English) forms of government dominate. Yet the fear of reverting to 'distant' Africa is always present. In the first part of the story the narrative voice takes care to keep its status as auditor intact, by the use of such phrases as 'I have often heard him say' (*O*, p. 177). The narrator is kept out of the story and appears as an impartial and unjudging observer and reporter. The attempt is to keep the text uninvolved and scientific, constructing Africa and its inhabitants as objects of curious observation. It is in the second part of the story that the narrator enters as actor (or actress) into the text, and has direct contact with Oroonoko (the 'object' of investigation). The narrator at this stage, as at the beginning, is self-conscious about the mediating role – 'I ought to tell you' (*O*, p. 186) or 'I had forgot to tell you' (*O*, p. 191). The role of 'native informant' is visible here and our understanding of the authenticity of the text then rests on the absolutely problematic positioning of such an informant.[8] The nature of the narrative voice thus further problematises the question of the historical veracity claimed by the narrative.

Oroonoko can be divided into three parts: (1) the early life of Oroonoko in his own country; (2) the capture and early residence in Surinam, affected through a change in name from Oroonoko to Caesar; and (3) the rebellion, or the gradual dehumanisation and defeat of the royal slave. The division into three parts also helps the text to operate at three levels of narration: the first, as already mentioned, exists as a narration – a telling of a story to an auditor – in the second, the narrator enters as actor or 'native informant', and is therefore in sympathy with the object under scrutiny; thirdly, the narrator/actor loses sympathy with the main protagonist, as rebellion and revenge drive the Black man away from the discourse of his white observer. Oroonoko remains the object of examination in all three sections, and it is his integration into the field of European commercial and political discourse that is under discussion. Bearing in mind that a woman is writing this novel, questions of femininity, sexuality and the Black man and, most crucially, the feminisation of the Black man, are brought to the forefront.

It will be useful, at this point, to go over the text of *Oroonoko* in some detail. The story opens in Surinam, with a description of its flora and fauna, its inhabitants and its commercial potential. The racial heterogeneity in Surinam is vividly brought to light: first, the slaves are not natives of this land. Unlike the slaves, the natives are free ('without daring to command 'em' [*O*, p. 148]), and the European settlers barter with them for fish, skins, furs, feathers, beads and trinkets. The exchange-value of these goods is enhanced by the racial exchange: Indian 'feather' habits being valued in England for their novelty – 'I had a set of these presented to me, and I gave 'em to the King's Theatre . . . [the feather habit was] infinitely admir'd by persons of quality; and was unimitable' (*O*, p. 148). Similarly, European beads were woven into ceremonial costumes and much valued by the Indians, who are portrayed as innocent, pure, beautiful and honest, presenting a picture of the noble savage prior to Rousseau. They stand witness to the fact 'that simple nature is the most harmless, inoffensive and vertuous mistress' (*O*, p. 149).

Surinam is at the service of its white colonisers. The value of the colony is judged by commercial considerations, and the beauty of the flora and fauna of the land is described with this in view. The land has not yet been fully explored: ''Tis a continent whose vast extent was never yet known' (*O*, p. 194). This 'unknown' nature of most fictitious colonies signals danger, and represents the uncharted and unmapped regions, outside the discursive purview of colonisation and 'civilisation'. The known, familiar, *colonised* parts of Surinam are described in terms of a tropical paradise: 'groves of oranges, lemons, citrons, figs, nutmegs and noble aromaticks, continually bearing their fragrancies' (*O*, p. 195). To this is contrasted the dangers of the unknown parts.

Slaves are separated from the native inhabitants, in both racial and geographical origin. They are 'transported thither' (*O*, p. 187). The flora and fauna have to be worked on to be converted to use-value, and slaves from Africa are brought over to work on the verdant beauty of Surinam. Both slaves and white masters are 'settlers', and it is felt that by cutting them off from the hinterland 'their numbers' could be contained, and they could be brought more effectively and completely under European domination. The text conveys a sense of the vast oceanic movements of the early modern period.[9] Slaves, like their white masters, had journeyed across the Atlantic to the new world. *Oroonoko* chooses Coromantien as a place in Africa from whence slaves were plentiful and profitable. The stress on the physical strength and durability of the people of this nation is made in the same spirit as the commercial potential of Surinam is brought to life.

It is in this context that Oroonoko is introduced. Seventeen years old and grandson of the King, he is at once simultaneously differentiated and brought on centre-stage. Immediately, Oroonoko's physical beauty is described in great detail – it is as if the Black prince, transformed into the 'object' of the Western gaze (as object of the discourse in *Oroonoko*), has to be set apart both in social and physical terms. This objectification is also a part of a process of feminisation and sexualisation. In this process, the position of the male hero of the novel becomes comparable to that of the female star as analysed by Laura Mulvey.[10] Let us go over the descriptions of this paragon of Black manhood – '[one of the] bravest soldiers that ever saw the field of Mars' (*O*, p. 152):

> he was adorn'd with a native beauty, so transcending all those of his gloomy race, that he struck an awe and reverence . . . as he did into me, who beheld him with surprise and wonder, when afterwards he arrived in our world.
>
> (*O*, p. 152)

He is 'different' from other people of his race – and the narrator cannot wait to say how beautiful he was to her sight, and interrupts her narration to reiterate this 'fact':

But though I had heard so much of him, I was as greatly
surpriz'd when I saw him, as if I had heard nothing of him,
so beyond all respect I found him. He came into the room,
and addressed himself to me, and some other women, with
the best grace in the world. He was pretty tall, but of a
shape the most exact that can be fancy'd: The most famous
statuary cou'd not form the figure of a man so admirably
turn'd from head to foot. His face was not of that brown
rusty black which most of all that nation are, but of perfect
ebony, or polished jet. His eyes were the most awful that
cou'd be seen, and very piercing; the white of 'em being
like snow, as were his teeth. His nose was rising and
Roman, instead of African and flat. His mouth the finest
shap'd that could be seen; far from those great turn'd lips,
which are so natural to the rest of the Negroes. The whole
proportion and air of his face was so nobly and exactly
form'd, that bating his colour, there could be nothing in
nature more beautiful, agreeable and handsome. There was
no one grace wanting, that bears the standard of true beauty.
His hair came down to his shoulders, by the aids of art,
which was by pulling it out with a quill, and keeping it
comb'd; of which he took particular care . . .

(*O*, p. 154)

Oroonoko's racial characteristics and features follow a long line
of tradition of the delineation of the Black man in English literature. The racially ambivalent or mixed person, such as the Moor,
is preferred. Othello's racial position is therefore hotly debated.[11]
The above description is exemplary in many ways: the carefully
marked distinctions between Oroonoko and other Blacks, the
little anthropological details (racial characteristics of the Negroes,
the way his hair is done, a coming to grips with 'other' realities)
and finally and predominantly the fact that the man is under the
purview of the narrative gaze, is being objectified and rendered
visible through the machinations of the dominant European
female's voice, and being brought under the gaze of a European
audience.[12] Notice the predominance of the authorial 'I' in the
passage, proof that the Black man is rendered the object of authorial and narrative gaze. Not only is his physical appearance suitably
Europeanised for the European readership, his mind, too, is suit-

49

ably trained – 'as if his education had been in some European court' (*O*, p. 153). His French tutor

> took a great pleasure to teach him morals, language and science; and was for it extremely belov'd and valu'd by him: Another reason was, to see all the English gentlemen that traded thither; and did not only learn their language, but that of the Spaniard also . . .
>
> (*O*, p. 153)

Note the branches of European knowledge that were considered desirable: morals, language and science. Morals and language had always been seen in conjunction, and as Olivia Smith (1984) points out, their combination, in the eighteenth century, plays a large part in the formation of class-divided notions of subjectivity. Science as a system of 'objective' investigation originated in the seventeenth century (with the establishment of the various Royal Societies). Its main task of classification and definition placed Black subjects and races as objects of investigation and research.[13] The representation of Oroonoko is typical of accounts of the colonised subject, where that subject, divided and ruptured by the processes of colonial domination, is fetishised and held up to view as an object of investigation, sometimes fearful and at others desirable. Duffy (1977) fails to point out the extent to which Oroonoko, in his economic and cultural activities, is Europeanised and serves imperial interests. However, she correctly compares the position of the Black man to that of women, showing how the notion of property and exchange turns both slaves and women into property: 'The slaves have become property, as women purchased in the marriage market were property' (Duffy, 1977, p. 268). Suitably Europeanised, speaking both French and English, so 'that I could talk with him' (*O*, p. 154) and even identifying with European commercial interests, Oroonoko is the prototype of the colonised subject, the Third World bourgeoisie of modern times, whose commercial, economic and political welfare are dependent on the fortunes of international finance.

The Black woman enters in the person of Imoinda – 'female to the noble male; the beautiful Black Venus to our young Mars' (*O*, p. 155). Instead of dwelling on the details of her beauty, the text introduces her irresistible charm with one sentence: 'I have seen a hundred white men sighing at her feet' (*O*, p. 155). The object of white male lust, she is nevertheless 'reserved' for

Oroonoko, too 'great' 'for any but a prince of her own nation to adore' (*O*, p. 155). However, ignoring this racial segregation, the text constantly refers to her as the 'fair' Imoinda (*O*, p. 156, 164). Of course, the word 'fair', in seventeenth-century usage, was synonymous with beautiful.

As *Oroonoko* is a novel by a woman, and celebrated by feminist literary history as such, the treatment of Imoinda within its pages is of crucial significance. The suppression of Behn's writings by the literary establishment has been used to show how women have been obliterated from literary history.[14] But the act of unearthing women's history performs another act of suppression by ignoring the representation of other feminine subjectivities within these early writings. Imoinda, in *Oroonoko*, remains a vague and hazy figure. Thomas Southerne adapted the play for the Restoration stage in 1696. In the play, Imoinda is a white woman. This change may have been guided by the fact that no actress could be made to 'blacken' up (a telling gesture in itself). Its effect was to provide another instance of miscegenation (in the manner of *Othello*) on the English stage.[15]

In this 'first' instance of a Black woman being treated by a white, the impression is of dismissal and effacement. There are many points at which the narrator identifies with the Black male, or expresses sympathy or admiration for him. But Imoinda remains in the background, and there is no direct contact between her and the narrative voice. Black female beauty is delineated only in terms of white male desire. There is a tendency to negate the fact of her colour. It is as though the text is unwilling to incorporate a notion of Black femininity, which is always represented as problematic. For example, *The Isle of Pines* had portrayed the Negro slave as a mere means of reproduction, and *not* as a desirable woman. Walter Raleigh, while gloating over the virginity of Guiana, expresses his admiration for a Black woman in the same missive, by comparing her to an Englishwoman: 'I have seen a lady in England so like to her, as but for the difference in colour I would have sworn might have been the same' (Raleigh, 1981, p. 485). Coming to grips with a notion of blackness and ascribing to it an aesthetic of sexual desirability proved to be very difficult. Dabydeen (1985a) quotes Sir Uvedale Price writing in 1801 (*A Dialogue on the Distinct Character of the Picturesque and the Beautiful*):

Variety, gradation and combination of tints are among the highest pleasures of vision: black is absolute monotony. In the particular instance of the human countenance, and most of all in that of females, the changes which arise from the softer passions and sensations are above all delightful; both from their outward effect in regard to colour, and from the connexion between that appearance and the inward feelings of the mind; but no Ethiopian poet could say of his mistress

> . . . Her pure and eloquent blood
> Spoke in her cheeks, and so distinctly
>   wrought
> That you might almost say her body
>   thought.

(Dabydeen, 1985a, p. 44)

This passage, besides indicating the difficulties of including Blackness within an aesthetic framework, also points to a notion of femininity and feminine desirability. The body of the woman is endowed with thought, and the thoughts of a woman sexualised into her body. The woman appeals to the softer passions, so that this body and its thoughts rest in an area of pleasure and play.

In *Oroonoko*, the love between the hero and Imoinda is jeopardised when she falls prey to the old grandfather's (the King's) lust. The 'royal veil' – a symbol of invitation to the royal bed – is sent to her.[16] The reader is regaled with a detailed description of the King leading Imoinda to his bed. Imoinda, on pain of death (for Oroonoko) declares her virginity, and waits unresisting for her fate. In the meantime, Oroonoko is driven to distraction over the loss of Imoinda, and is wondering how best to confront his old grandfather with his anger and resentment. The story proceeds with the many little conspiracies and stratagems that the lovers devise, and the intrigues typical of any court.[17] Finally, Oroonoko manages to enter Imoinda's chambers one night and 'ravish(ed) in a moment what his old grandfather had been endeavouring for so many months' (*O*, p. 169).

Now begins a tussle between the dominant signifying systems and 'reality': a tussle between the signification of the veil and Imoinda's preserved virginity. Imoinda had been sent the veil, and was within the system a wife or mistress of the King. Thus Oroonoko touched her at the danger of his own life, and the 'real' love between the two was forbidden because of the supposed relationship that the veil had forged between the old King and the young princess. Although Imoinda had remained a virgin, that signification is decisive. Imoinda, wife to the King, ravished by the grandson, cannot now be legitimately possessed by either, and is therefore banished and sold into slavery. The selling of Imoinda into slavery is a result of the negation, of the rejection, of the woman with an ambiguous sexual positioning, whose status within the social framework becomes difficult to define. Unable to be contained within the established order, Imoinda is sold by the Black man to the white man, and in a way represents the situation of the colonised woman. Imoinda is thus lost to Oroonoko.

Oroonoko, in the meantime, believes Imoinda to be dead and is prostrate with grief, with the result that the hitherto noble and courageous army is confused and awry in his absence. The excess of grief is in keeping with the nature of his love, and is associated with Eastern passion: as that love was pure and innocent (unlike Western passion), so is the grief excessive. The 'amorous slumber' enjoyed by a 'love-sick slave' (*O*, p. 176) is seen as part of a process of feminisation.[18]

In time Oroonoko awakens to a sense of responsibility and to the dangers that face his nation. He resumes his trading career, selling slaves to white merchants. The fortunes and status of the colonised subject are determined within the boundaries of commercial colonisation, and the difficulty of ascribing stable positions to native subjects is well demonstrated by Oroonoko's trading practice. As trader, he is on the coloniser's side, but his position as such is precarious and cannot be sustained. When an English ship appears in the port, the captain and Oroonoko become friends. The friendship proves to be treacherous; Oroonoko, along with 'about a hundred of the noblest of the youths of the court' is captured in a state of semi-drunkenness and the ship sails off with 'this innocent and glorious prize' (*O*, p. 179). A commercial partnership is thus transformed, and the European acquires full power over the fate and lives of his native friends. These instances have led readers of the novel (such as Duffy) to presume that it is a celebration of native or 'Black' values over European and 'civilised' ones. The deception does not end here – the whole voyage is punctuated by promises of freedom at the other end, thereby quenching any potential rebellions and other protests. It is interesting to see how the whole voyage reads like a seduction of an unwilling maid: the form of protest that Oroonoko and his friends resort to is to stop eating. The Black man is envisaged as the reluctant sultry female and his white captor as the cajoling, persuading, deceiving man. The captive Oroonoko is helpless and under complete control. The irons may be taken off, preferential treatment may be given, but the expectations raised are always false. And Oroonoko, though suspicious of his jailers, nevertheless acquiesces in the belief that his is a special case, and that his specialities should somehow preclude him from the fate suffered by the other slaves. Class divisions between the captured Blacks are emphasised and used to keep white dominance intact. However, Oroonoko is not freed, but is taken into captivity.

Oroonoko is sold as a slave to Trefry, who is impressed by his royal bearing. The emphasis is always on Oroonoko's difference from the other slaves, an underlining of the fact that he is a *royal* slave. At this point, the narrative is concerned to show the closeness and brotherhood between the two men. Despite the unmistakable stamp of royalty in Oroonoko's demeanour – 'they venerated and esteemed him; his eyes insensibly commanded respect, and his behaviour insinuated it in every soul' (*O*, p. 185) – he is, at the same time, a slave. This transformation in his identity is ratified by the act of naming him Caesar – a new baptism whereby the slave is given a royal name and is made to bear the emblem of a power and nobility in which he can have no share.

The act of naming is of prime significance and is related to a notion of possession. Todorov (1984, p. 27) has a wonderful description of Columbus taking possession of the islands as he baptises them anew, ignoring their old names, after the Christian god, saints and the Spanish king and queen – San Salvador, Santa Maria de Concepcion, Fernandina or Isabella. In tracing the distinguishing features of the novel, Watt (1957) commented on the significance of naming characters. Novels are distinguished from romance and allegory by the fact that characters are marked off from each other by a name. In *Robinson Crusoe* (the text that *that* history identifies as the first novel) names and the act of naming have a lot of importance. *Robinson Crusoe* begins by establishing the narrator's identity – by ascribing him with a name: 'I was born in the year 1632, in the city of York, of a good family . . .' (*RC*, p. 17). The name or the inscription of the main narrative voice in the social fabric is sure and defined. Despite this firmness of social placing, there is no fixity, but flux and change, as exemplified in the change in names: Robinson Kreutznaer becomes Robinson Crusoe. Robinson Crusoe is carried away – literally ('that wave having driven me, or rather carried me a vast way . . .' [*RC*, p. 48]) – to a place where he is unable to name things around him. Robinson subsequently seeks to establish his mastery over the island by this act of naming.

Naming and addressing is an act of possession – to be performed by the dominant subject. It can also be seen as an act of classification and ordering, bringing deserted (is)lands to life. Crusoe's initial bewilderment is evoked by diary entries like the following: 'On one of those three days I killed a large bird that was good to eat, but I know not what to call it' (*RC*, p. 70). Robinson needs to classify the flora and fauna around him, and, in turn, wants *them* to address him, that is, wants to inscribe himself within the system that he himself is creating on the island. Thus the pet parrot is taught to address itself and Robinson; later Friday is named by Robinson, and is in turn made to address him as master.

In *Oroonoko*, it is at this point of naming that the author/narrator enters the text as an actor and addresses Oroonoko by his new name: 'For the future therefore I must call Oroonoko Caesar; since by that name only he was known in our Western world . . .' (*O*, p. 186). Notice the way in which the sentence works: the emphatic first-person pronoun 'I' refers to Aphra Behn (white, female narrator) while Oroonoko/Caesar is the object of the sentence and acts as predicate to the verb 'call'. 'Our Western world' draws in the boundaries of the colony, and effectively keeps the Black subject outside its parameters. The tension between 'reality' and 'appearance' is brought back here: Oroonoko's status in the colony is determined by the system of slavery. As with Imoinda, who, once caught in the signifying chain of the royal veil, had to suffer banishment and slavery, Oroonoko, caught in the system of slavery, having crossed the Atlantic, having been sold and bought, having been rechristened, is indeed a slave, whether he goes 'towards that part of the plantation where the Negroes were' (*O*, p. 186) or not. Playing about with Oroonoko's subject-positions does not preclude him from the status of a slave, as that is the only role that the discourse of colonisation and slavery had to offer the Black, captive man.

Initially, the text tries to erase the hierarchical divisions between master and slave by insisting on the 'individual' superiority of Oroonoko. The 'she-slave' is introduced and the woman is made to play the role of exchange and mediation. Imoinda, now Clemene, the 'fair' slave, has won everyone's heart, including Mr Trefry, who claims 'that all the white beauties he had seen, never charm'd him so absolutely as this fine creature had done . . .' (O, p. 188). When Clemene's identity is revealed, Mr Trefry steps aside and Imoinda and Oroonoko are reconciled in the New World. The heaven that had been denied them in their old home becomes theirs to enjoy in this New World, unfettered by bigoted and antiquated social customs. Thus, though there is a celebration of Other 'primitive' cultures, it is nonetheless the products of the European Enlightenment who are celebrated. Trefry stands as representative and symbol of the new order in Europe. However, the economic prosperity of that order is based on commercial and colonial expansion. It is ironical that the eighteenth-century doctrine of the 'rights' of man should be established within a system which legitimised trade in human bodies.

The author/narrator presents herself in terms of this concept of rights, entering suddenly to tell the readers that she had already constituted herself an advocate for Caesar's liberty, and making herself as interested as Trefry in the couple. This authorial interjection introduces a new note into the text – one of 'narrative pleading': 'I was interested in Oroonoko only on humanitarian grounds' – implying that this interest could be otherwise construed, perhaps as a sexual interest; and secondly, Oroonoko's chief support is moved to the shoulders of a woman, and there is a separation from his master, Mr Trefry.

This movement into the *zenana*, or women's quarters, has a number of effects. It is accompanied by a renewed interest in the physical and exotic details of Oroonoko's appearance and dress. Oroonoko has already been differentiated from other slaves by his class status, and he is now being kept away from other *men* by his 'social habits'. It also foregrounds or calls a new form of attention to the voice of the narrator in the text. While with the women, our shrewd narrator (with her background in spying) ferrets out information from Oroonoko only to discover that thoughts of escape and revenge are never far from his mind. The text here is confused regarding which 'deception' it ought to highlight: the one being effected by the narrator on the hero (acting as spy while purporting to be a friend) or by Oroonoko (harbouring thoughts of rebellion and revenge while being given favourable treatment). The author's admiration for the hero is replaced by suspicion, and a re-establishment of white authority becomes necessary. Oroonoko has no friends, as he is accepted, admired and loved only so long as he remains within the conditions laid down by his white masters. The women remain more frequently in his company to quell and 'soften' his rebellious notions, and Oroonoko diverts himself and them (and they him) with various feats. Oroonoko/Caesar and his harem (or the harem and their slave) go hunting, fishing, trekking over the island, and the once noble prince becomes a tourist guide and an entertainer. To Oroonoko's status as a tourist guide is added that of intermediary between the native Indians (who suddenly break out in rebellion) and the white colonisers.[19] Black populations are divided along ethnic lines, and service to the white master becomes the function of Oroonoko's life. The sudden uprising of the Indians is uncalled for and unexplained in the text, part of the 'unknowableness' of the continent.

Oroonoko's final rebellion remains incomprehensible to the narrator (perhaps explaining the removal of her sympathy) and shows how the Other subject evades the representational form. The friendly, admiring European narrator is bewildered at Oroonoko's rebellion. The revolt is reported in terms which make it clear that the rebellion (and the rebel) are doomed to failure. Oroonoko's speech to the Black community is described as a 'harangue', and his followers shown like a motley rabble, without organisation, who do not need to be crushed, as they themselves disintegrate in confusion. The governor-general proceeds with an armed band of men, and Trefry, once Caesar's friend, is part of this band, though he goes along 'rather to be a mediator than a conqueror in such a battle' (*O*, p. 210). Pursuit and discovery are easy, the slaves forging their own trail, burning and cutting through the thick forest, clearing a path as they flee. The other Blacks give in easily, but Caesar and Imoinda are more difficult to track down. Finally, Caesar is caught and persuaded to surrender. Again, it is through the agency and mediation of Trefry that Caesar submits: belief in a white friend inevitably results in captivity for the Black man.

The warning issued in friendship by the author is seriously carried out, and Oroonoko is beaten and whipped to break his spirit. Foucault sees the changes in punitive systems in France from the end of the eighteenth century to the beginning of the nineteenth as being marked by the death of the 'gloomy festival of punishment' (Foucault, 1977b, *Discipline and Punish*, p 8). The concentration on the *body* of the criminal as site of torture is transferred into a system of discourses that centre around the *administration* of the body of the criminal: penal laws, prisons, solitary confinement and other forms that mark modern punitive systems. Interestingly, Foucault shows how the establishment of penal colonies transferred some of this punitive responsibility to the shoulders of the ministries of navy and colonies. Those elements that could not be incorporated into the emerging democratic bourgeois order in Europe were violently ejected into these tropical islands.

In *Oroonoko*, the graphic description of torture and suffering is not punctuated by any comment from the author, who has by now completely identified herself with the European community. The sympathy of the authorial voice is left in no doubt: the 'we' refers to the European community as a whole, but especially to the women. This gives a sexual dimension to the fear. The women, once his friends, are terrified of Oroonoko, now that he is no longer under the gaze and control of the European rulers. Aphra Behn emphatically interjects as author at this point and suddenly shifts her loyalties and fixes her admiration on a Colonel Martin:

> We met on the river with Colonel Martin, a man of great gallantry, wit, and goodness, and whom I have celebrated in a character of my new comedy . . .

> (O, p. 214)

Oroonoko, rebellious and humiliated, is definitely losing his position, giving way to a more intrinsically 'civilised' man, who is, like the author, sympathetic to Oroonoko. Imoinda, in the meantime, had injured the evil governor, Byam, with a poisoned arrow, but he survived, the poison being sucked out by his *Indian* mistress.

Despite the goodwill of his friends, Oroonoko's situation continues to be hopeless, so that he contemplates suicide. This is to be preceded by the killing of Imoinda and their unborn child, and his enemies. The death of Imoinda, being the first in the series, is described in great detail and in ennobling and glowing terms. As she meets death at the hands of her husband, Imoinda is transformed into a martyr: it is a form of *suttee* being performed. The Negro kills his wife and child, effacing his future in an act of desperation. Remember that the promise had been to kill his enemies next: but this time he is so prostrated with grief (as he had been previously) that he is incapable of carrying out his resolve. In the meantime, search parties are sent out to look for him.

The cause of worry, though attributed to concern for Oroonoko's safety, may well be traced to fear. They finally find Oroonoko, guided by the smell of a putrefying carcass. His own body, wracked by hunger, is on the point of collapse, and he is incapable of carrying out his threat of revenge on his enemies (who by now have dwindled to one, the Governor Byam). The one last action still open to him – that of taking his own life – is denied as he is taken, captive, to the public square and hacked to pieces:

> And then the executioner came, and first cut off his members, and threw them into the fire . . . they cut off his ears and his nose, and hurl'd them . . . then they hack'd off one of his arms . . .
>
> (*O*, p. 223)

and so on and so forth in great anatomical detail. The body of the Black man, once held up for admiration and fetishised as perfect manhood, is dismembered, tortured and destroyed. So ends the story of Oroonoko, prince of a Black kingdom, hacked and quartered by white colonisers in Surinam.

Feminism's rereading of the history of the novel prioritises the position of *Oroonoko*, as a novel written by a woman, and gives its author the status of a heroine, whose works had been deliberately forgotten by a male-dominated literary critical establishment. Despite its celebration, *Oroonoko*, about the life and death of a Black slave, does not further the feminist project of establishing the novel as a woman-to-woman discourse. The female first-person authorial voice interjects into the textual terrain merely to highlight racial divisions, which, rather than gender differentiation, is the primary concern of the novel.

The power relations are used, at one level, to create a distance between the subject and object in the narrative, separating the white female narrator from the Black male as the object of the discourse. Along with the Black man, a colonial settlement is being brought under purview. Here, ethnic relations divide the whites and the Blacks, while native Indians and imported Blacks are also kept separate. The Black woman, in this representation, is completely effaced, appearing as a hazy figure in the background, tossed between different systems which place her in positions of passivity and powerlessness. There is no sisterly attempt to 'understand' her.

Finally, the text also addresses the question of a colonised subject and the attempts to find a discursive space for such a subject. The complete annihilation of Oroonoko, described in graphic physical terms, reveals the futility of this project. *Oroonoko*, seen as an originating instance for the novel, provides the genre with a history that deals with examinations of power and sexuality, combined with class and racial differences.

3

DANGEROUS IDENTITY
The many disguises of Roxana

At first glance it may seem difficult to make the transition from the distant tropical island, the world of sea adventure and trade to the host of eighteenth-century novels written in the female first person and dealing with problems of women's status and sexuality. These novels appear more as confessions of sexual adventures and have, on the surface, little to do with the literature of travel and exploration. However, by keeping the 'history' of the novel in mind (Watt; Davis, 1983) the leap from *Robinson Crusoe* (1719) to *Pamela* (1740–1) or *Clarissa* (1748–9) marks the transition of the novel into the more domestic and homely domain. This is not to say that excitement and adventure are eschewed, but that they are transferred into the sexual terrain, and by making the female protagonist and the female narrator central to the discourse the status and position of women and sexuality become increasingly the main concerns of the novel. The nature of adventure in the novel changes. Again, the shift to the domestic does not keep the novel confined within familiar structures: the realm of the domestic is extended to show how even familiarity can be rendered strange, exciting and dangerous. The female protagonist and narrator come to occupy a central position, as it is within the domain of the sexual that these changes take place.

The shift marks a change in the discursive terrain from the status of savages, the origin of civilisation and systems of government to the position of women and sexuality in society. However, the concern is still with the establishment of a system of control or government and colludes with the creation and maintenance of hierarchies, and the intellectual pursuit concerned with

61

'origins', 'beginnings' – of civilisation and the passage from nature to culture.

The reading of *Roxana* that ensues traces this shift in the novelistic terrain from a romanticised land to an idealisation of femininity and identity within a more domestic, European setting. This movement follows a notion of 'origins', whereby the woman is placed centre-stage, made to tell her own story (supposedly), and a search for 'true' identity – an exact location for femininity and female sexuality – is made. I have chosen to read *Roxana* (1724) rather than *Moll Flanders* (1722) because *Roxana* uses an Orientalist motif to delineate and project a female subject. Written by Defoe (usually held to be the first English novelist), *Roxana* can be read as the first English novel where the subject is split between an inner and outer world: between a state of secret mental agony and physical and economic well-being. Juliet Mitchell reads *Moll Flanders* as the first example of a female *Bildungsroman*. Moll Flanders, the female counterpart of Robinson Crusoe, is seen as representative of the 'rise of the capitalist woman' and as tracing the development of an individual character:

> the novel is structured around her growth. What happens to Moll as a mature woman, depends on the conditions of her birth, her infancy, childhood and adolescence. The child is mother to the woman. As with a concept of social history, an idea of development is a *sine qua non* of a concept of the history of the individual.
> (Mitchell, 1984, *Women: The Longest Revolution*, p. 217)

By concentrating on *Roxana* I will show how a female first-person narrative is not always a *Bildungsroman*, but can instead be executed within, and placed on to, a terrain in which the unravelling of this identity becomes highly problematic. *Roxana* does *not* trace its female protagonist back to her childhood or roots, but places her within a fissured terrain where no idea of roots is tenable or within reach. Identity and subject-positions are sought and constructed in conjunction with images of the Other, who, in *Roxana*, occupies fluctuating positions. Stabilising the protagonist's position involves the removal and obliteration of other positions, which are represented by means of a racial and class hierarchy. The triumph of the narrating subject rests on mobility and a large space for manoeuvre. However, these constant movements and fluctuations also entail loss. Finally, the desire for recovery of the lost site of innocence and happiness unsettles the narrative, and blurs the distance between the subject and the Other. Subject and the Other merge in the figure of the daughter, who surfaces as that lost site, that Other position. The violent murder of the daughter obliterates the Other. But, because this Other is no longer separated, and is, in fact, part of the subject, the simple narrative position that *Oroonoko*, for example, embodies, is no longer tenable. The externalised manifestations of the Other, brought into being by the processes of colonial and class hierarchies, as shown in the previous chapter, now converge in the figure of the narrating subject. With the merging of the subject and the Other, the narrative positions in the text are disturbed in a more fundamental manner, and the easy, schematic separation of the two is blurred and cannot be maintained.

FEMININITY AND SLAVERY

Before beginning the reading of *Roxana*, I would like to draw comparisons between the status of women and of Black races to show how both categories existed as an 'underside' against which a notion of the sovereign subject was created and to point to the existence of a discursive field in which these issues were debated. This discourse puts women and slaves on a similar footing, and contemporary feminist writings reiterate this comparison to plead for the rights of women. Mary Astell, for example, bases her advocacy of the freedom of women and their equality with men on a comparison between the status of the Black man and of women in contemporary European society:

> *If all Men are born free*, how is it that all Women are born slaves? as they must be if the being subject to the *inconstant, uncertain, unknown, arbitrary Will* of Men, be the *perfect condition of Slavery*? and if the Essence of Freedom consists; as our Masters say it does, in having a *standing Rule to live by*? And why is slavery condemn'd and strove against in one case, and so highly applauded, and held so necessary and so sacred in another.
> ('Reflections upon Marriage', 1706, in Hill, 1986, *The First English Feminist*, p. 76)

Women, deprived of their full human status, are seen to be the slaves of men, and women's education and training have to be guided towards enabling women to take on their position as independent and free agents.

Mary Wollstonecraft, in her *Vindication of the Rights of Woman*, (1792), written nearly a century later, compares the position of women with the conditions prevalent within an 'eastern' state, specifically Turkey. The Orientalist assumptions of such a system of hierarchisation and representation are thereby highlighted:

> In a seraglio, I grant that all these arts are necessary, the epicure must have his palate tickled, or he will sink into apathy: but have women so little ambition as to be satisfied with such a condition? Can they supinely dream life away in the lap of pleasure, or the languor of weariness, rather than assert their claim to pursue reasonable pleasures, and render themselves conspicuous by practising the virtues which dignify mankind? Surely she has not an immortal soul who can loiter life away merely to adorn her person, that she may amuse the languid hours, and soften the cares of a fellow-creature who is willing to be enlivened by her smiles and tricks, when the serious business of life is over.
> (Wollstonecraft, 1978, *A Vindication of the Rights of Woman*, p. 112)

An Eastern harem is envisaged as the place where women are completely at the service of the male potentate. The dignity and humanity of the Enlightenment subject is in polar opposition to this other image, where a feudal overlord owns human beings. In this schema, the harem woman is completely sexualised: she is portrayed not only as a slave, possessed by another, but as sexual property, a body devoted to the service of her master. The subject of Wollstonecraft's *Vindication*, middle-class and European, is contrasted to this other woman. However, by transferring images of bondage and slavery to another terrain, the presence of 'real' Black slaves in English society is overlooked. Moreover, the practice of slavery – the slave trade, the use of slave labour – was a prominent feature of the worldwide political and economic empire being set up by the British. Feminist polemics ignores these factors, while it Orientalises the terms in which it argues for the rights of women.

Later in the century, Hannah More (writing in 1799), wants women's education to be aimed towards the creation of a perfect Christian lady, who would be different from Other women: 'that we are neither to train up Amazons nor Circassians, but to form Christians' (More, 1987, *Strictures on the Modern System of Female Education*, vol. 1, p. 76). Further, Asian excesses are to be avoided, as it is contact with the 'luxurious dissipations brought in by their Asian counterparts' (ibid., p. 84) that had brought the downfall of the Roman Empire.

The argument for women's education (which, in fact, is the main point of all these feminist tracts), rests on a notion of innate equality of the sexes. For women to take up their rightful position as the equals of men, they must be given similar educational opportunities. While gender equality is pleaded and argued for, the position of women is carefully differentiated from that of Other societies: Eastern or Black. The imperialist underpinnings of the demand for female equality cannot be ignored. The appeal adopts and creates an Orientalist discourse in which Eastern feudal societies are used to portray the complete subordination of women. The appeal is to an ethnocentrism which seeks to establish the difference between women and Blacks. After all, European women are part of the Enlightenment, and it is scandalous to keep them in a position comparable to that of slaves.

Women are compared to slaves in discourses other than women's polemical writings. As we saw in Chapter 2, the hierarchy produced by the process of sexualisation placed both Black races and Black and white women as sites of sexual fantasy and pleasure. David Dabydeen's comments on the significance of the Black female slave beating hemp in the Bridewell scene of Hogarth's *The Harlot's Progress* are significant in this context. The sexual subordination of women and slaves is used for the settlement of colonies. The Black woman's presence in the painting is seen to be 'part of the imagery of enslavement which runs through the work' (Dabydeen, 1985a, *Hogarth's Blacks*, p. 107). Female inmates in prisons and Black slaves in colonies occupy comparable positions. Both are under the total domination of the white overseer or gaoler, and embody the tragic side-effects of the viciousness of the capitalist enterprise. Most significantly, both are used to satisfy the sexual demands of the male coloniser. Their reproductive potential creates the colony's future – thus the importance attached to the figure of the pregnant slave or prisoner:

The female slaves were 'breeder women': the slave-owner had his fun of them secure in the knowledge that his sexual recreation was profitable since it led to an increase in the stock of slaves. The transported white whore did also serve sexual and economic purposes; gratifying the sexual longing of wifeless planters as well as bearing children who would constitute the future labour force so necessary to the economic development of the day.

(Dabydeen, 1985a, *Hogarth's Blacks*, p. 107)[1]

The novel traverses these two worlds, and creates its narrative structures by placing the narrating subject in positions where its desired sovereignty and autonomy are created in conjunction and opposition to these other sites. Racial and sexual categories provide a fantasised site, sometimes of origin and at others of difference, against which the emerging narrative subject is created and placed. The sex of this stable subject is not in question: whether male or female, the subordinated categories provide the basis from which a notion of the 'self' of the dominant subject can emanate.

MOTHERHOOD AS SITE OF ORIGIN

Feminist demands in the eighteenth century revolved between two poles: (1) the demand for women to be recognised as autonomous, individual *sovereign* subjects (Astell, Wollstonecraft); or (2) the 'instrumental feminist' demand, i.e., a feminism that places its demands for autonomy and rights without seeking to transform women's structural position as wife and mother.[2] Again, taking the correspondence between femininity and Blackness, the two categories are similar as both are used to provide a picture of an essential or original area which at once evoked fear and desire in the 'civilised' subject in confrontation with it. The nature/culture divide ascribed natural positions to certain groups, who were then subjected to exploitation and violence. This is why *education* – the cultivation of the mind – formed such an important focus for eighteenth-century feminists, who wanted to take women out of the natural sphere, and make them active participants in the creation of culture.

This emphasis, highlighting the difference between nature and culture or between civilisation and primitivity, brought out, yet again, the similarities between women and savages.

The stress on women's education questioned the notion of an

essential, natural difference between the sexes. It took the Lockean position that the mind was formed by training and experience. The host of writings during the seventeenth and eighteenth centuries on the subject of women's education are based on this position.[3] Both in Mary Astell's *A Serious Proposal to the Ladies* Parts 1 and 2 (1696 and 1697) which perhaps inaugurates the subject from a woman's point of view, and in the influential *A Vindication of the Rights of Woman*, written nearly a century later (in 1792) there is a demand for the recognition of women as independent and autonomous *subjects*, and the need for education to be directed towards enabling women to take on the full dignity and responsibility of that status. Both are suspicious of the appeals to 'nature': women's so-called natural tendencies are shown to be the result of a faulty education, which needs to be changed if women are to take their rightful place as citizen-subjects in the new political and economic order heralded by the European Enlightenment.

Mary Astell's *Proposal*, for example, is very sure of the distinction between nature and nurture: women's faults are traced to the inadequacies of education and instruction:

> The Cause therefore of the defects we labour under is, if not wholly, yet at least in the first place, to be ascribed to the mistakes of our Education, which like an Error in the first concoction, spreads its ill influence through all our Lives.
>
> (Astell in Hill, 1986, p. 143)

These appeals for the better education of women were not only guided towards equipping them for their rightful status as free and autonomous subjects but also kept in mind their function as mothers and therefore as prime educators of children. Wollstonecraft's argument against Rousseau stems from the realisation that the educational programme that he chalks out for Sophie is not only detrimental to the cause of women, but is faulty even in its own purpose – the fashioning of a perfect companion for Emile. Wollstonecraft develops the 'instrumental feminist' stand that women's role is as the primary educational provider for children. She views education from a Lockean perspective, and sees the mind and understanding as the result of the various influences that are brought to bear on them: 'The formation of the mind must be begun very early, and the temper, in particular, requires the most judicious attention' . . . (Wollstonecraft, 1978, p. 265).

Given that the early influences are derived solely from the mother, her mind and personality are of prime importance in giving the child the right early stimuli:

> To be a good mother, a woman must have sense, and that independence of mind which few women possess who are taught to depend entirely on their husbands . . . I now only mean to insist, that unless the understanding of women be enlarged, and her character rendered more firm, she will never have sufficient sense or command of temper to manage her children properly.
>
> (Wollstonecraft, 1978, p. 266)

The harping on women's maternal role underlines her sexed position. These arguments, based on the Lockean formula of a gradual brick-by-brick building process, fall on uneasy ground when faced with the biological dimensions of the women's role of mothering. The instrumental feminism referred to by Alice Browne (1987) bases itself on the sociological implications of this biological fact.

But the question of motherhood – the image of the woman as mother – cannot be confined to the sociological role of mothering. Childhood had been envisaged in eighteenth-century thought (specifically in Locke) as a *tabula rasa*, a state of pure innocence, on which life's experiences were to write their chronicles and narratives. As we saw earlier, the dividing line between savagery and civilisation was drawn on the basis of a use of language, and a search for that moment of origin was undertaken to provide 'civilisation' with a sense of roots and beginnings. Woman, by providing that originating moment – the moment of birth – came to be invested in as a site where the pristine, pure childhood of man could be glimpsed. The figure of the mother came to provide a site for the fantasy of origins.

There are a number of analogies here with psychoanalytic theory. Freud himself has compared women and nature, referring to female sexuality as the 'dark continent' or to the Mycenaean–Minoan stage of Greek civilisation. Motherhood is envisaged as that original, imaginary ideal site, whence the human child has been forcefully and tragically propelled on its journey to human subjectivity. Psychoanalysis identifies the Oedipal stage as the moment at which the separation takes place. Sexual differentiation is the result of the difference in positioning between boys and girls at this stage. This difference is put into motion through the relationship with the mother and the Law of the father – the third factor that interjects into the dyad of mother and child. The Oedipus complex for girls manifests itself as penis envy (desire for that which she does not possess) and in boys in the fear of castration (fear of losing the sign that identifies him with the paternal, phallic Law). The figure of the mother remains crucial in all these processes. She comes to represent an idealised, but repudiated, site. For example, Freud's grandson in the *fort-da* game (*Beyond the Pleasure Principle*), is coming to terms with the necessary absences of his mother. In similar fashion, the Lacanian stage of the Imaginary is composed of the ideal mother/child dyad and it is only through a violent rupture of this by the symbolic phallus that the human child enters into the symbolic order and its own tenuous positioning within it. The woman is doubly implicated – as the figure of the mother (idealised and then repudiated), and also, in her own turn, as the Oedipal child, who can resolve her crisis only by transferring her desire for the mother to coveting a penis, and then to the baby that a penis can bestow on her – in short, the desire to become a mother herself. Motherhood comes to represent woman's position where she is held and located. It is allied to the 'before' of human subjectivity – the image of the ideal mother, the fantasy of the ideal union that existed in another time and another place – and so on. Thus the figure of the woman becomes one with nature: before the irruption of the human order, before civilisation and before a notion of lack and absence has been acquired.

Motherhood is seen as the site in which the semiotic and symbolic meet and clash to create the role of the woman, who, at the Oedipal stage, had to repudiate the mother's body in order to take her place within the symbolic order.[4] Julia Kristeva sees the woman's positioning at the Oedipal phase to be determined by whether she represses the maternal *jouissance*, and identifies with the Law to take on the position of the symbolic order, or whether she remains that silent Other within what she terms the semiotic. The girl's desire for a baby (her resolution of the Oedipus complex) recreates within her, from a different position, the ideal mother/child dyad. The irruption of the semiotic into the symbolic is seen to occur at certain sites, when the human subject reverts to or recaptures that original moment. Motherhood is seen to provide one of those sites for the female subject:

By giving birth, the woman enters into contact with her mother; she is her own mother, they are the same continuity differentiating itself . . .

('Motherhood according to Bellini', in Kristeva, 1980, *Desire in Language: A Semiotic Approach to Literature and Art*, p. 239)

While the interjection of the symbolic separates this contact with the mother, reunion with the mother is seen to be possible by recreating motherhood in one's own person. Kristeva has identifed various sites from where the semiotic can emerge – Renaissance art, *avant-garde* poetry, Christian theology and now the process of motherhood/infancy.[5] Renaissance art, with its emphasis on paintings of the Madonna and Child, also recreates that ideal moment. In the same article Kristeva continues to talk about the 'language of art':

The language of art, too, follows (but differently and more closely) the other aspect of maternal *jouissance*, the sublimation taking place at the very moment of primal repression within the mother's body, arising perhaps unwittingly out of her marginal position. At the intersection of signs and rhythm, of representation and light, of the symbolic and the semiotic, the artist speaks from a place where she is not, where she knows not.

(Kristeva, 1980, p. 242)

The artist speaks from that limning position of the original semiotic pre-Oedipal self. Is this interface between the symbolic and the semiotic to be read as an authenticity or reality – a return to roots?[6]

If we go back to our examination of the origins of the novel in the first chapter, we will remember that Marthe Robert's analysis of the genre had seen it as a replaying of the roles ascribed to the child in Freud's Family Romance. Laplanche and Pontalis (1986) point out how the subject in a narrative (the fantasy sequence of a father seducing a daughter in their example) ranges over the whole fantasised scenario. In the light of these readings, female-narrated novels present a discourse in which the search for identity by the female subject plays around with the mother/child union and the idealised body of the woman from two vantage-points: that of the mother and that of the child. Both *Moll Flanders* and *Roxana* present women who have lost their identities and conceal this loss with a plethora of disguises. Their narratives and histories are *about* the muffling and covering up of self. In both cases it is a confrontation with the mother, from the position of the mother or the child, that threatens to *reveal* identity, but which does not bring about security or solidity for the subject. The image of the mother is given the status of an impossible desire, and as representing an unattainable site. As site of origin, motherhood represents the impossible and fearful desire hitherto invested in the figure of the noble savage. Motherhood acquires an added significance in female-narrated novels, as the narrating subject and the Other site of identity merge.[7]

My reading of *Roxana* bears in mind the signs that the text marks out as indicative of subjectivity and the processes within it directed towards the revelation of the identity of its female narrator. The significance of names, Roxana's relationship with other women and the final threatened discovery of original identity by her daughter operate in an equivocal manner, never really locating 'Roxana' anywhere as stable within the textual terrain. *Roxana* is also read in conjunction with *Moll Flanders*, as a comparison with that text shows how Defoe's female-narrated novels create ambiguous and dangerous identities, which remain protean, changing and evasive. Most crucially, the creation of a first-person female text rests on the invocation of other women, differentiated by class (Amy, the maid) and by race (Roxana, the imaginary figure). The central subject is made to construct itself around these other women, while effacing and erasing their direct entry into the text. Finally, the upward mobility of 'Roxana' is threatened by her daughter – the *female* child – who is dispensed with in order for the inexorable capitalist movement to continue.

THE SIGNIFICANCE OF NAMES

The use of proper names is crucial in the history of the development of the English novel (cf. Watt, 1957). Derrida's *Of Grammatology* highlights their significance. Chapter 1 of Part 11 discusses Lévi-Strauss's *Tristes Tropiques*, and looks at the anthropologist's machinations to probe behind nicknames and appellations. Derrida is mainly interested in the 'violation, ruse, perfidy or oppression' that is involved in the process of discovery. The significance he attaches to the interdiction of the utterance of the proper name is crucial in this analysis:

What the interdict is laid upon is the uttering of what *functions* as the proper name. And this function is *consciousness* itself. . . . The lifting of the interdict, the great game of denunciation and the great exhibition of the 'proper' . . . does not consist in revealing proper names, but in tearing a veil hiding a classification and an appurtenance, the inscription within a system of linguistic and social differences.

(Derrida, 1976, Of Grammatology, p. 111)

The proper name is associated with a system of classification, and its utterance seen as a revelatory act – 'tearing the veil'. The use of the proper name in the English novel (in contrast to the older Romance traditions, where the naming of characters is closely allied to allegory) is important. Besides creating an atmosphere of realism, it performs a revelatory, confessional function. The avoidance of the use of proper names in texts such as *Moll Flanders* and *Roxana* is significant, making the problem of identity crucial within them. *Moll Flanders* begins by avoiding mention of the name:

> My *true name* is so well known in the records or registers at Newgate, and in the Old Bailey . . . that it is not to be expected I should set my name or the account of my family to this work . . .
>
> (MF, p. 15)

She goes on:

> It is enough to tell you, that as some of my worst comrades who are out of the way of doing me harm . . . know me by the name of Moll Flanders, so you may give me leave to go under that name till I dare own *who I have been, as well as who I am.*
>
> (MF, p. 15, emphasis added)

This revelatory text, where the 'Author's Preface' has stated that every aspect of a criminal's life is to be unravelled, says at the very outset that it dare not reveal its true identity. The veils are kept intact. The ignorance of her name and parental origins (here the parent referred to is, significantly, the mother) gives the narrator the freedom to move casually from one subject-position to another. It is as though being outside the social classificatory system the subject is undefined, and free to wander at will.

The problem with proper names surfaces even in the prefaces that accompany most of Defoe's novels. They have given rise to a lot of comment, especially in the light of Gildon's attack on *Robinson Crusoe* (see Davis, 1983, pp. 156–8). Most of these prefaces protest the veracity of the ensuing texts, keeping intact the illusion of truth in the novel. In *Moll Flanders* and *Roxana* they are of special interest, as both present female autobiographies signed by their male author. Prefaces to eighteenth-century novels are used to establish the factual underpinnings of a discourse which is read as fictional. Before going on to the preface of *Roxana*, a look at the prefaces of Mary Delarivière Manley's novels will be useful as they show the practice to be common among other novelists of the period. These prefaces provide the reader with a theory, as it were, of the novel in the eighteenth century. The preface to the *Secret History of Queen Zarah*, for example, spells out the points of difference between the novel and romance. Verisimilitude, both in plot and characterisation, is presented as the main point of difference. Not only are formal stylistic devices shown to be directed towards realistic portrayal, but a claim for the historical veracity of the ensuing account is also made. Notions of fact and fiction are blurred in this account, as the fictional representation in the novel is shown to be based on reality – not imagined, but real.

Manley's novels (specifically *The Secret History of Queen Zarah* [1705] and *The Adventures of Rivella* [1714]), are about the sexual and political intrigues of the Restoration Court. The fact/fiction intermingling in these texts refers to actual personages, and their contemporary popularity was based on their 'gossip' appeal: actual court scandal appeared behind a thinly veiled plot. The novels, written by a woman, pleading veracity and a basis in facts, came to be associated with the author herself. The theme of sexual adventure and intrigue was read as the sexual confessions of the author, who was then identified with the scandals reported in these *romans à clef*. *The Adventures of Rivella* is still read as an autobiography, by Fidelis Morgan, for instance.[8] The text lays the woman open for readers' perusal: her eyes, teeth, lips and body. The sexualisation of woman's writing is expressed in lines like the following: 'Do her eyes love as well as her pen?' (Morgan, 1987, p. 25). The text becomes the body through which the female writer invites her audience to view her. The equation of text and author resulted, in the case of the eighteenth-century female novelist, in an identification of the events of the novel with her personal life story. Behn, in *Oroonoko*, keeping such an identification in mind, had carefully denied any sexual interest in the Black male protagonist of her text. On the other hand, Manley exploits the author/text identification of the genre for the sexual delectation of the audience, and draws audience, text and author together in a game of exhibitionism and voyeurism.

Defoe uses the prefaces of his female-narrated novels, (as indeed he does in *Robinson Crusoe*) to establish their authenticity.[9] Despite this claim, the first thing the prefaces do is to say that the true name of the protagonists will not be revealed. The identity of the author of the text (the novel is presented as somebody else's retrieved manuscript), is muffled and manipulated by the author/ editor, Defoe. This mediation acquires an added significance in the accounts of female lives. As with Manley's novels, the association of the text – the retrieved manuscript – with the body of its original author, is maintained. The manipulation by a male writer then presents female autobiographies, edited and crafted by a male novelist. A woman's narrative voice, spinning the tale of her life – holding her body up to public view – is presented at one remove. The autograph of the male author in this presentation remains dominant, as, despite its claims, neither *Moll Flanders* nor *Roxana* is read as the account of the woman portrayed.

In *Moll Flanders* a sense of modesty has entered to curb and censor the true words of the woman:

> All possible care, however, has been taken to give no lewd ideas, no immodest turns in the new dressing up this story. . . . To this purpose some of the vicious part of her life, which could not be modestly told, is quite left out . . .
>
> (*MF*, p. 9)

In *Roxana*, the preface merges the voice of the woman with the narrative: 'The History of this Beautiful lady, is to speak for itself' (*R*, p. 1). The flaws in the text, its failure to equal the beauty of the lady, are explained as the 'Defect of his Performance'. The problem, then, is related to the notion of the gap between reality and representation, and to the question of whether words, the relating of the life of the lady – the narrative – can, in any way, equal the 'reality' of her life. Also, the use of the male pronoun – 'his' performance – muddles the notion of female authorship, the 'his' referred to here being presumably the author, Daniel Defoe.

The gap between reality – 'the beauty of the lady' – and the representation is not attributed to formal representational limitations alone. A more deliberate manipulation is soon manifested as the 'diverting parts' are 'adapted to the Instruction and Improvement of the Reader' (*R*, p. 1). The crucial word here is *adapted* – the history of the beautiful lady cannot be launched forth on its own, but has to be fashioned to suit the tastes of the public to whom it is addressed. The author interjects to create another hiatus between the life and the story. The author/text/ reader community is recreated in this address to the reader, and the story of the life – the narrative – is an address from the author (of the novel and not of the manuscript) to the reader, who is to read the story for entertainment (the beauty of the lady), and for instruction (improvement).

The preface of *Roxana* names no names: 'it was necessary to *conceal* names and persons', and, 'It is not always necessary that the Names of Persons should be discover'd' (*R*, p. 1). This tinkering with the name is indeed crucial in a narrative that is *about* identity and subjectivity. The narrative starts with the following statement:

> I was Born, as my Friends tell me, at the City of Poictiers, in the Province, or County of Poicteau, in France, from whence I was brought to England by my Parents, who fled for their Religion about the Year 1683, when the Protestants were banished from France by the Cruelty of their Persecutors.
>
> (*R*, p. 5)

The *facts* are clear enough – the country and city of birth, including the expulsion of the Huguenots from France in the latter part of the seventeenth century. However, the phrase 'as my Friends tell me' muddles the 'reality' of the presentation, and the reader can no longer be sure, just as the emphatic first-person pronoun 'I' is not very sure, of the place and time of birth. A dual nationality is established – the narrator is born in France and brought up in England – 'I retain'd nothing of France, but the Language' (*R*, p. 5) – inherits 25,000 French *livres* from her father (the patrimony) and is married to an English brewer. The ambiguity of nationality and the duality of tongue enables her to flit from one country to another, sometimes English and sometimes French, adding to her chameleon disposition. The French connection is used to bring in an air of sensuality and foreign grace into the text: 'Being French Born, I danc'd, as some say, naturally, lov'd it extremely, and sung well also' (*R*, p. 6). Besides, the confusion of nationalities also plays a part in the progress of the plot. For example, when a marriage becomes difficult to prove, the narrator takes refuge in the duality of her nationality:

> but how such things were carried on in France I knew not; I told him, the greatest Difficulty would be to prove our Marriage, for that it was done in England, and in a remote part of England too . . .
>
> (*R*, p. 117)

Singing, dancing – the deceiving arts (like eloquence) – are transferred outside the shores of England. The text proceeds by extending the boundaries of this alien, but pleasurable, terrain to include Italy and Turkey, all the time muffling the central first-person voice, deflecting and disguising it.

ROXANA/AMY: IDENTITY, SEXUALITY AND CLASS

Let us briefly describe the text. *Roxana* (1724) uses a first-person female narrator, who recounts her life and loves. Ensconced within a completely European world, the text does not make the journey across the Atlantic – that rite of passage – unlike the novels so far examined. The Other enters into this European world, in terms both of race and of class origins, not only as metaphor but as actual persons and incidents through which the identity of the narrative voice is unravelled. Roxana and her maid Amy appear in close conjunction and cooperation throughout, and despite all the playing around with subject and social positions, the maid/mistress relationship remains intact. Similarly, Roxana achieves the pinnacle of her career as 'Roxana', a name that is of Persian origin, symbolising strangeness, adventure and exotic freedom. She holds out, and is in turn presented with, an endless world of sexual and social promise in this guise. Finally, the unravelling of identity results in a sense of doom – murder, mystery and death enter into the text. It is her own daughter who finally threatens to reveal Roxana's identity and thereby to disturb the freedom of the subject, who had hitherto, nameless and rootless, been free to wander all over Europe and from lover to lover. Roxana's hounding by her daughter throws her world and existence into confusion, breaks her relationship with Amy (the only consistent one in the book) and plunges the textual surface from ironic comedy to despair and tragedy.

The construction of a 'sisterhood' can be seen in the constancy and intimacy that pertains between the narrator and her maid, Amy. Despite this seeming oneness, there are, I would like to maintain, factors that create a hegemonic, even an imperialist, relationship between the two. Most significantly, Amy is the only named character in a text that functions by concealing names and identities. By naming Amy and keeping the female narrator as a first-person pronoun, the text is affecting an objectification of Amy, who becomes the object of the gaze, plays the role of Man Friday, as it were.[10]

The mistress/servant relationship is seemingly broken at many points, but through all their mutual adventures, the hierarchy in their relationship remains intact. While 'Roxana' creates and constructs her own story, Amy acts as her *alter ego*, aiding, abetting and persuading. The narrator trespasses beyond her sanctioned sexual position and by sleeping with her landlord becomes a whore quite early in the narrative. Amy plays a large part in the prostitution of her mistress and she is, in turn, subjected to the same kind of persuasion and turned into a whore. Amy is constantly present as the landlord (later to be known as the jeweller) proceeds to woo her mistress. The simultaneous presence of the two women makes it difficult to identify the wooed object: Amy joins them in their meals, puts on her best clothes, and is very much a part of the sexual bantering and foreplay:

> Well, Amy, says he, I intend to Lye with you to Morrow-Night; *To-Night, if you please Sir*, says Amy very innocently, *your Room is quite ready:* Well *Amy, says he*, I am glad you are so willing . . .
>
> (*R*, p. 33)

The maid and mistress are equally courted. Amy, object of the man's desires, and both willing and instrumental in the seduction of her mistress, diverts the responsibility of the sexual and social transgressions on to herself, the servant. The mistress (upper class) is led by the servant (poor working class) into the paths of

vice and debauchery. The class position of the narrator has already
been put into jeopardy: now she is brought to the sexual position
of the maid. The eliding of social positions (is Amy still her
servant? – note that her salary is not being paid and later is paid
by the male benefactor, in other words, Amy as recipient of
money and goods from the landlord can also be seen as his whore,
being 'kept' by him) has set askew the economic and social underpinnings of the maid/mistress relationship. This ambiguity allows
Amy to be persuaded and coerced into bed with her master. The
master/mistress/whore relationship is completely befuddled as the
two women occupy different positions, even while in bed with
the same man. Amy's seduction is violent: 'so I fairly strip't her,
and then I threw upon the Bed, and thrust her in' (R, p. 46).
Roxana's own seduction had not been described in such forceful
terms, but Amy is violently 'strip't' and 'thrust' into her mistress's
position. Amy's seduction gives the narrator a chance to review
her own social and sexual status:

> I need say no more; this is enough to convince any-body
> that I did not think him my Husband.
>
> (R, p. 46)

or

> Had I look'd upon myself as a Wife, you cannot suppose I
> would have been willing to let my Husband lye with my
> Maid, much less . . . but as I thought myself a Whore,
> I cannot say but that it was something design'd in my
> Thoughts, that my Maid should be a Whore too, and should
> not reproach me with it.
>
> (R, p. 47)

'My maid' cannot remain chaste while the mistress prostitutes
herself: class barriers must remain, servants cannot hope to be
better than their masters and mistresses. But, whether he sleeps
with Amy or not, it is the narrator who is treated as wife, and,
after his death, reinscribes herself into the social scene (in Paris)
as the jeweller's widow. Amy remains a servant and a maid,
plotting on behalf of her mistress. Social rules have collapsed,
but the social hierarchy remains intact: the widow of Poicteau (as
she is now known) becomes mistress to a prince, while Amy
seduces his valet:

I might have interspersed this Part of my Story with a great many Pleasant Parts, and Discourses, which happen'd between my Maid *Amy*; and I; but I omit them, on account of my own Story, which has been so extraordinary: However, I must mention something, as to *Amy*, and her Gentleman, I enquired of *Amy*, upon what terms they came to be so intimate; but *Amy* seem'd backward to explain herself; I did not care to press her upon a Question of that Nature, knowing that she might have answer'd my Question with a Question, and have said, Why, how did I and the Prince come to be so intimate, so I left off further enquiring into it, till after some time, she told me it all freely, of her own Accord, which, to cut it short, amounted to no more than this, that *like* Mistress, *like* Maid; as they had many leisure Hours together below, while they waited respectively, when his Lord and I were together above; I say, they could hardly avoid the usual Question one to another, namely, Why might they not do the same thing below, what we did above?

(*R*, p. 83)

This passage, read in conjunction with the preface, can be seen to reiterate the connection between the text and the narrator's life. The status of Amy, the other woman in the text, is defined. Amy, though occupying a central position in the events of the narrative, remains incidental to it. Roxana's 'extraordinary' story is the focus of the narration. Class hierarchies between Amy and Roxana, despite their mutual adventures, are maintained in the text. The mistress becomes mistress to a prince, while Amy seduces his man; the mistress and the prince are above stairs while the maid and the man remain below. Sexual barriers apparently break, but social hierarchies remain intact. This is revealed in the text not only by means of plot, but in the very identification of the text with the main narrator's life. The narration of a woman's life story and the construction of a female narrative identity brings forth other women through which that identity and its narrative are framed. But that Other woman (differentiated by class in Amy's case) is evoked only to bring the central character into being, and the Other woman's story is 'cut short'. Thus, in *Roxana*, Amy's story remains unheard, and Roxana's life history is followed.

THE COLONIAL RISE OF THE NOVEL

ROXANA: SEXUALITY AND THE OTHER

In *Roxana*, therefore, Otherness is expressed as a class difference, where transgressive sexuality, or sex as adventure, is 'taught' to the narrator, who is schooled in the ways of her maid. Roxana learns this sexual laxity and freedom, and sets off on her upwardly mobile career. The questioning of race is also central to this mobility and self-differentiation. The racially and geographically differentiated Other woman is, interestingly enough, introduced into the pages of this text through a dress, a costume. We have seen how the text, while seeking to establish the identity of its narrator, actually muffles that identity by playing around with and concealing that name. In a similar way, dress is used to categorise and define identity, and as the narrator flits from one persona to another, her clothes keep changing. Let us have a detailed look at the Turkish costume that bestows on her the title of 'Roxana', which then provides the title for the story of her life:

> the Habit of a *Turkish Princess*; the Habit I got at *Leghorn*, when my *Foreign Prince* bought me a *Turkish* Slave, as I have said, the *Malthese* Man of War had, it seems, taken a *Turkish* Vessel going from *Constantinople* to *Alexandria*, in which were seen Ladies bound for *Grand Cairo* in *Egypt*; and as the Ladies were made Slaves, so their fine Cloaths were thus expos'd; and with this *Turkish* Slave, I bought the rich Cloaths too: The Dress was extraordinary Fine indeed, I had bought it as a Curiosity, having never seen the like; the Robe was a fine *Persian*, or *India* Damask; the Ground white, and the Flower blue and gold, and the Train held five Yards, the Dress under it, was a Vest of the same, embroider'd with Gold, and set with some Pearl in the Work, and some *Turquois* Stones; to the Vest, was a Girdle five or six Inches wide, after the *Turkish* Mode; and on both Ends where it join'd, of hook'd was set with Diamonds for eight Inches either way, only they were not true Diamonds; but no-body knew that but myself.

> (*R*, pp. 173–4)

We are back in the world of *Robinson Crusoe*, with slaves, captives at sea, ships and pirates; in other words a displacement of peoples from one culture to another. The habit belongs to a Turkish princess, but the persona who enters the text is a Turkish slave. Displacement of people results in class displacement, as positions are completely manipulated in the process – 'ladies' are made into 'slaves'. This displacement, sexual bartering and the trade in human bodies are part of the commercial exploitation that accompanied capitalism and colonisation. The world of trade and commerce is graphically brought to light in the costume – 'fine *Persian*', '*India* damask', made in the 'Turkish mode'. The foreign goods on offer are luxury items – fine cloths. The fashion is also foreign – a dress in the Turkish mode. The Turkish mode of dress is enhanced by Turkish customs: 'and of her [the Turkish slave] I learnt the *Turkish* Language; their Way of Dressing, and Dancing, and some *Turkish*, rather *Moorish* songs' (*R*, p. 102). Initially, her French origins had accounted for her graceful dancing; now wider horizons provide the text with an image of exotic beauty, in dress and dance. The Other woman's dress and habits are adopted by the narrator, just as she had learnt the sexual habits of her maid.

This new costume gives the narrator a new persona. She is named Roxana:

> upon which foolish Accident I had the Name of *Roxana* presently fix'd upon me all over the Court End of Town, as effectually as if I had been Christen'd *Roxana*.
>
> (*R*, p. 176)

The name Roxana, evocative of foreign Other lands, from which her costume had been procured, blends the foreign and the exotic into the identity of this European woman. However, the difference between the Other and the narrating subject is blurred, similar to the way in which the origins of Roxana's dance are made unsure: did she learn it from the Turkish slaves, or was it 'invented by a famous Master at Paris' (*R*, p. 175)? This mongrel dance, Turkish/Moorish but with French overtones, emblematises the mixture of the foreign, the Other within Europe, and the use of it to create areas of pleasure, leisure, sexuality and luxury. Eastern Other nations are ransacked for their goods. This process is accompanied by the production of Orientalist motifs for the creation of an arena of leisure, pleasure and exciting sexual play. The white woman is constructed in this arena, and she adopts the goods made available by the commercial expansion to invest in her own person. Roxana's sexual career is accompanied by an amassing of wealth, making her the prototype of the capitalist woman, whose entry into the expanding commercial world is effected through the decoration of her body with foreign goods. The body of the woman is adorned with the goods that the oceans yield (Roxana's costume had been found by pirates who had captured a 'Malthese man of war'), and this body is then projected by the woman to build up her fortunes. The aim of the text (as stated in the preface), had been to equal the 'beauty of the lady'. The body of the woman, identified with the text, bedecked with commodities extracted from other lands, itself becomes a commodity, to be invested in, and to become as desirable as the goods with which it is adorned.[11] The text is that fetishised figure, adorned, decorated, decked up, held up to view. Roxana, at the acme of her career in Pall Mall, is an amalgam of all the different factors that the text has effaced: the easy sexuality is learnt from Amy, working-class woman, and the exotic beauty culled from distant foreign women, who themselves are enslaved, and have no role in the text.

The merging of class and cultural difference to produce the ideal image of Roxana is accompanied by a blending of factual and fictional material in the text, keeping alive the illusion of reality or the myth of an original manuscript. The introduction of a 'real' figure such as Robert Clayton allies the commercial motif in the text with the 'real' world of capitalist money-making. Similarly, the figure of a tall masked man is introduced to tease both Roxana and the reader with the hope that this may be the King himself. Disguise is used to play around with the notion of kingship (real authority) and pretence, sham, make-believe. Again, this is emblematic of the way that the text functions: teasing the audience with its dual status as factual and fictional. The masked man is not the King at all, only the Pretender to the Throne, and Roxana herself does not turn out to be a great lady but a 'mere Roxana' (R, p. 182). Dreams come true and yet not true, as the narrative unfolds its various strands, as more and more guises are put on and as the masks become the realities. When Roxana finally does become a Countess, it is a sham one, as the title is bought for her, so that in the final instance she becomes a Countess in commercial terms alone.

DANGEROUS MOTHERHOOD

The amassing of wealth and the placing of the central narrating subject in a position of greater stability is accompanied by the search for her lost children. *Roxana*, when read, like *Moll Flanders*, as the development of capitalist woman, shows the subject gathering personal wealth and investing this financial fortune wisely. Her other search is for a family, as she seeks to bestow her fortune on her progeny. *Roxana* had begun with the breakdown of the first marriage, which had unbalanced Roxana's position as wife and mother, and initially propelled her on the journey recorded in the text. When settled financially, Roxana begins a hunt for the children she had been compelled to put out to care, in order to bestow on them a portion of her wealth. The mother's search for her children brings familial establishment into focus, as lost wandering subjects seek stability through a notion of family and inheritance.

Interestingly, this mother's search for her children is transformed into the daughter's (the *female* child's) search for her mother. This search is presented as a desperate game of hide-and-seek, by means of which the proper name, hidden under every device and form, seems to be torn out of the narrative and uttered. It is a dangerous utterance: 'and in a word, Amy and Susan (for she was my own Name)' (*R*, p. 205). Susan is Roxana's daughter, whom she had abandoned in childhood, and who is named after her. Roxana wants her children back, but she is desperate to hide her courtesan status from them. Susan recognises her as the Roxana of Pall Mall, and hounds her mother down, making it impossible for her to live her subsequent life as a respectably married woman. Despite threats and fears, it is not the daughter but the narrative that accidentally, jerkily – *unconsciously* – reveals the real name. A slip of the tongue reveals what the text was meant to conceal.[12] Mother and daughter share the same name, and the repetition of the name has a mirror effect by which the image of the subject is reflected on to another figure. The doubling effect can be seen as productive of an Other position, tied to the subject by means of this mirror–image. Susan's image is reflected in Susan, her daughter. The daughter's search for her mother is a dangerous enterprise, the site of confrontation with the Other which, at one level, would *place* the wandering protean subject, whose very drifting was a source of strength, while, at another, presenting the subject with its unsettling double, or image. So far, the text had used images of Other women (Amy, Roxana) to furnish the narrator with a variety of subject-positions. The daughter's name – her mark of identity – echoes and repeats that of the mother's, and a mirror-image is created by which the identity of the one is irrevocably tied to the other. However, rather than producing stability, this confrontation is threatening. Susan, the daughter, is presented as the dangerous Other, as if the problem previously projected on to class and racial difference now works its way into the personal, subjective narrative of the text. Once placed in that position, Susan is similarly dispensed with, to allow the protagonist to remain in a position of certainty and stability.

This confrontation between mother and daughter can be read in psychoanalytic terms. A daughter's search for a mother is evocative of the original mother/child dyad, and of the special significance of that moment for the female subject. The desire for the recreation of that site is tied to a search for origins, through which human subjects seek to establish their own identities. While both *Moll Flanders* and *Roxana* recreate that lost moment, they do not use it to provide the narrative with positions of comfort or ease. In *Moll Flanders*, the female narrator, placed in the position of daughter, meets her mother in Virginia, a colonial penitentiary. A Family Romance is created in this site of displacement: in a plantation in the 'South of the Newfound Colonies of America'. The long journey across the Atlantic takes us outside the confines of known society, and, in that alien place, brings about a meeting with the mother (site of origin) and seeks to establish the real, and hitherto concealed, identity of Moll Flanders. Virginia, though separated from England, is closely related to Newgate. Both are penitentiaries, sites to which 'civilisation' banishes those subjects it cannot incorporate. Newgate was Moll's birthplace, and, as a place of detention, a nightmare image of her ultimate destination. The image of Newgate has a petrifying effect. On the other hand, colonies as penitentiaries freed the criminal, and provided a new site where lives could be started afresh. Europe, unable to contain its 'criminals', put them on board ships and transported them, literally, to other worlds. Criminals were enabled, in their turn, to doff new identities and to create other lives in these new worlds. Thus:

many a Newgate bird becomes a great man, and we
have . . . several justices of the peace, officers of the trained
bands, and magistrates of the towns they live in, that have
been burnt in the hand.

(*MF*, p. 86)

that is, bear the mark of Newgate. Differences between criminality and lawfulness are completely broken down. Moll's
mother's story is one of sexual reform: of someone who

had been both whore and thief; but I verily believe [she]
had lived to repent sincerely of both, and that she was then
a very pious, sober, and religious woman.

(*MF*, p. 87)

It is in this site and through the relation of this story that Moll
Flanders, whose true identity had been veiled by various textual
devices, recognises her mother. The utterance of her Newgate
name reveals the mother's identity to the daughter. This utterance
is dangerous, and does not operate to reunite mother and child.
Instead, it reveals the truth of the relationship between Moll and
her new husband, who is, in fact, her brother. The Family
Romance takes on a grotesque proportion, and the breaking of
the incest taboo is shown to be really unsettling.

Illness and irrationality are one of the first effects of this discovery: so much so that the brother/husband even threatens to
send our heroine to a madhouse. The fear of incarceration surfaces
yet again. Criminality and madness are both classified as dangerous, and the regulation of criminals and mad people is similar:
subjects classified as either were put aside, hidden or thrust away.
However, madness was associated with emotional and mental
states, and the regulation and diagnosis of madness not so easily
effected. *Moll Flanders* shows its narrator in positions where she
is in danger of classification as both mad person and criminal,
and the fear evoked by this is allied to the real possibility of
exclusion and ejection from society.

However, it is in Virginia that the narrator of *Moll Flanders*
finds a final resting place. This is effected, at the end of the novel,
through another meeting and another mother/child reunion – this
time a mother/son reunion. The son, settled in Virginia, recognises his mother, and returns her *colonial* property to her. Displacement, movement and journey *away* from the native country

provide that point of stability and rest. *Moll Flanders* reports two mother/child reunions: one where the narrator as female child meets the mother (the place of origin and identity), and the other where the narrator as mother meets her male child. The first meeting is unsettling, bringing the narrator close to madness, jeopardising her position, whilst the meeting with the son (the male child, inheritor of the phallus), bestows on her property, position and stability.

So female subjectivity and the problems of a mother/daughter reunion help to keep intact barriers between women, and no notion of rest is provided by that image. The central female subject is concerned to keep herself in a position of stability and prosperity. This position is available only at the cost of effacing and eradicating other subjects, through which the central narrator enriches and enhances her self. However, the daughter is not so easily ejected or annihilated. These confrontations between mother and child introduce a site of unmanageable instability, one which cannot simply retranscribe the Other in race or class terms. To this extent, they could be said to be the point at which the novel's own project of cohesion breaks down. In *Roxana*, Roxana/Susan's daughter occupies the position of double, sharing and repeating the same name. Her murder breaks the mother's heart, and the novel ends on a note of tragedy and great personal suffering. The romantic heroine is born. The Other, that which has to be effaced in order for stability to be achieved, cannot remain in easily identifiable and *external* positions. A Family Romance is created to show the Other as part of self, and the impossibility of a complete separation of self and Other. Susan kills Susan, and the emotional turmoil, loneliness and despair of the last pages of the novel portray a truly suffering subject, locked in her own world of suffering and penitence. Newgate and Virginia have been incorporated, as it were, into the identity of the narrator.

Roxana records the transference of the world of adventure of the novel from remote islands and deep tropical forests to adventurous sex. This shift also shifts the terrain of the novel to centre on women. The capitalist amassing of wealth is accompanied by sexual pleasure, and women range over this domain, as both objects and seekers of pleasure. Flux, fluidity, danger and excitement are now centred on the figure of the woman. A female-narrated novel becomes an exciting and dangerous site, evoking pleasure. Remember how Locke had explained the failure of the exact word/object schema as the result of deception and play, of the creation of an area where words became self-referential, and playing with words the object of their use. In that formulation, eloquence, the deceptive and pleasurable use of words, had been compared to the female sex.

Novels, appealing to both fact and fiction as their reference points, soon merged with that deceptive sex to create the dominance of women as producers, theme and consumers of the genre.

Roxana explores structures that define identity, to finally create a subject whose inner emotional self is radically separated from her social position of prosperity and ease. The split female subject has emerged. The search for identity had posed other female identities against whom the narrator had placed herself. Amy, the maid, had provided sisterly companionship and a sharing of adventures, but the text had never worked to bring the two women together. Other women emerge only to separate this 'core' relationship. Roxana, a fantasised Turkish woman, lends to our English heroine an exotic and exciting persona which raises her to a height in the sexual/social sphere. The 'real' Roxana – the woman whose costume alone appears in the text – is effaced, lost at sea or enslaved. The imaginary exotic persona becomes, ironically enough, the strongest identification mark for our heroine, who is then recognised by her daughter (the female child) in that garb. The original mother/child dyad is evoked through that Other woman. No other sites are available, and every image is destroyed, while the heroine goes on to rise as the capitalist, bourgeois woman.

Roxana provides no site of rest or peace: it is truly about the impossibility of authentic identity.

4

CHARLOTTE BRONTË/
CURRER BELL

Sexuality, the text
and the woman novelist

The readings of *Oroonoko* and *Roxana* give a background for a new reading of the nineteenth-century novel. Read as 'origins', these texts – the first English novel (*Oroonoko*) or a female-narrated novel by the first 'recognised' English novelist (*Roxana*) – show together how themes of gender, race and class intersect to produce the central subject who weaves the narrative. It is against this background that I would like to place Charlotte Brontë's novels: that is, to show that she inherited and worked within a form of writing that had been set up around the notion of a coherent, consistent narrating subject, often female, who was constructed by the effacement of *Other* subjects. That many of these narrative voices were female has detracted critical attention from the imperialistic and oppressive factors within the genre. The novel does not work in a simple way: female-narrated or authored, speaking to other women. It is part of a discursive terrain in which the ideal, unified Enlightenment subject is placed, where a fantasy of unity is created by the invocation and subsequent obliteration of the Other subject, differentiated by class, race and gender.

Charlotte Brontë's novels have provided, for feminist literary criticism, a point for the launching of the search for the original feminist novel, in which female desire or the voice of femininity speaks out. The shifts and movements in the feminist appropriation and celebration of the Brontë writings reflect a shift in the reading of the novel as a realistic genre to the more recent reading of it as a blend of factual and fictional modes. They also reflect a shift in feminism's own changed and changing attitude towards the status of female narratives as realistic delineations of women's actual lived situations, as well as to the status of fantasy and desire within these discourses.

Let us look at the critical history of the reception of the Brontë writings before going on to the actual readings of the texts. This history is linked to the eighteenth-century novelistic mode, and shows how the genre is mainly concerned with the narrating subject and the ways in which its homogeneity may be established and maintained. I have looked at this history as divided into two broad categories or periods. First, the contemporary, nineteenth-century responses to the novels of Charlotte Brontë are used to provide a link with eighteenth-century modes of novel writing, and to foreground the notion of a central narrating subject. While providing these links, these critiques also reveal the changes in the relation between the text, the author and the narrative voice.

Woolf's famous diatribes against Brontë will provide the background for the second period. The feminist celebration of the Brontës (exemplified in writings by Showalter, Moers, Gilbert and Gubar) appear as a response to Woolf's castigations of the Brontë writings. Modern-day feminist writings about the Brontës mark the third stage of the feminist response, and can be traced to the Marxist–Feminist Literary Collective's 1978 presentation to the Essex Conference. This response challenges the earlier celebration, which had unquestioningly drawn a realist link between the narrative novelistic voice and the lived realities of women's lives. The writings of Gayatri Spivak and Cora Kaplan, by bringing in concepts of class and racial division, have made a significant addition to the field of Brontë criticism. A subsidiary tradition that merges with the feminist is witnessed by the Marxist writers – Raymond Williams and Terry Eagleton – as well as the writings of Judith Lowder Newton.

The richness of the history of Brontë criticism affirms the significance of these writings within the historical and political framework that determines the reception of literary texts. This critical tradition, however, overlooks the imperial framework that informs the writing. Imperialism in the Brontë writings is part of the novelistic genre, and when placed against the background from which these writings emerged, the imperialism does not remain limited to colonialism as a *theme* in the novels, but becomes part and parcel of the genre itself. Moreover, the ignoring of this theme is a symptom of the limitations of feminist literary criticism, which needs to be (and is, in fact, in the process of being) redefined along these new lines.

The eighteenth-century novel set itself up as a discourse spun by a narrator, and as relating the 'truth' of a 'real' person's life. The status of the narrative as fictional or factual was dependent on the status ascribed to that narrating subject. In the nineteenth century – 'the great age of the novel' – the notion of reality was transformed into the more formalist concept of realism, and this realism, in turn, was made to rest on an author's personality and experiences. The authentic voice of the writer was now sought within a discourse which openly displayed itself as fictional. Life's 'truths' were somehow to be gleaned through the fictional prism.

Charlotte Brontë entered this arena disguised as 'Currer Bell'. The first published work, a collection of poems written by Currer, Ellis and Acton Bell, went more or less unnoticed (1846), but *Jane Eyre* (1847) made a great stir in the literary world of the day, and acquired what can today be called bestseller status. With this success came the search for the identity of the author. Questions of femininity and masculinity were brought to the fore, as the sex of the author was debated. Alongside this speculation was placed a notion of the 'sex' of the text as being dictated by that of the author. Author and text are thus equated, harking back to the eighteenth-century prefaces which had merged, through a convention of authorial disavowal, the text and the so-called 'real' person whose life they delineated.

This chapter uses a chronological sequence to divide the history of Brontë criticism into two parts: first, the contemporary response to the Brontës and second, the 'feminist' appropriation of Charlotte Brontë. The aim, in these readings, is to see the similarities and changes in the notions of sexuality, gender and a disruptive textual terrain. In each section I will be concentrating on *women's* responses, in order to bring out a sense of the community of women who can be seen to be reading these texts. What this process reveals is that delineations of female reality are not necessarily read with sympathy by *all* women, and neither does the textual realism of a woman's text appeal to all women. In the first section I shall mainly look at Elizabeth Rigby's celebrated *Westminster Review* essay on *Jane Eyre* (December 1848) in conjunction with Anne Mozley's *Christian Remembrancer* review of *Villette* (April 1853). The second section will read through the writings of avowedly feminist responses to Charlotte Brontë's works, drawing similarities and marking changes with the earlier contemporary responses.

A REVOLUTIONARY WRITER?

We do not hesitate to say that the tone of mind and thought which has overthrown authority and violated every code human and divine abroad, and fostered Chartism and rebellion at home, is the same which has also written *Jane Eyre*.

(*CH*, pp. 109–10)

This famous sentence considers the text dangerous for two reasons: as regards its contents, which are potentially subversive and revolutionary; and because the author's personal views are linked with the dangerous ideological standpoints expressed in the text. The text's 'tone of mind and thought' is related to the author, and the novel seen as the medium through which the author's political and social position is revealed.

A new notion of realism is visible here. Let us look briefly at the changes in the way that the relationship between reality and the text has been construed. The eighteenth-century concept of *vraisemblance* had operated to separate the novel from the romance. This concept highlighted the truth or 'reality' of the novel, which was then differentiated from romance on this basis. The appeal to reality was substantiated by the convention of the author's preface, used to disavow any but editorial responsibility for the ensuing manuscript, which could then be presented as a 'true' story told in the actual words of the protagonist. The blend of factual and fictional modes that the novel embodied emerged from this masquerade as 'reality'. By the middle of the nineteenth century, the notion of the 'reality' within a novel had been replaced by a notion of 'realism': that is to say, the reader and the writer are both aware that the novel is fictional – not real – but its value and excellence are judged on its nearness to reality. The identity of the author acquires a different significance, but nevertheless remains crucial. The excellence (or otherwise) of a novel is now judged on its closeness to the actual experiences of the author, so that a notion of reality – *vraisemblance* – remains central in determining the value of novels. The novel is still seen to be the authentic expression of the author's real experiences.

At the same time, however, and in a way which situates

Charlotte Brontë in the transition between these two concepts, the contemporary response to her novels is marked by constant allusion to their eighteenth-century origins. The two main concepts that this contemporary criticism draws on are (a) a notion of reality as it applies to the novel; and (b) a notion of adventure which characterised the central subject of novelistic discourse, an exploratory spirit that was constructed by the overcoming of known boundaries (in the sense of geographical exploration) and by transgression of established boundaries (in the image of the sexually promiscuous and 'free' woman). However, in the progress of the genre from the eighteenth to the mid-nineteenth century, both terms are transformed. Despite this change, the eighteenth-century roots are visible and constantly evoked in contemporary discourse around the novel.

The critical discourse around the publication of Charlotte Brontë's novels seems to place these texts within this shift. These novels are read for their expression of passion, and whether celebrated or castigated, this passion is related to the author's personality and biography.

This brings us to the second consideration: the author/experience/text equation, which, in the case of the androgynously named Currer Bell, is extended into a search for the sex of the author. The search for the author's identity, based on controversy over the author's gender, brings into the critical discourse a questioning of masculinity and femininity. The text, used to provide a clue to the sex of the author, is read to produce definitions of male and female. In the identification of the author with the text, the text becomes 'sexed', in that it provides evidence that unravels the mystery of the author's sexual identity.

Exploration, adventure and travel had been the main motifs in the early English novel. The progress of the novel, however, records a change of interest, and transforms that sense of adventure to adventurous and transgressive sexuality. Female-narrated and authored novels therefore became sites where sex as adventure connected female protagonists to the world of capitalist and colonial development of the time, while using that notion of a dangerous sexuality to put at risk the central narrating subject (mostly female). The dangers of sex are not limited to the external realm, which, unknown and unmapped, led the exploring subject to perilous areas, but are internalised: shown to exist *within* the subject herself. The disturbing and transgressive pollution Rigby condemned has been seen by other reviewers as a celebration of the outward-moving, adventurous and exploring spirit, and compared to the novels of Defoe (cf. *CH*, p. 101).

Rigby also compares *Jane Eyre* to an eighteenth-century novel – Richardson's *Pamela*. The *Quarterly* essay begins its analysis with this comparison, condemning both novels for their 'coarseness and laxity', which in Richardson could have been excused because of 'the manners of Richardson's time' (*CH*, p. 106). The dangerous revolution in the text is a social and sexual one, embodied in the marriage between a servant girl and her master. The review places *Jane Eyre* within a history of the novel which sees it as a form where sexuality is recalcitrant, disruptive and inimical to social order.

Pamela has also been read as a 'first' novel. Rigby's comparison draws *Jane Eyre* into the world of eighteenth-century writing. Ian Watt's *The Rise of the Novel* sees in *Pamela* the *first* instance of the conflation of 'high' and 'low' forms. A notion of sexuality and sexual morality, Watt shows, had been the mainstay of the romance. However, the honour, chivalry and female chastity of romance literature referred only to the upper classes. 'Opposed traditions' (the ballad, perhaps) dealing with people of humbler social origin, did not stress chastity and honour. The importance of Richardson's *Pamela* therefore lies in this

historical and literary perspective . . . Richardson's novel presents the first complete confluence of two previously opposed traditions in fiction: it combines 'high' and 'low' cultures, and, even more important, it portrays the conflict between the two.

(Watt, 1957, pp. 165–6)

The novel has been seen as a heterogeneous form of writing, straddling 'fictional' and 'factual' discursive terrain. Pamela, by combining two forms which differ in their class-based attitude towards sexual norms and rules, adds to this heterogeneity. The *Westminster Review* essay displays an uneasiness with this combination, and its dismissal of *Jane Eyre* rests upon ideas of class, sexuality and an upper-class scorn and disgust at the breakdown of social forms and decorum. This idea of a potential breakdown is also present in the emerging concept of the formal realism of the text.

REALISM AND THE NOVEL

Let us go back and review the changes in the notion of an author/ text/reality correspondence scheme between the eighteenth-century novels we have considered and the emerging notion of realism in nineteenth-century critical discourse. Female-authored and narrated eighteenth-century novels claimed verisimilitude and were presented as real by insisting that the stories they told recorded real events in the lives of real characters. This convention, in nineteenth-century terms, was transferred to a concept of realism which based its claims to reality on an appeal to the events of the author's life. In this formulation, despite fictional mediation, author and text remain one. While author and text are separated – the novel is no longer seen as an autobiography (author's or otherwise) – nonetheless, the text is still supposed to mirror the author's life, or his/her understanding of life.

The text, the author and society are now related to each other along lines of correspondence which are different from the eighteenth-century notion of an 'authentic' manuscript. This reflects a critical transformation in the perception of the blending of fact and fiction in the novel. Contemporary critical discourse around *Jane Eyre* reveals the changes in this position. First, the author/ text identification remains as a link between the author's biography and the text. Second, the novel, read as the narrative of an individual subject, makes that subject represent a 'real' character, and aspects of social reality are seen to be portrayed within the pages of a novel. Finally, the notion of the text as dangerous brings into focus the multi-faceted connections between the text and social, political reality. The text is dangerous because, while it reflects real events, it also contains the power to influence them.

Lukács's essay, 'Narrate or Describe?' (1936) perhaps best illustrates the changes in the author/text/reality correspondence scheme outlined by the nineteenth-century critical discourse. He links the more complex characterisation of the nineteenth-century novel directly to the more complex arena of social relations in which such a subject was placed:

> The relationship of the individual to his class had become more complicated than it had been in the seventeenth and eighteenth centuries. Formerly a summary indication of the background, external appearance and personal habits of an individual (as in Le Sage) had sufficed for a clear and com-

prehensive social characterisation. Individualisation was accompanied almost exclusively through action, through the reactions of characters to events.

(Lukács, 'Narrate or Describe?', in Kahn, 1978, *Georg Lukács, Writer and Critic*, p. 117)

The more complex social terrain in the emerging industrial order during the nineteenth century is seen to have found its perfect representational form in the realist novel, which was successful in penetrating the visible phenomena of social relations to decipher and delineate their underlying laws. In Lukács's formulation, the nineteenth-century novel is also seen as an integrative text where history is internalised in the 'consciousness' of the main character, who has not yet become prey to the alienation of subject and object characteristic of the modernist novel. Novelistic form emerges as a response to the changing social and political scene: 'Every new style is socially and historically determined and is the product of a social development' (Lukács, 1978, p. 119).

Lukács reads Walter Scott's *Old Mortality* as an example of a transitional text from the old feudal to the new industrial order, and of its corresponding social relations. Scott's artistry is a result of an understanding of the political and historical conjuncture which the text reconstructs: 'The artistry in his composition is thus a reflection of his own political position, a formal expression of his own ideology' (Lukács, 1978, p. 141). Author, text, character and social reality are placed along a continuum, and 'true' artistic expression results from the author's ability to mould and modify the form in a manner that reflects and 'truly' represents changing social and economic conditions. For Lukács, the nineteenth-century realistic novel provides an example of a successful blend of artistic representational form and a changing social order.[1]

Lukács's formulation thus places the subject of the novel (narrator and/or central character) as the repository of the ideological contents of the text. The critical discourse of realism re-establishes the centrality of the subject in the novel as the formal carrier of its ideological position. However, and paradoxically, the realist text itself is seen to be the product of a change, of the transition from feudalism to industrial capitalism. It is placed within a historical moment that is replete with contradictions, heterogeneous, containing both feudal residue and embryonic capitalist forms.

What nineteenth-century realism reflects and represents is social and historical contradiction and difference. The homogeneity of form and content refers to a heterogeneous arena of content, and so the desired coherence of form is not attained.

SEXUAL IDEOLOGY AND THE CONTEMPORARY CRITICAL SCENE

Lukács's concept of realism relates the ideological positioning of the novelistic text to the position of the central subject, who, as narrator, relates the events of the narrative, or, as central character, is its chief protagonist. Contemporary critical discourse attributes a sexual ideology to the writings of Charlotte Brontë. Her texts are used to provide clues to the solution of the mystery of the androgynous *nom de plume*, and for deciphering the real identity, sex and name of the author. The sexual ideology and the gender position of the subject of the novel, especially in *Jane Eyre*, is extended to include the author, and the author and text are connected in a linear scheme whereby the views presented in the text are directly related to her. Text and author are now linked to a notion of sex that is seen as subversive and dangerous for its transgression of social boundaries.

It is interesting to note how the many descriptions of masculinity and femininity that the search for Currer Bell generates are related to a class-based definition. The text is read as dangerous for its subversion of sexual decorum. The notion of sexual decorum is closely related to, and springs from, definitions of class. To quote Elizabeth Rigby again:

> no woman trusses game and garnishes dessert-dishes with the same hands, or talks of so doing in the same breath. Above all, no woman attires another in such fancy dresses as Jane's ladies assume . . .

> (*CH*, p. 111)

Social forms and graces – culinary etiquette and fashion – are brought to bear on this definition of womanhood. Women are limited to cooking and dressing in this description, and the desired propriety of forms presupposes prior agreement regarding them. A class-based snobbishness dismisses off-hand those women who are unaware of such forms.

Other women critics not only dismiss Charlotte Brontë because of her neglect of social mores and forms, but see this lack of propriety as extending to the portrayal of women's emotional lives. Anne Mozley, writing about *Villette* in the *Christian Remembrancer* (April 1853), compares the baring of women's emotional lives to the public revelation of a woman's sex life and secrets. Women writers, says Mozley, betray their own cause when they show 'that women give away their hearts unsought as often as they would have us believe' (*CH*, p. 207).

Passionate effusiveness is dismissed as unfeminine, and contrasted with dominant Victorian notions of passive and demure femininity. Women's novels are transgressive in that they overlook these proscriptions and, most unashamedly, lay the female heart open to public view. Moreover, this unravelling is likened to a public undressing, which is inimical to female subjectivity as a whole – for the author, the character and the woman who reads the text. The novels of Manley and Behn had been scandalous in the voyeuristic invitation they extended to their readers. Now a similar unease is expressed at the baring of a woman's emotional life. This is what leads the *Christian Remembrancer* article to castigate women writers for revealing the secrets of the female heart. The expression of female emotion and passion is dangerous for the woman. In relation to femininity, therefore, the formal concept of the novel as correspondence or revelation is seen to contain its own element of risk.

Femininity, in Rigby's article, is associated with decorum and restraint, echoing dominant definitions of Victorian womanhood. Yet at the same time femininity is posited as the unconscious, original, even undifferentiated state, and identified as passion and emotion – an 'authentic' and undiluted, although risky or transgressive, mode of expression. Rigby condemns *Jane Eyre* for its neglect of the first kind of femininity; the presence of the second notion of femininity is manifested as a lack of artistry, so the 'spontaneity' of the writing is not appreciated:

> It bears no impress of being written at all, but is poured out rather in the heat and hurry of an instinct, which flows ungovernably on to its object, indifferent by what means it reaches it, and unconscious.
>
> (*CH*, p. 110)

Anne Mozley similarly takes up the idea of feminine spontaneity

as disruptive and criticises the novel as too raw and autobiographical:

> The defect of the plot is a want of continuity. In fact, the
> style is rather that of an autobiography – and, perhaps,
> excusable as adopting that form – than a novel.
>
> (*CH*, p. 204)

It is rather as if femininity sets the limits to the formal realism
of the nineteenth-century novelistic text. The novel should delineate a life but in a form which *contains*, as much as *reproduces*, it.
The novel is on a continuum with the author, but too close a
proximity, when linked to femininity, produces not verisimilitude
but a lapse from the established ideals of femininity. This idea is
related to, while contrasting with, a developing conception which
reappropriates the link between femininity and spontaneity as part
of a realist conception of the novel as the privileged form for
capturing 'true life'.

The project of realism celebrates emotional appeal in novels,
and associates this appeal with the emotions and passions of both
writer and readers, who are, in turn, related to a sensibility that
observed, and therefore could describe, every aspect of human
life. The congruence of author and text was then extended to
include the reader, whose appreciation of the novel was based
on his/her ability to understand and identify with the emotions
delineated. Novels expressed 'the philosophical skills . . . and the
experience or sagacity of the hand that delineates (W. P. Scargill,
'Novel Writing', *The Athenaeum*, 9 November 1833, in Olmsted,
1979, *A Victorian Art of Fiction*, vol. 1, p. 143). Novel-readers
were appealed to on the basis of shared human experiences and
emotions: novel reading is seen to have 'reference to mind and
human feelings, emotions, interests, or passion; and it is in this
class that are found common novel readers in abundance' (*The
Athenaeum*, 14 September 1833, in Olmsted, 1979, p. 138).

The shift from eighteenth-century novelistic concepts of reality
to the nineteenth-century emphasis on social realism, is extended
to include the reader in active collusion with the writing. The
fiction becomes a means of direct communication between the
writer and reader, drawing on the experience of both. Despite
the *formal* difference, the eighteenth-century appeal to reality lives
on in the realist conception of the novel in the mid-nineteenth

century, as this concept is based on an equation of author with text.

Charlotte Brontë found in George Henry Lewes a consistent admirer of her writings.[2] His reviews show this concept of realism most clearly: here the excellence of the novels is judged by reference to a notion of realism which springs out of the author's circumstance of life:

> Reality – deep, significant reality – is the great characteristic of the book. It is an autobiography, – not, perhaps, in the naked facts and circumstances, but in the actual suffering and experience. . . . This gives the book its charm: it is soul speaking to soul; it is an utterance from the depths of a struggling, suffering much-enduring spirit . . .
>
> (*CH*, p. 84)

This is in direct contrast to Rigby or Mozley, who had condemned the autobiographical qualities of the writing as revealing a lack of artistry and sophistication. Lewes's own earlier advice (both in his letter to Charlotte Brontë and in his *Jane Eyre* review), was that the 'authoress' should look unwaveringly on reality. That earlier recommendation for an all-seeing objective vision is transformed into an unproblematic merging of the author's thoughts and feelings with the reality of the text.[3]

LOVE AND THE WOMAN NOVELIST

Nineteenth-century critical discourse defined femininity as delicacy, passion and most significantly, as spontaneous and uncontrolled expression. Masculinity, on the other hand, was defined as strength, coarseness or rational control. Uncontrolled spontaneous writing, allied with femininity, was further identified with the perils of textual utterance, which are seen to originate in areas which spelt danger for the coherence and consistency of both the text and its narrator.

Contemporary literary critical discourse at times attributed a revolutionary potential to this transgressive femininity. In Currer Bell's case, the identity of the author was associated, crucially, with the gender of the person hidden behind the pseudonym. The critical debates veered around the connections between femininity and writing, and the mystery of the androgynous pen name gave a new and sexual dimension to the search for the author's identity. As a result of this, Charlotte Brontë's writings, especially *Jane Eyre*, attracted many women readers, who responded to these writings as a discourse that spoke specifically and directly to them. Twentieth-century feminist responses have taken a similar attitude towards these writings, and engage with the text with a sense of emotional and personal identification. However, women's responses (as in the contemporary critical arena) are not necessarily approving, and vary from a celebration of the feminism (seen in the demand for the greater rights and autonomy for women) to a problem with the delineations of female desire within the Brontë texts. Virginia Woolf's famous remarks are the most apt point from which to begin a review of feminist responses to Charlotte Brontë:

> The drawbacks of being Jane Eyre are not far to seek. Always to be a governess and always to be in love is a serious limitation in a world which is full, after all, of people who are neither one or the other . . .
> (Woolf, '*Jane Eyre* and *Wuthering Heights*', in Woolf, 1979, p. 128)

An excess of passion and an inordinate dwelling on the emotional aspects of life are condemned as being limiting and not truly representative of female lives. Woolf's reading of Brontë is meant to draw attention to the limitations of the text and its neglect of wider social and political interests. However, this accusation of neglect springs from Woolf's overemphasis on the sexual and romantic theme of the novel in general, and *Jane Eyre* in particular. Charlotte Brontë is also accused of an unwarranted obsession with female deprivation. Woolf's description of *Jane Eyre* as a partial delineation of woman's condition has been similary criticised, and seen by Adrienne Rich, for example, as a result of a partial reading that 'often recalled and referred to [the Thornfield episode] as if it *were* the novel *Jane Eyre*' (Rich, 1980, *On Lies, Secrets and Silence*, p. 96). Rich extends her attention beyond the love story to other episodes in the novel, specifically those relating to female friendships, to discover and delineate a 'sisterhood' in the text.

It is interesting to note how both Woolf and Rich express a similar unease with the passion in the novel as Rigby or Mozley. Woolf expresses the same reservations as Rigby: Jane Eyre's passion (always in love) and her marginalised social positioning (always a governess) results in a flawed narrative, which is suffused with personal anger and longing. Adrienne Rich looks away from the Thornfield episode and concentrates on the establishment of the female subject in the novel. In her reading, the love story is important as it brings the female protagonist closer to a recognition of her self – her 'Jane Eyre-ity'. Rich's reading, though expressing the same unease about the transgressive sexuality, is different from that expressed by Woolf or contemporary nineteenth-century female readers, in its celebration of the social protest in the text. However, its denial of centrality to the love story expresses the same discomfort with female sexuality and desire.

The text, oscillating between an expression of revolutionary feminist demands and a complicit desire, poses a problem for its feminist readers. Rich's reading detracts from, while Woolf concentrates on, the love story. Both are, however, uncomfortable with it. Later critics are equally disturbed by this oscillating movement, and see Jane Eyre's success in its resolution of these opposing tendencies. The happy ending is often read as the resolution of the heroine's conflicts. Sexual desire, often equated with madness and symbolised by the figure of Bertha Mason, is forcefully and violently removed, to bring about the happiness and repose of the last scene. Elaine Showalter's influential reading of *Jane Eyre* thus reads the Ferndean scenes as a union between the romantic hero and heroine, which is based, crucially, on the eradication of the 'madness' in Jane (Showalter, 1977).

Showalter's reading necessitates the eradication of female sexual passion, which is associated with madness. Madness and sexuality are, in turn, invested in the figure of the Other woman. Sexuality, equated with madness, creates unease and tension, and is forcefully ejected for social and personal harmony to reign. Sexual passion has thus to be denied to enable the woman to emerge as triumphant and coherent.

This phase of feminist criticism was concerned to establish the female subject-under-construction in Charlotte Brontë's novels in a harmonious and cohesive position. Kate Millett's discussion of *Villette* provides a good example of this. *Villette* is the only novel, in fact the only text of any kind, written by a woman to be considered in *Sexual Politics* (1969). Millett sees *Villette* as an impassioned plea made by a woman living in a male-dominated society. The text is the expression of a deprived and subordinated person. The speaking voice is seen as directly addressing the reader, drawing his/her attention to the 'condition of woman' in the nineteenth century. Millett's celebration of *Villette* rests on the centrality ascribed to the 'I/eye' of Lucy Snowe:

> She is a pair of eyes watching society; weighing, ridiculing, judging. A piece of furniture whom no one notices, Lucy sees everything and reports, cynically, compassionately, truthfully, analytically.
>
> (Millett, 1971, p. 140)

The narrative voice in *Villette*, identified with Lucy Snowe, is seen as impartial and objective. However, the marginalised position of the narrator must be emphasised: she is 'a piece of furniture', outside the main focus of the narrative world. This marginalisation is read as emblematic of women's position in Victorian England. *Villette*, written *by* a woman, using a female narrative voice, is then read as a direct and simple reflection of the author's understanding of her social/sexual position.

Male literary criticism is criticised for its unsympathetic treatment of the Brontë texts and for including biographical references in its reading. Male critics concentrate on the lack of artistry, and are set on proving that 'they can't write and are hopeless primitives'. The male critic is seen in the role of 'a schoolmaster' who castigates these 'case histories from the wilds', but who is actually afraid that 'Charlotte might "castrate" them or Emily "unman" them with their passion' (Millett, 1971, p. 147).

The terms in which Millett lashes out at the male literary critical establishment echo the factors that characterise colonial encounters. The woman novelist is looked upon as an unsophisticated, uncivilised 'primitive', who needs training and education – the envisaged role of the critic as schoolmaster.[4]

The educational project directed towards the female novelist – the Brontë sisters in this case – is based on a colonial fear, of being unmanned and castrated. Millett herself falls into a biographical way of looking at the texts, in her reference to the 'house of half-mad sisters with a domestic tyrant for a father' (Millett, 1971, p. 147) as her vision of the place where the novels were written. More crucially, in the celebration of the impartial gaze of Lucy Snowe, Millett inherits many of the formal concepts on which these earlier criticisms were based. The realism in the novel is connected to the author's experience, translated into the world of the text and then read by the sympathetic reader as the true account of a Victorian woman's life. The notion of realism posited by G. H. Lewes and the contemporary Victorian critical reception of the Brontë novels has not really changed in this reading.

Some of the terms that mainstream feminist criticism inherited from the nineteenth-century response are visible in the discomfort with the expression of female sexuality and transgressive desire. Even the celebration of these writings (in Rich, Showalter, Gilbert and Gubar) cannot easily deal with the expression of feminine passion. Thus, Showalter insists on the obliteration of *dark* passion and sexuality as a prerequisite for the triumph of the female subject.

The centrality given to the female narrator in early feminist critiques and the homogeneity presupposed between female author and text are questioned by later feminists, who concentrate on the fluctuations in the narrative position. Psychoanalytical theories about the construction of the human subject are used to look at the fragmented and divided voice, which, ranging over contradictory positions, can never be seen as cohesive and harmonious. The Marxist–Feminist Literature Collective's presentation to the Essex Conference in 1978 focused on the processes of fragmentation and break-up that bring the central narrative voice in the Brontë novels into operation. The speaking voice in *Villette* is now noted not only for its expressed positions, but also for what is repressed and not articulated – the silences and gaps in the text.

The recognition of the impossibility of a coherent subject-position has led to an examination of the split subject, and the class and race significance of such a subject-position for feminism. This is illustrated in Cora Kaplan's article, 'Pandora's Box' (1986), which draws together and differentiates between two feminist readings of *Villette* (by Mary Jacobus and J. L. Newton) in terms of their attitudes to the romanticism in the text. Kaplan reads this difference in attitude as symptomatic of the differences in feminism's efforts to define the category of woman.

The two letters that Lucy Snowe writes to Graham Bretton form the basis for Jacobus's reading of *Villette*, which follows on from the Marxist–Feminist Literature Collective's 1978 presentation.[5] One is written for the recipient, while the other, written secretly, is buried and read by no other eyes than the sender's.

This buried, hidden letter is identified as the Other, the site that is repudiated, but which, nevertheless, remains intact, erupts into the text, breaks, and most crucially, *effects* the enunciation. The text is seen to be divided along lines of romanticism and realism, and to exist within a split, fissured and fragmented terrain. *Roxana* had been read as the discourse of a subject split between an inner, secret world of grief and a life of ease, plenty and comfort. Similarly, *Villette* is read as a text where the inner, secret self interrupts and disturbs the public, rational discourse being written. Thus, textual fissures are associated with gaps in the subject-position of the narrator.

Newton's more materialistic reading of *Villette* also sees the text as divided along lines of romanticism and realism. However, it tends to see the romanticism as dangerous and subversive, and as inimical to the position of the female heroine, an expression of regressive desire. The disruptions in 'the progress of the narrative' result from the contradiction between felt oppression and a complicit desire. 'It is this contradiction', writes Newton, 'which makes of *Villette* a lesson in the virulence of the enemy within and a demonstration of the fact that intuition of oppression does not make for easy protest' (Newton, 1981, *Women, Power and Subversion: Social Strategies in British Fiction 1778–1860*, p. 99).

Romanticism is seen as the enemy within, the factor that has to be destroyed for the triumphant female heroine to emerge. While the two readings differ along the lines that Kaplan has pointed out, both nevertheless testify to the difficulties in obliterating Other positions, as these are *internalised* to form the identity of the subject as well as of the narrative. Thus the inner secret enemy, the romantic self of the Gothic heroine, cannot be completely extricated, and constantly pushes against the textual surface to disrupt and interrupt the narrative of her growth. The either/or-ism of each of the readers could be said to illustrate the failure of a straight linear progression in the Brontë text.

CLASS, RACE AND THE FEMINIST CRITIC

The woman writer who allows her femininity full rein 'will write in a rage where she should write calmly', writes Virginia Woolf. Further, 'She will write foolishly where she should write wisely' (Woolf, 1977, *A Room of One's Own*, p. 67). The rage and passion in her work – the 'spasm of pain' (ibid., p. 70) – are a result of an undue concentration on the marginalised and sexual position of women. This divisiveness, writes Woolf, disturbs the attention of the reader:

> The desire to plead some personal cause or to make a character the mouthpiece of some personal discontent or grievance always has a distressing effect as if the spot at which the reader's attention if diverted were suddenly twofold instead of single.
>
> (Woolf, 1979, p. 47)

The desired unity of reading that Woolf suggests can only result from a writing that ignores or remains unaware of social divisions and grievances.

That is why Brontë's expression of female anger and rebellion can be compared to that of the working-class or the Black man. No man 'unless, indeed, he happens to be a working-man, a Negro, or one who for some other reason is conscious of disability' (Woolf, 1979, p. 47) would write in this manner. This startling comparison is not drawn to show how social structures create these subordinate groups, but lays the onus on the groups to overcome their positions of inferiority and to attain that unified position that is available, according to Woolf's own arguments, to men of the ruling class only.

The comparison between the writings of Blacks and women brings back into focus the relationship between the writing, narrating subject and language, as well as the notion of the formation of the subject within language and other representational systems. A hierarchised social system places its subject in positions of inferiority and subordination. The expression of this subordinate subject, by calling too much attention to his/her deprivations and injustices, would create disruption and disturbance rather than effect a comfortable, easy and harmonious form of expression. The insistence on unity, of narrative theme and subject, seeks to obliterate the expression of texual and social divisions.

Ellen Moers, writing in 1963, also makes a comparison between the concepts of race and gender in fictional writing. However, she bases her comparison on writings *about* Blacks and women, rather than *by* them. By comparing *Jane Eyre* and Harriet Beecher Stowe's *Uncle Tom's Cabin*, she links the 'language of rage' that characterised anti-slavery writings to the feminist protest in women's writings. The dangers of *Jane Eyre*, as perceived by

Woolf, inhere in the language of social protest, and are therefore akin to the 'panoramic pamphleteering' of *Uncle Tom's Cabin* (Moers, 1980, *Literary Women*, p. 15). The metaphor of slavery is transferred to femininity and the condition of women. The comparison with *Uncle Tom's Cabin* might, however, suggest a similar form of social unsettling in the two novels.

Uncle Tom's Cabin, first published in serial form in an abolitionist journal, the *National Era*, in 1851, is comparable to *Oroonoko*.[6] Written by a white woman, it is a sentimental delineation, informed by Christian notions of charity and humility, of the lives of slaves in antebellum America. The plot is replete with accounts of runaway slaves, cruel and kind white masters, instances of miscegenation, and so on. What remains in the minds of the reader, and symbolises the text in the popular imagination today, is the episode in which Uncle Tom (the Black slave) rescues little Eva (the rich, virtuous, little white girl) from drowning. The figure of the Black man is juxtaposed with that of the white girl and painted in terms of paternalism. However, the novel makes clear that this paternalism emanates not from the man, but from the girl who reflects, in a benign and feminine fashion, the authority of her father. Ambiguity of gender roles reinforces the racial motif. *Uncle Tom's Cabin*, despite its popularity, has never been read unproblematically as an abolitionist novel. The problems with that genre have been amply pointed out (by Wylie Sypher and Maureen Duffy); comparison with *Jane Eyre* serves to demonstrate how a 'feminist' text operates in the same manner as one that rests on the polemics of the anti-slavery movement in America. The problems with that delineation cannot be ignored and crop up whenever the novel is discussed (cf. Sundquist (ed.), 1986, *New Essays on 'Uncle Tom's Cabin'*). Rachel Bowlby, in a more recent article ('Breakfast in America' in Bhabha, 1990, *Nation and Narration*), looks at the novel for the notion of femininity portrayed within it, and to show how this notion is divided along lines of racial origin. Thus, Eva is contrasted to Topsy, and the differences between the two girls are seen to represent 'two irreconcilable theories of what makes a human being' (ibid., p. 201). Definitions of woman and femininity are divided along racial lines, and a notion of 'original' difference posited as dividing the two races.

Stowe's *Key* to *Uncle Tom's Cabin* unquestioningly accepts prevalent attitudes towards Blacks, and is based on a biological explanation of racial difference:

> The vision attributed to Uncle Tom introduces quite a curious chapter of psychology with regard to the negro race and indicates a peculiarity which goes far to show how very different they are from the white race. They are possessed of nervous organisations peculiarly susceptible and impressible. Their sensations and impressions are very vivid, and their fancy and imagination lively. In this respect, the race has an Oriental character, and betrays its tropical origin . . .
>
> (Stowe, 1975, *A Key to Uncle Tom's Cabin*, p. 276)

This description of Blacks as emotional and sensitive contrasts them with the 'cool, logical and practical' (Stowe, 1975, p. 277) Anglo-Saxon. Again, this drawing of Black and white in oppositional positions has the effect of feminising the Black man, thereby justifying his subordination. Ellen Moers's comparison of *Jane Eyre* with *Uncle Tom's Cabin* places the former within a mode of writing where social differences, though the object of protest, remain unquestioned, and are therefore far from transformed.

Both comparisons (by Moers and Woolf) of Charlotte Brontë's novels with those written by or about Black men/people link sexual and racial subordination. *Jane Eyre* remains central in this context, as it has provided the most potent and powerful fictional portrayal of the Other subject, in terms both of gender and race. The figure of Bertha Mason, repository of a sexuality whose *darkness* is read as dangerous, has recently been reread, by a discourse informed by colonial history, as the obliteration and obfuscation of the Other woman within the pages of a famous female-authored novel. Rhys's rewriting of *Jane Eyre* as *Wide Sargasso Sea* tries to bring the Other woman into the speaking position. As Spivak points out, that Other woman cannot be given the central role in the novel, which remains a discourse of the Enlightenment subject. I shall extend this reading of Bertha Mason as Other to show how the Other, present in *all* Brontë texts, is given different status: sometimes as savage, sometimes as savage woman, sometimes as madness and at others as a transgressive sexuality.

Feminist literary criticism has used Charlotte Brontë, and specifically *Jane Eyre*, to formulate a feminist notion of a female

107

subject. A recognition of the revolutionary potential in the text has often rested on a misrecognition. On the one hand, there is the direct feminism of the novel, which, given the historic time of its publication, corroborated a class revolution that was already disturbing the social and political arena. The Marxist–Feminist Literature Collective therefore compares the Brontë texts to the spectre of social unrest and revolution (1978). On the other hand, the notion of a transgressive, dangerous, exciting and adventurous female sexuality had been a part of the discourse since the eighteenth-century novels of Behn, Manley and Defoe. An uneasiness with female sexuality and desire had marked the reception of these novels, at the same time as many contemporary critics valorised the spontaneity and authenticity through which it was expressed. This notion of authenticity, now applied to femininity, has reverberations on the ways in which Blackness and savagery are represented in these texts.

I am going to read the Brontë novels as part of the imperialist motif of a genre in which a central subject seeks to establish itself through the eradication of Other subjects. Whether the narrative subject is male or female, the movement is always towards the obliteration of the Other, represented in terms of class, race or sex. Yet while it seeks to obliterate the Other, it is only in a dialectical relationship with that Other that it can define its own subject-position. The Other therefore impinges on the subject, creating disturbance and disrupting the stability it seeks. It is in the tension between these two moments – disturbance and obliteration – that I situate the fictional writings of Charlotte Brontë.

5

THE BRONTË CHILDREN
AT PLAY

The novel has progressed from an initial fascination with adventure in far-off lands and a portrayal of other cultures to sexual and social formations within the domestic setting. The Brontë writings partake of this trajectory, and traverse the same area as the novel. More crucially, they employ the primary narrative technique that is associated with the genre, that is, the use of a narrative voice, sometimes in the third and sometimes in the first person, weaving the representational form together. As such, the question of subjectivity remains central. Written by a woman, 'about' women, Charlotte Brontë's writings bring to the forefront issues concerned with the construction of a female subjectivity. These novels, while concerned with the independence and autonomy of their heroines, reveal areas of disjuncture and dislocation that such an establishment entails.

I will begin my examination of the Brontë writings with the juvenilia. From the host of complete and incomplete, published and unpublished material that forms the Brontë juvenilia, I will select some stories written by Charlotte Brontë. Lying prior to the published and mature work, the juvenilia throws up, most startlingly, the question of origins; on the one hand it provides an example of the development of an individual instance of writing (the growth of an author) and on the other, by its sheer heterogeneity and density, it provides the historian or biographer with a laboratory – a work in progress – from which different strands have to be untangled for the finished product to emerge. There is rich material here for the biographical critic exploring Brontëana, or for developmental theorists of childhood to look for growth patterns. Much Brontë criticism is marked by the excitement of finding another little scrap of paper containing yet

another story penned by these gifted children. Collections of the
Brontë juvenilia are usually accompanied by a biographical
account of the Brontës' childhood. For example, Fannie Ratchford's *The Brontës' Web of Childhood*, written in 1941, connects
the Brontë writing to events in their lives. This project is characterised by the unearthing and discovery of new and more authentic facts about the Brontës' lives. Christine Alexander has, more
recently, been on the rounds of the libraries looking for older
manuscripts, while rendering better versions of the ones already
published. The first volume of her *Edition of the Early Works of
Charlotte Brontë* (1987) contains manuscripts dating from the year
1826, going three years further back than Symington and Wise's
Shakespeare Head edition of the Brontë juvenilia (1936), which
had been the definitive collection of early Brontë manuscripts.
While this search for the 'real' Charlotte Brontë has provided the
Brontë scholar with invaluable material, it has not undertaken the
task of looking at these writings other than for their biographical
value.

The Brontë juvenilia shows, in microscopic form, the development of an individual practice of writing concomitant with the
development of the novelistic genre as a whole. It also brings
into doubt the notion of straightforward development, either of
a form of writing or of the individual subjectivity of the writer.
The juvenilia operates in a much more complex manner, mud-
dling the identity of the writers. Its characters have unfixed identities and dwell in unreal lands, where they meet with fantastic
adventures. It is difficult to glean autobiographical references from
these writings. Instead, they reveal the ways in which subjectivity
is mediated, and the processes and transformations that affect the
relationship between narrativity and subjectivity.

Biographical references can be used to show how this happens.
For example, Elizabeth Gaskell's description of the way Mr
Brontë made his children 'speak' is of direct relevance to the
notion of authorial identity and its connections with speech/
writing:

> When my children were very young, when, as far as I can
> remember, my oldest was about ten years of age, and the
> youngest about four, thinking that they knew more than I
> had yet discovered, in order to make them speak with less
> timidity, I deemed that if they were put under a sort of

cover I might gain my end; and happening to have a mask in the house, I told them all to stand and speak boldly from under the cover of the mask.

(Elizabeth Gaskell, 1914, *Life of Charlotte Brontë*, p. 58)

Mr Brontë's technique bears a striking resemblance to the methods used by Victorian social reformers and journalists as they probed into the disturbing aspects of nineteenth-century society. Mayhew's interviews with the needlewomen spring immediately to mind, as disguise and secrecy are felt to be necessary to unlock the flow of speech – 'to make them speak with less timidity'. The power relations in this 'incitement to speak' remain comparable: the adult male is given the powerful role of questioner, looking into the minds of his six young children, five of whom are female.[1] The above paragraph not only illustrates the ways in which speech is elicited from the power structures that constrain the speech act, it highlights another factor in the Brontë story which crucially allies it with fictional discourse as a whole. This is the element of disguise in speech, uttering forth 'from under the cover of the masks' – pointing towards the constraints of the enunciation, which, rather than being completely revelatory, has to hide behind masks and veils. This provides an early instance of the disguises the children donned before commencing their play. The elaborate and fluctuating pseudonyms the children apply to themselves, as well as the changing names they give their fictional characters, are later transformed into the pseudonyms the Brontë girls adopt for their published poems and novels. The Victorian female novelist takes on male pseudonyms not because she is shy about her writing, and wary about the opprobrium that it may bring her; more crucially, this disguise forms part of the foundation of her discourse, and her entry into the literary sphere is negotiated in a manner that compels her to hide, seek disguises, change names and baffle her audience. This, we have seen, is what happens in the history of the novel itself, where the eighteenth-century author had presented her/himself as a transcriber or editor, relating other people's true-life stories or editing somebody else's manuscript, and where the subject-positions of fictional characters are unfixed and moving.

The Brontë children at play provide an instance of the development of a practice of writing based on a juggling of the identities and subjective positions of both author(s) and characters portrayed. The children begin to write together in a joint venture, then split into pairs (Charlotte/Branwell, Emily/Anne). Finally, the women 'emerge' as 'individual' authors. The pairing according to contiguity in age is dropped during the publishing enterprise, as the women form a new collaboration to launch their first publishing venture. Gradually, this 'sisterhood' is dropped, and Charlotte 'emerges' as the 'individual' author.

The aim of the following examination is not to decipher, from within the density of the material, the growth of a practice of writing and of an author, i.e. Charlotte Brontë, but to see these stories as part of the novelistic project, similar to the novels that have already been looked at. The African theme will be highlighted with emphasis on the ways in which this fictional material and 'imaginary' land are located in physical and geographical terms. The stories are set in West Africa, enabling the texts to incorporate African and Oriental images, which can also be seen in Charlotte Brontë's mature work. African and Oriental images create textual heterogeneity. Of the various categories of difference, race operates more directly in the earlier juvenilia, whereas in the later writings, social difference and a notion of class positioning acquire importance. Both categories produce areas of ambiguity. Instead of creating neat hierarchical divisions, they work in an equivocal manner and produce, on one level, a feeling of anxiety and fear of the unknown and, on another, a feeling of triumph, based on a conquest of the Other.

The juvenilia will be divided into two parts to facilitate examination. A chronological sequence will be maintained, along with a simultaneous critique of the notion of development. First we will look at the early juvenilia, ranging between the years 1829 and 1833. The beginning of this period is marked by the first story that can be easily attributed to Charlotte Brontë. This period continues to the year 1833 – the 'halcyon period of her early juvenilia' – when her first fully formed stories were written. The second section will look at the later juvenilia – covering the years from 1835 to 1838, including some stories written in 1839, after which Charlotte Brontë stops writing stories based on the sagas inaugurated by the Glass Town adventures and the Angrian legends.

A COLONISING MISSION

The Early Juvenilia: 1829–33

Before looking at individual stories, some of the various strands that contribute to the composition of the dense material of the Brontë juvenilia will be untangled, to facilitate an understanding of the sequence of the texts, characters and events contained within them. Right at the inception of the play/writing, different games merge, making it difficult to untangle distinct stories. The final Glass Town Saga that emerges between the years 1829 and 1830 is an amalgamation of three separate plays: *The Young Men's Play* (June 1826), *Our Fellow's Play* (July 1827) and the *Islanders' Play* (December 1827). Similarly the collaborators change partners: Charlotte Brontë's first written and neatly hand-sewn piece of work is a story written at the age of ten and read to her sister Anne. It begins: 'There once was a girl and her name was Anne' (Alexander, 1981, p. 3); 'bed plays' which she shared with Emily are also mentioned: 'Emily's and my bed plays were established December 1, 1827; the others March 1828. Bed plays mean secret plays; they are very nice ones' (*SHCBM*, vol. 1, p. 1).

The games are played at varying levels of secrecy: the bed plays are completely secret, while the Glass Town Saga is a shared family secret. Again, the Glass Town Saga began as a communal game, with all the children participating. They gradually split into pairs according to age, Charlotte and Branwell and Emily and Anne forming the two pairs. However, as the bed plays reveal, this does not prevent the formation of other partnerships and games.

Both Branwell and Charlotte Brontë describe the commencement of *The Young Men's Play*. There is a discrepancy in the dates given by the two children: Charlotte dates the games as beginning from June 1826 (when Mr Brontë bought the soldiers from Leeds), whereas Branwell sets these events two years earlier, with the purchase of a different set of toy soldiers from Bradford. The difference in dates points to the tenuous nature of the collaboration. Though writing together, brother and sister differ on vital points. The games, later transformed into stories, were recorded in a magazine. To begin with, Branwell Brontë was its editor (from January to July 1829). This journal was first named *Branwell's Blackwood Magazine*. Charlotte Brontë changed its name in August 1829 to *Blackwood's Young Men's Magazine*, and in the following year, August 1830, it was renamed *Young Men's Magazine*.[2] The fluctuating names of the games and the magazines are echoed in the fluctuating names that the authors give themselves and their characters. In the beginning they take on the role of the Genii, naming themselves Anni, Emmi, Branni and Tanni. This gives a supernatural dimension to the game. Their names as authors follow this pattern of change. As editor of *Branwell's Blackwood Magazine*, Branwell's name is Sergeant Bud. As the editorship passes into Charlotte's hands, the signature UT or WT begins to appear – 'us two' or 'we two'.[3] Though recording the close collaboration between brother and sister, the ascendancy of Charlotte as editor, under the name of 'Captain Tree', is visible. By 1829, the chief characters in Charlotte Brontë's plays, the Duke of Wellington and his two sons, the Marquis of Douro and Charles Wellesley, are fairly well entrenched.

A Romantic Tale

One of the earliest stories that can be attributed to Charlotte Brontë is entitled *A Romantic Tale*, written on 15 April 1829. This tale is about Africa and about the problems of establishing colonial authority. It is signed Charlotte Brontë, and is not part of the magazines:

> This story is contained in a small manuscript booklet of 11pp entitled: 'Two Romantic Tales by Charlotte Brontë, April 28, 1829.
>
> (*SHCBM*, vol. 1, p. 13)

Consciously presented as Charlotte Brontë's 'individual' production, it nevertheless remains a part of the Glass Town Saga, and contains a description of the building of Glass Town/Verreopolis/Verdopolis, and an account of the heroic nature and exploits of Arthur Wellesley. At this point the collaboration is still strong, and it is difficult to disentangle the contributions of the brother and the sister. Joint and individual writings merge, and one remains a part of the other.

The fact/fiction blending in this story is also interesting. It purports to be based on another book: 'But I have read a book called the *Travels of Captain Parnell*, out of which the following is an extract' (*SHCBM*, vol. 1, p. 3). The book has not been located. Scholars such as Christine Alexander do not comment upon it, while Raymond and Hélène Bellour are not sure whether the book is real or fictitious.[4] References to other books and sources, as well as cross-references to their own or each other's writings, are a characteristic feature of the juvenilia. This makes it difficult to connect the children's reading material directly with the world of their writing. Ratchford, for example, lists *The Arabian Nights*, and 'titles by Bewick, Johnson, Scott, Byron and Southey' 'worn shabby by so much reading' (Ratchford, 1941, p. 4), as obvious sources for the children's world of fantasy. Moreover, the Keighley Public Library and the library of Ponden House also provided the children with books and reading materials, and *Blackwood's Edinburgh Magazine* is seen as the main source of inspiration and model, as evidenced in the name and the format that Branwell Brontë gave the early magazines.

A Romantic Tale records the journey of the twelves (represented by the twelve wooden soldiers), under the leadership of Arthur Wellesley, across the Atlantic, the landing on African shores and the settling of a colony there. The careful delineation of geographical facts imitates the articles appearing in contemporary issues of *Blackwood's Magazine*. The young authors map out, in physical terms, their fantasies and dreams, which then become the subject-matter for their games. The main characteristics of the early juvenilia are similar to those of the early novels: both are distinguished by stories of adventure, exploration, discovery and excitement.

Nearly every issue of the 'real' *Blackwood's Edinburgh Magazine* during the late 1820s and early 1830s contained articles dealing with the colonial question: debates regarding the efficacy of British territorial expansion, trade, slavery, on the phenomenon of displaced and mixed races and peoples and explorations in natural history and geography. The letters of one James Macqueen, published in the journal throughout the year 1831, defended the colonists against the malignant slanders by 'anti-colonists'. Macqueen's main argument was for the establishment and growth of British trade and wealth. Geographical explorations were crucial to this and were therefore dealt with in these letters in great detail. The interest in exploration is related to the task of bringing hitherto unknown areas into the realm of the mapped, identified and observed arena.

The significance of such explorations is well evidenced by *Blackwood's* sustained interest in the theme, starting perhaps with its June 1826 review of a book entitled *Narrative of Travels and Discoveries in Northern and Central Africa in 1822, 1823 and 1824*, written by Major Denham, Captain Clapperton and Dr Oudney (*BM*, no. cxii, vol. xix, June 1826, pp. 687–709). Moreover, the September 1829 edition contained an article entitled 'The British Settlement in West Africa', geographically locating the land of the Ashanti:

> Ashantee is a powerful and barbarous country situated in the interior of Guinea, to the south-east of Cape Court Castle.
>
> (*BM*, no. clvi, vol. xxvi, September 1829, pp. 341–50)

Geographical and historical resemblances between the fictional world of the Brontë juvenilia and its journalistic sources are easy to draw. Their wholesale incorporation into the juvenilia (albeit in a fictionalised form) not only illustrates a direct link between influences and writing, but also shows the participation of the juvenilia in the fact/fiction dichotomies of the novelistic genre. The adventure at sea takes place in the South Atlantic Ocean, as the twelves are blown from Trinidad to the land of the Ashanti. The geographical details are significant:

> Far off to the east the long black line of gloomy forests skirted the horizon. To the north the Gillel Kumnion [? Gibbel Kumnion] Mountains of the Moon seemed a misty girdle to the plain of Dahomey; before us to the west lay the desert.
>
> (*SHCBM*, vol. 1, p. 8)

Branwell Brontë's account of the settlement allies it with a romanticism and a magic based on its geographical remoteness and a notion of a 'lost' past glory. The memory (or image) of the vanquishing of a once-glorious African kingdom becomes symbolic of an impending and unavoidable sense of danger that the present kingdom is threatened by – a fear that this carefully built colony may relapse into the 'darkness' from whence it had emerged. The description of Glass Town harps on this sense of doom.

Enchantment and distance are allied, and are embodied in the Genii, who are the magical elements invoked to keep this impend-

116

ing danger at bay, and who help the twelves in the war against the Africans, in the building of Glass Town, and most importantly in the return of Arthur Wellesley to England. Links with England remain: Arthur Wellesley, now Duke of Wellington, is 'a fit and proper person to sit on the throne of these realms' (*SHCBM*, vol. 1, p. 13). This commingling of the fictional character with the 'real' Arthur Wellesley, Duke of Wellington, is effected through the use of names and titles. The juvenilia thus traverses and oscillates between contemporary Europe and the fictional African colony, keeping the fact/fiction dichotomy in the manuscript intact. This blend shows that one foot has to be kept in England for the success of these colonial adventures.

In *A Romantic Tale*, a great tower is built to secure the conquests of the twelves – the city (Glass Town) is supplied with a Hall of Justice and an Inn. Branwell Brontë describes this town as 'firm, complete and able *to resist all intruders*' (*SHCBM*, vol. 1, p. 77; emphasis added). Despite the architectural paraphernalia, a fear of the dangers that lurk beneath is ever present. The colony is beset by such fears. Thus Arthur Wellesley wonders, 'Does the King of the Blacks view our prosperity with other eyes than ours?' (*SHCBM*, vol. 1, p. 7). The pronouns in this rhetorical question stare the reader in the face – '*our* prosperity', '*other* eyes than ours'. Ties between the motherland and the newly established colony are irrevocably established – the riches of the '*new* world we have discovered' have to be secured with the help of an army from England. The security of the white settlers on the African continent is tenuous and held by various paraphernalia which are then identified as the forces of civilisation.

Charlotte Brontë's short description of the war with the Ashanti, gives the impression that the war was a swift and decisive affair. The Ashanti are portrayed as a strong and destructive force – they 'came on like a torrent, sweeping everything, and laying waste the rice-fields' (*SHCBM*, vol. 1, p. 10), so their easy and swift defeat seems a wish-fulfilment. The war cry – that 'terrible yell' – signals danger for the colonisers, wishing them to 'be consumed from the face of the earth' (*SHCBM*, vol. 1, p. 10).

External dangers are invested with a strange and unknown magic, and the buttresses against them have to be equally magical and supernatural. Magic is thus associated with both the alien Other and the friendly, supportive Genii. Branwell Brontë, who deals with the war in much greater detail than his sister, also portrays the victory of the twelves as decisive. The first encounter between the European adventurers and the natives of the land is described by Branwell. This encounter is recounted in terms that have been culled from the prevalent discourse of colonial conquest:

> they observed advancing from a distance a large party of savages, the first they had seen in the country. They were tall, strong, well-made and of a black or copper colour.
>
> (*SHCBM*, vol. 1, p. 78)

The instantaneous use of the word 'savage' defines the Ashanti, followed by a nearly anthropological description of their physical stature and colour.

The strange peoples met with in these new lands were always described as savages in the contemporary discourse, and set in positions of polar opposition to the white European explorer/trader/coloniser. In this scheme, India and America came to occupy opposite poles on the scale. Stone buildings, literacy or an 'ancient' heritage in India were used to classify the natives as 'civilised', while in the American encounter the absence of such artefacts was translated as classifying the inhabitants as uncivilised or savage. The criteria employed for making these judgements were fluid and attenuated at will. But as Peter Hulme points out, the notion of savagery, accompanied by the gradation of civilisations, was always brought to bear at every instance of colonial encounter, and territorial occupation, control of trade and the establishment of a colonial administration was accompanied by classification of the people met within these encounters (Hulme, 1986, *Colonial Encounters: Europe and the Native Caribbean*).

The colonial encounter in the Brontë juvenilia recognises the Ashanti as savage, and thus follows the pattern established in the contemporary colonial discourse. The 'factual' delineation of the Ashanti in the *Blackwood* article had focused on the 'savagery' of the people, who were classified as cannibals.[5]

In the juvenilia a supernatural element is added to highlight the distance between savagery and civilisation, as the Genii are called upon to defeat the Ashanti. Magical forces are invoked out of a feeling of insecurity, and from a sense of hidden threats and dangers. Branwell Brontë records an eight-year interval of peace, while in his sister's account the peace is shown to have lasted ten years. During this period, the Ashanti honour the truce under the mild and benevolent leadership of their King Cashna Quamina. Glass Town is built in this interval, a kingdom is founded and a colony set up. But underlying dangers continue to disturb: the old King dies, and the new King, his son, Sai Tootoo Quamina, is 'young, headstrong and revengeful' (*SHCBM*, vol. 1, p. 79). Sai Tootoo Quamina becomes transformed, in later stories, into the figure of Quashia, those 'eyes other than ours', who disturbs the peace and prosperity of the Glass Town heroes and heroines.

A Romantic Tale contains the major distinguishing features of the Brontë juvenilia. At the heart of the story lies a colonising enterprise and a triumphant tale of conquest and victory over alien and strange forces. However, behind this obvious buoyancy there is a feeling of unease and disturbance, marked by a fear of danger from outside (the unexplored and unsubdued natives) and from within (internal dissension, rivalries and corruption). The external danger is located in the strange terrain, and is gradually concentrated into the person of Quashia Quamina, who becomes emblematic of the recalcitrant savage. But external and internal factors do not remain so schematically marked off from each other, as the subsequent story of Quashia Quamina will show.

In the meantime, collaborative and individual writings continue. *Characters of its Celebrated Men* (December 1829) gives a list of the names of the more important personages in the Charlotte Brontë juvenilia. The most important characters listed are the Duke of Wellington, his sons the Marquis of Douro or Arthur Wellesley and Lord Charles Wellesley (often, at this stage, a pseudonym used by Charlotte Brontë), Captain Bud, Rogue, Naughty, Bady, Pigtail and sundry characters like Delisle, Le Brun, Dundee and Vennett (the list is in order of importance). As the year progresses, the pseudonym Captain Tree (which is also the name of one of the soldiers) is used most frequently by Charlotte Brontë. The two narrative personae she uses are male, but neither is the main protagonist in the stories. It is difficult to see the juvenilia as unadulterated and unedited outpouring. Charles Wellesley, as narrator, is merely an observer, while Captain Tree occupies the more formal position of editor. The narrative stance is that of reporting or observing 'other' stories. We have seen how such an editorial position had been taken by eighteenth-century novelists as well. In these stories, Glass Town and its environs are explored by Captain Tree in 'A Visit to the Duke of Wellington's Small Palace situated on the Banks of the Indiennes' (January 1830) or in 'The Frenchman's Journal' in the *Young Men's Magazine* (no. 4, August 1830).

The unveiling of the mystery surrounding the Brontë juvenilia hinges on the status of the signatures appended to the juvenile manuscripts. Fannie Ratchford talks about the gradual ascendancy of Charlotte Brontë and uses 'evidence[s] of Charlotte's improving hand' (Ratchford, 1941, p. 19) as the stories are shown to progress in chronological sequence and time. Christine Alexander follows this notion to extricate Charlotte Brontë's manuscripts to make the case of an author in progress. Despite these efforts, the collaborative nature of the production makes it impossible to separate manuscripts according to author. Tom Winnifrith even hints at possibilities of forgery on the part of Wise, one of the editors of the original Symington and Wise collection of the Brontë manuscripts (Winnifrith, 1973, *The Brontës and Their Background: Romance and Reality*, p. 16). Charlotte Brontë's signature on many of the manuscripts may have been superadded by the editor, as her work was considered more valuable than that of her siblings. The identity of the author of the manuscripts provides an interesting and absorbing literary puzzle, at the same time as it functions as a debating ground for the nature of the connections between the literary text and the author's identity.

Albion and Marina

The theme of romantic love and sexual longing is a part of this world of adventure, power play and the clash between two civilisations. Charlotte Brontë's novels are often read as the spontaneous overflow of female desire. The sexual theme in the juvenilia is seen as a source of Charlotte Brontë's mature love stories and as an even more undiluted utterance of female desire than is available in the novels. John Maynard, for example, claims that the juvenilia had escaped the Victorian censor – 'Brontë could and did write with freedom on issues of sex and scandal [in her juvenilia] that she . . . dared not exercise in published works (Maynard, 1984, *Charlotte Brontë and Sexuality*, p. 40). Sexuality is read as the subterranean region in her writings, which surfaces only for private publication.

The sexual elements and the colonial theme are related in the juvenilia as they both act as a point of dislocation and bring in questions of Otherness and desire, as well as of power and domination. Charlotte Brontë's first love story is *Albion and Marina*, written on 12 October 1830. This story separates her literary and imaginative efforts from those of her brother Branwell, whose contemporary writings, *Letters from an Englishman* (1830–3) dealt with military and state affairs. This separation follows a gendered pattern, the sexual interest and the love theme being attributed to the sister, while accounts of military exploits are Branwell Brontë's domain. However, the problems of identifying these writings as Charlotte Brontë's alone should be kept in mind. Also, the notion of development of an individual author, which guides most research into the Charlotte Brontë juvenilia, is more useful if applied to an examination of the imperialist motif, and the development of that motif within these writings.

The preface of *Albion and Marina* muddles the identity of the author. It claims that the story was written spontaneously, and even unconsciously: 'Many parts, especially the former, were composed under a mysterious influence that I cannot account for' (*SHCBM*, vol. 1, p. 24).[6] This preface is signed C. Wellesley, to which has been added a one-line comment: 'I wrote this in four hours – C.B.' (*SHCBM*, vol. 1, p. 25). Again, Captain Tree, the 'editor' of the *Young Men's Magazine*, appears within the text, commenting on the literary efforts of the Marquis of Tagus. The author enters in various guises – as Charlotte Brontë, Charles Wellesley or as Captain Tree. This uncertainty of identity also applies to the principal characters, whose names undergo a similar process of change. Thus the heroine's name Marina 'nearly resembles her true name' (*SHCBM*, vol. 1, p. 27). Albion, the hero, is also the Marquis of Tagus, and the text alternates between referring to him by his name and by his title. In this process an ambiguity of identity is created, as the young hero Albion simultaneously occupies the persona of the more stately Marquis of Tagus. The use of titles instead of names is a common device used by both Branwell and Charlotte Brontë in their childhood. The novelistic genre ascribes a lot of importance to names and naming, while it recognises the impossibility of ascribing definite names, symbolic of stability and sureness of identity, to the central narrative subject. A similar ambiguity is created by playing around with names in the juvenilia.

Albion and Marina enacts the love story at two levels. The separation between Albion and Marina is manifested as the distance between Africa, to which the hero is exiled, and England, where his lover resides. Africa is a strange and magical land, while comfort and ease are associated with England. Moreover, the love story does not represent or celebrate 'true' monogamous love, but is concerned with a triangular situation, in which the hero, Albion or Arthur Wellesley, Marquis of Douro, is torn between his love for the fair Marina and the attractions of the dark lady, Zelzia.

This dichotomy between the two women remains a constant feature, as later the Duke of Zamorna flits between Mary Henrietta and Mina Laury. The division is made along racial lines – Lady Zelzia, though not African, is dark and lives in that continent. In later stories, this difference is expressed in terms of class division. The varied and divided sexual terrain is always at the service of the male protagonist, who is free to cross racial and class barriers in search of sexual pleasure and excitement. Despite the emphasis on the difference between the 'dark' exotic pleasures of Lady Zelzia, and the peaceful comforts to be enjoyed in the company of Marian Hume, no *Black* woman actually enters the pages of the text. The same difficulties are met with as regards the portrayal of Black femininity as in *Oroonoko* or *The Isle of Pines*. The Black woman cannot be incorporated within representational forms, and she is made 'fair' to make her more recognisable and palatable. *Roxana* completely obliterated the Black woman, and used a white European woman to embody the mystery and sexual excitement normally attributed to the unknown and the foreign. Similarly, *Albion and Marina* refuses to look at the black woman and uses a white woman to represent that area. As we have seen, Imoinda in Southerne's dramatised version of *Oroonoko* had to be portrayed as a white woman, no actress being willing to 'blacken' up. Here we have another example of the 'whitening' up of the Black woman.

Albion and Marina is primarily a story of love and longing, of separation and desire. Marina remains in her little pastoral home in the south of England, while Albion is exiled to Africa. England and Africa are portrayed as polar opposites: a 'sweet little pastoral village in the south of England' whose homely qualities – 'little peaceful valleys, low hills crowned with wood, murmuring cascades and streamlets, richly cultivated fields, farmhouses, cottages, and a wide river' – hardly 'figure to advantage in a novel' (*SHCBM*, vol. 1, p. 25). The familiar is definitely precluded as an apt subject for a novel. Albion goes away to Africa, to far-off Glass Town, whose magnificence appears (to English people) as a 'dream or gorgeous fiction': 'It seemed as the cities of old: Nineveh or Babylon' (*SHCBM*, vol. 1, p. 29). The African town is like a dream, unreal, like the Oriental cities of ancient times – because in a way it is unreal, built by magic, to be wiped away eventually by the forces of darkness.

The love story related in *Albion and Marina* is enacted on two levels and echoes the polarity between the familiar and the strange. First there is Albion's undying love for the absent Marina. This spiritual and romantic love is contrasted to the physical charms of Lady Zelzia Ellrington. The 'darker', foreign qualities of Lady Zelzia are emphasised (as in the 'exotic' name). She is described as having 'jetty black' eyes and hair, and a 'dark glowing complexion' (*SHCBM*, vol. 1, p. 31).

In contrast, Marina is calm, pure, serene – the 'fair' Marina, with 'silver tresses' and a neck and forehead of snow' (*SHCBM*, vol. 1, p. 27). A dark, sensuous sexuality is associated with Lady Zelzia. She is fascinating and challenging, as is the African continent, while Marina, more homely and tractable, symbolises comfort and familiarity. The racial contrast gives a sexual dimension to political domination, where notions of racial difference and inequality play a central part. The security of the conquerors is constantly seen to be at risk. The jungle, the desert or the sea loom beyond fortified areas and provide a fearsome backdrop for these newly found colonies. Similarly, the notion of an unconfined, dark but highly desirable area of sexual pleasure holds an ambiguous promise. These fears are then embodied in, and projected on to, African lands and people, who, though easily conquered, cannot be contained, and therefore continue to disturb and distress. John Maynard's reading of the juvenilia as a way of expressing 'the complexity of her [Charlotte Brontë's] understanding of sexual experience' (Maynard, 1984, p. 3), overlooks the complexities of the textual processes that create this divided sexual terrain.

These two early stories establish the groundwork for our reading of subsequent narratives. Sexuality, racial difference, displacement, travel and conquests form the main ingredients of Charlotte Brontë's juvenile writings. The stories provide the reader with a unique glimpse of a genius in progress, but their greater significance lies in the colonising enterprise with which they are concerned. Eighteenth-century novels had been connected to the contemporary colonial enterprise. This same concern is reflected in the writings of the Brontë children, who frame their narratives around a colonising enterprise. The arena of adventure and sexuality or of an adventurous sexuality created by these narratives presents a savage Other as evocative of fear and desire, and proceeds to create an arena of sexuality, dangerous, transgressive and exciting, in which these fictional characters are immersed. The way that fluctuating pseudonyms are used to inscribe the children as authors and editors into the text brings in, but also troubles, the image of the writer as directly participating in the fictional terrain created.

Fluctuations in place names and names of characters remain a constant feature of the Brontë juvenilia. By the time *Visits in Verreopolis* is written (18 December 1830, two months after *Albion and Marina*), Glass Town has become Verreopolis, Lady Zelzia Ellrington has become Lady Zenobia Ellrington, and the characters introduced in *Albion and Marina* have also undergone a transformation. Marina is now Marian and alive (she had died during the course of the former story). Albion is still the main hero, but is now called Arthur Wellesley, Marquis of Douro. Young Soult (one of Branwell Brontë's pseudonyms) enters into the work. Lord Charles Wellesley, the author of the first volume (7–11 December 1830) takes on the florid appellation of the Honourable Charles Albert Florian Lord Wellesley (on 18 December 1830). Both Charlotte and Branwell Brontë play about with the names of authors and characters, sometimes applying to the author the name that appears within the text as a character, or using each other's pseudonyms for the fictitious characters in the stories. This process, together with the fluctuating pseudonyms they give themselves as authors, makes it impossible to identify the 'real' author of any specific story.

Given that the twelve toy soldiers were 'real', and that the first account in *The Young Men's Play* was perhaps a recounting of 'real' events, the connection with autobiography remains central in the search for the authors' identity. However, the fluidity of the genre – the novel being characterised by a reference to both

fictional and factual sources – dooms this search. Charlotte Brontë's first story, 'There once was a little girl . . . ' refers to her
'real' sister Anne, but the following story is fictional. The tenacity
of the search for the 'real' Charlotte Brontë shows the way in
which the personality of the author is made to portray an authenticity of expression. The juvenilia is often read as a source for
the mature novels, but can more usefully be read as another
instance of the blending of fact and fiction in the novelistic terrain,
which area is then further fissured along lines of race, gender and
class. Authorial identity is completely subsumed under textual
devices.

Charlotte Brontë went to Roe Head as a student in 1831,
bringing a temporary halt to her contribution to the Glass Town
Saga. The resumption of the writing (around 1833) inaugurates
the second period of the juvenilia.

QUASHIA QUAMINA: THE NOBLE SAVAGE

The Brontë juvenilia contains, hidden amongst its fragmented
morass, a vague and threatening Black figure – Quashia Quamina.
Son of Sai Too Too Quamina, the deposed Ashanti King, Quashia represents the 'untamed' savage, impervious to Angrian education and rule. Resentful, recalcitrant and rebellious, Quashia
continues to disturb the peace of the Angrian kingdom.

More crucially, the figure of Quashia is emblematic of the
tensions and contradictions that had characterised colonial encounters. To read him simply as the recalcitrant native would be to
recuperate the savage/civilised binary formula in a simple stance
of opposition. But, as the ambiguity of colonial encounters
shows, the distinction between savagery and civilisation cannot
be drawn so easily and unproblematically, as a notion of the
difference lies in a search for origins, which in itself is riddled
with contradictions. Quashia is a figure replete with all the reson-
ances of legend. The legend of Quashy, or Quazy, portrays a
noble and sensitive native. Part of the tradition of the noble
savage, this legend is full of the contradictions that help to keep
such a notion in place.[7] The legendary Quashy, overseer of a
plantation, had risen in rebellion against his white masters in
order to avenge and recompense the insults heaped on his person
and race. His rebellion, like Oroonoko's, is doomed to failure,
and Quashy is finally made to kill himself in the face of abject

125

defeat. The figure of Quashia is thus part of a discourse that carries with it the contradictions and tensions that beset the representation of the savage (the Other) as both noble and dangerous.

At one level, it will be true to say that Quashia is presented as a residuum – as a representative of that which could not be brought under the purview of European rule. That is why 'notwithstanding the care with which he had been treated by his conquerors, he retained against them, as if by instinct, the most deeply rooted and inveterate hatred' (*Legends of Angria*, p. 65). The hatred is deeply rooted and instinctual, impervious to the care with which he had been brought up. Despite the unregeneracy, it is impossible to see in the figure of Quashia a form of authentic savagery, as the education received in the Angrian court cannot be overlooked. The comparison with Oroonoko becomes obvious and is followed in the descriptions of the physical appearance and desirability of Quashia, who is 'good-looking' – 'a tall handsome youth, black as jet, and with an eye full of expression and fire' (*Legends of Angria*, p. 65). Quashia cannot be incorporated into Western systems of representation, and remains hidden in the forest, envious and dangerous.

Education and the upbringing in an Angrian court make Quashia an emblem of the Other as *colonised* subject. Colonial power was established and its commerce expanded by a forceful and violent annihilation of Other subjects and their worlds. Processes of colonial dominance placed the native Other in positions of savagery and inferiority. This placing had another, unplanned-for effect: the creation of (colonial) desire in the now colonised Other. European education and training, designed to 'impress' the natives (as Macaulay had envisaged in his 1835 minute (cf. Chapter 1)), works, in turn, to create an impossible desire in the colonised subject. Homi Bhabha takes up Fanon's reformulation of Freud's question 'What does a woman want?' into 'What does a (Black) man want?' to highlight the threat contained in the desire of the colonised for the coloniser. The fear Quashia represents is part of the dialectic through which the self and the Other are bound: the (mis)recognition of self in the specular image which is nevertheless necessary for a formation of subjectivity. In the colonial situation

the image of the post-Enlightenment man [is] tethered to, not confronted by, his dark reflection, the shadow of colonised man that splits his presence, distorts his outline; breaches his boundaries, repeats his action at a distance, disturbs and divides the very time of his being.

(Bhabha, 1986a, p. xiv)

As Homi Bhabha points out, it is the act of mimicry, the imitation, the reflection, by the colonised which spells danger for the coloniser. The desire for the coloniser's power makes the Other a fearful presence, and his aspiration and designs have to be controlled and contained. Fortified Angrian cities are duplicated in the mountain fastnesses of the Jibbel Kumri forests, where Quashia gathers forces that can match those of Douro.

Quashia's equal facility in both the English and Ashanti languages is emphasised, bringing to the forefront the role of language in the formation of the colonised subject. The split subjectivity visible in this straddling two worlds is not allowed to surface, as the subject itself is fetishised as an ambiguous figure of fear and desire. His martial prowess is similarly considered the result of his training in the Angrian court, as well as an inheritance from his father's warlike spirit. Again, it is in the duplication of colonial systems that the danger of native duplicity inheres. While the 'hatred' is seen to be 'deeply rooted' (essential, part of the savage condition), it is not simply that. It arises out of and is enhanced by envy for the coloniser:

there is no native who does not dream at least once a day of setting himself up in the settler's place. It is always in relation to the place of the Other that colonial desire is articulated.

(Bhabha, 1986a, p. xv)

The care given to Quashia's upbringing in the Duke of Wellington's court therefore works not towards erasing and eradicating (educating?) savage instincts, but, by colonising the native, produces the desire which threatens, by desiring to possess, colonial power and authority. Colonisation produces its own adversaries, as colonised subjects, caught within the system economically (the bourgeoisie of the present-day Third World) and culturally (the bilingual subject veering uncomfortably between native 'mother' tongue and the 'official' languages of government and commerce) struggle to recreate – 'mimic' – colonial forms.

In the Brontë juvenilia, the African colony set up by the twelve

127

THE COLONIAL RISE OF THE NOVEL

adventurers and ruled by the Duke of Wellington is constantly under threat of attack by Quashia and his followers. Quashia, adopted son of the Duke of Wellington, is therefore portrayed as vicious and treacherous, and above all, ungrateful. But in the reiteration of his ingratitude is an overlooking of other factors: as in *Oroonoko,* the question of ingratitude is linked to the racial position occupied. Who is ungrateful? The forceful ejection of these Black figures forcefully smooths over the questions that they may evoke. It is through the violence perpetrated against them that the peace and harmony of the new-found colonies is established.

I will trace the 'history' of Quashia through three main stories: *The African Queen's Lament* (12 February 1833), *The Green Dwarf* (2 September 1833) and *Leaf from an Unopened Volume* (17 January 1834). The stories are written under the pseudonym Lord Charles Wellesley, making the narrator the adopted brother of the hero/ villain. The discovery or adoption of Quashia by the Duke of Wellington is recorded in the first story, while *The Green Dwarf* talks about his rebellion. The last story shows us his death. 'The Life and Death of Quashia', however, is not the theme of these fragments. I have extrapolated them (in the same way that Char-lotte Brontë's contributions have been extrapolated from the mass of the juvenilia to trace the growth and development of an author), i.e. forced them out – prised them open – to highlight and draw attention to the colonial enterprise that lies at the heart of the juvenilia and to draw the case for it (along with that of the novelistic genre as a whole) as part and parcel of an imperialist project based on the creation of sovereign subjects, a project which necessitated a violent and brutal negation of the Other. The dominant theme in this cycle of stories is crucially tied to the 'object' of investigation. The theme is that of the lost child, brought up in 'other' environs, in search of 'identity', the real roots of its origin. Identity, subjectivity and racial intermixture operate to create the dense, fluid and changing terrain of these stories. The year 1833 is, moreover, marked by a gradual separ-ation of Charlotte and Branwell Brontë, a separation usually seen to be connected to the growing emphasis on romantic and sexual love in the writings of Charlotte. This emphasis, besides being based on a simple and simplified notion of the development of a single author and a practice of writing, ignores the African theme in the stories, thereby missing the colonial enterprise that informs the whole cycle.

The African Queen's Lament

Quashia, who disturbs the peace of the newly found colony occupies a central position in these narratives. *The African Queen's Lament* is about his adoption by the Duke of Wellington, who, walking on the banks of the river Sahala after the war which spelt the complete destruction of the Coomassie (the kingdom of the Quaminas), hears a song wafted from afar by the breeze that 'sounded like a requiem for the dead, or a song which it is the custom of some African Nations to chant over the dying' (*SHCBM*, vol. 1, p. 216). Following the sound to its source, he discovers a

> very handsome black woman richly dressed reclining in the shade. She was evidently much exhausted, and famine, sickness or some other equally powerful cause had brought her to the very door of death.

(ibid.)

The richness of the woman's dress contrasts with the state of starvation in which she is found. Once-glorious and rich African royalty has been reduced to poverty and destitution, and the figure of the African Queen symbolises this change in African fortunes.

The image is of a white man (King, conqueror of the race) watching a lamenting African Queen (Black woman, defeated, abject). This image is frozen – petrified – and recurs at unexpected moments in the juvenilia. For example, *The Foundling* describes a 'black marble monument, surmounted by a gracefully sculptured personification of Africa weeping under her palm-tree' (*SHCBM*, vol. 1, p. 286). Sexuality, race and the hierarchies of power and domination are starkly represented in this image. The position of the gaze is strongly delineated: the Black woman is the passive object of the white man's gaze. This man takes away her child, using his power to separate child and mother. The Black mother is associated with the lost territory, which can never be recovered, and remains as representative of the ideal and blissful state of the mother/child dyad. The third paternal factor is embodied in the person of a white man. Patriarchal power – the Law – belongs to the colonising power. Imperialism thus is part and parcel of the processes that determine subject-positions in the narrative tableaux that Charlotte Brontë etches in her juvenilia.

The Black woman appears as the passive object of the white man's gaze, making this narrative event comparable to the way in which other texts had brought in the figure of the Black woman. This novelistic effacement may be symptomatic of the effacement of the Black woman's voice from all representative forms. Does she appear in a speaking position in other forms of discourse? Gayatri Spivak's powerful example of the Rani of Sirmur's desire to commit suttee images the Black woman in positions of subalternity from where she never emerges to formulate a speaking voice and position for herself. Objectors to this stance (for example Benita Parry) take an anthropological viewpoint, aiming to recover the 'real' woman. This approach, in turn, places woman in 'traditional' areas, and ascribes her to a lost and irrecoverable arena of innocence and virginity.[8]

This woman can, perhaps, be placed in more radical positions. Such a position, however, is so covered and veiled that it is difficult to decipher. It is like the song that the African Queen sings in *The African Queen's Lament*, which, far from being a dirge, is really a call to arms and revenge. The 'Duke of Wellington' is led to the Queen by her song. In this context, Homi Bhabha's interpretation of Fanon's example, of the veiled Algerian woman, carrying a bomb in her handbag, is significant. This veiled woman shows how the image and the mask become a 'mockery' of what they are supposed to represent. The veiled Algerian woman no longer symbolises the traditional Algerian woman, but is a militant Algerian revolutionary. As the state machinery interrogates and intercepts every veiled native during the Algerian revolution, the significance of the veil is radically transformed. The *covered* Other woman, placed under a multitude of oppressive systems, cannot be revived in the field of representation as long as she is viewed as a lost territory, and her voice is sought within an essential, virginal, irrecoverable terrain. The uncovering of this woman is possible only through a recognition of the specific historical situations in which she occurs.[9]

The Black woman, in the historical moment of the writing of the juvenilia, was not absent from the field of representation. The manner of her entry, however, was affected by processes guided towards her obliteration. While her figure – the image – is fetishised, the woman herself is kept out of the margins of discourse. A contemporary example from *Blackwood's Edinburgh Magazine* illustrates the way that slavery, Blackness and the figure of the woman are used to debate and decide issues of individual autonomy and rights. This example, of course, also extends the autobiographical project that is concerned with the 'factual' sources of the Brontë writings. But, given the intermixture of 'facts' in the fictional world of the writing, the use of this example is warranted. The point is not to create a moment of authentic textual origin, but to indicate the shared range of references and images which these different discourses represent – the presence of fantasy images in historical writing, the incorporation of historical discourse into the fictional world and, in the example used, a debate about history and fictionality itself.

James Macqueen, still writing to *Blackwood's Edinburgh Magazine* on the colonial question (no. clxxxvii, vol. xxx, November 1831), (re)tells the story of one Mary Prince, Black slave from Jamaica. Her story, told 'in her own words', had been used by the anti-slavery lobby to bolster their demands and to give a 'factual' illustration of the cruel effects of colonisation. Macqueen, supporter of colonialism and especially of its commercial enterprises, opines that the story used by the anti-slavery lobby was a fabrication, and that the young woman was very well treated in her white master's establishment.[10] Mary's own voice is obliterated, while her figure is tossed between two opposing camps, as they spar with each other. White men use the figure of a Black slave woman to debate the limits of the Enlightenment concept of freedom and humanism.

To come back to *The African Queen's Lament*: the image is that of a Black woman, reclining, singing over a baby, being watched by a white man, destroyer and victor over her people. This abject figure sings of 'bloody recompense' and 'final victory' (*SHCBM*, vol. 1, p. 215). By adopting the child to whom this song is sung, the Duke of Wellington not only acts as the powerful representative of patriarchal white Law, but also lets other, unknown and potentially dangerous elements into the kingdom. The threat in his mother's song is remembered and feared: 'His mother's last advice will not . . . be entirely lost upon him' (*SHCBM*, vol. 1, p. 215).

The threat posed by Quashia, when it is shown as instinctive, refers to his mother's counsel, and his rebellion is envisaged as a

desire for a return to origins. Such a reading can only see a
futility in the native rebellion, as it is marked by a desire for
reversion towards a lost moment – a lost territory. The rebellion
is meaningful only when seen within the precincts of colonial
desire, when seen in the light of the production of the Other,
dispossessed colonised figure making a bid to recreate, imitate
and possess colonial authority.

The African Queen's Lament, while narrating the story of Quashia's
adoption, plays with the theme of adoption to show how the
process works both ways, as the adopted Other child adopts the
desire for the seizure of colonial power.[11]

The Green Dwarf

The Green Dwarf tells a love story (between Lord St Clair and
Emily Charlesworth) into which is interpolated the account of
the rebellion of Quashia Quamina. The love story follows a
familiar pattern, where the unravelling of a disguised identity
results in an affirmation of love and a happy ending.[12] Lord St
Clair is disguised as a poor artist, and, despite winning her heart,
is unable to marry Emily Charlesworth, who is engaged to the
socially superior Alexander Percy. The final and triumphant
removal of his disguise is preceded by events recording a confusion of identities and a mistaken elopement. 'True' identity and
'true' love seem to go hand in hand.

In this story, the war with Quashia remains in the background.
'The mountain glens and caverns of Jibbel Kumri, . . . the unexplored regions of inner Africa, and . . . the almost boundless
desert of Sahara' (Legends of Angria, p. 66) (the unexplored regions
of Africa), harbour the formidable African army. This war,
though a crucial element in the plot, never occupies the centre of
the narrative in Charlotte Brontë's stories.[13] Charlotte Brontë's
greater concentration on the romantic elements is read as differentiating the sister's contributions from the brother's. The schematic
division of manuscripts which associates the stories delineating
martial exploits with Branwell Brontë and the love stories with
his sister also divides the writing along sexual lines, making a
sharp difference between a woman's interests and a man's.

Leaf from an Unopened Volume

The war is concluded in the next piece of writing *Leaf from an Unopened Volume*. The formation of the kingdom has changed: Glass Town has been left behind to introduce the more glamorous and complicated world of Angria. Douro is now called Adrian, and his capital is Adrianopolis. He has also been given the new title of the Duke of Zamorna. Alexander Percy, Lady Zenobia's husband, rules over Verdopolis, and is known as the Duke of Northangerland. Northangerland is also Zamorna's father-in-law, and the Duchess, Mary Henrietta, is his daughter. The dismemberment of Angrian unity results in dissension between father and son-in-law, who now rule over the Western and Eastern provinces of the African kingdom respectively. Another generation of African adventurers is now being presented. Despite this, many of the personages overlap with the characters in the earlier stories. The main difference is that the world described is now much more sophisticated and complex, as to the external dangers are added the divisive forces within the European kingdom.

Leaf from an Unopened Volume begins with a description of the extermination of Quashia Quamina:

> Deep and fixed must have been that hatred which could have induced him [Adrian] to reject every suggestion of clemency in favour of a man in whose person all the virtues of a savage life were so nobly united, even although it cannot be denied that he possessed likewise many of its concomitant vices.
>
> *(Leaf,* p. 3)

The Black man (like Oroonoko) cannot be allowed to survive unless he capitulates completely to the European colonisers. His forceful ejection is necessary. The simultaneous existence of 'vices' and 'virtues' within the savage state reflect the contradictions that were brought to bear on the image of the savage. But the violence of the destruction of the savage Other bespeaks a fear and an anxiety associated with that image which must be defeated for the coloniser to reign supreme. The constant building of fortifications that marks the colonial enterprise is symptomatic of an inability to completely eradicate and annihilate other races and signs of other civilisations. But the anxiety remains, and in a manner similar to the sense of doom expressed in Branwell Brontë's

A History of the Year, a sense of impending danger is shown to lie over Adrianopolis. This is embodied in the decayed glory of the once-magnificent Northangerland House.

Other adopted children are introduced in *Leaf from an Unopened Volume*, making adoption its central theme. Zorayda, a strange beautiful lady, and a misshapen dwarf, play the role of lost children in these stories, in search of their real parents. An emphasis on the complexion of the female figure brings out the centrality of race as a determinant of 'original' identity:

> The corset of this tunic fastened as high as her throat, where it opened and showed a portion of the neck, whose whiteness was much more dazzling than the sunny tint of her cheek and brow could warrant anyone in expecting.
>
> (*Leaf*, p. 11)

Racial ambivalence is underlined – the 'dark' hair and eyes coupled with a 'white' neck. A loveliness that is difficult to ascribe to the Black woman is reserved for this seemingly Black, white woman. Beautiful and musical, Zorayda is easily accepted in the Angrian court.

Racial ambivalence is central in the story of deception that *A Leaf from an Unopened Volume* narrates. Zorayda declares herself as 'Quamina's Daughter. . . . Avenger of the unjustly slain' (*Leaf*, p. 57), justifying her sudden attack on Adrian. The woman embodies the danger once posed by the Black man. Adrian is saved, protected by 'the strength of the invulnerable steel corselet that covered his chest' (*Leaf*, p. 57). Protective coverings against all possible attacks have to be strong, invincible and invulnerable. Further, Zorayda's whiteness and racial ambiguity enhance the uncertainty of subject-positions in the text. Descriptions of 'The eloquent flush [that] . . . faded to a corpse-like paleness' or the 'dead-white in [her] cheek and brow' (*Leaf*, pp. 57, 58) draw the reader's attention to the paleness of her skin.

Zorayda is finally placed in the position of a white woman, and identified as another lost child. William Etty, the painter, had lost his wife, who had disappeared during an excursion in 'a wild and lonely part of the country far East' (*Leaf*, p. 49). Mother and child had been found by men of Quashia's tribe, and the little girl (the mother having died) had been adopted by Quamina as his own daughter. Her inability to avenge Quashia's death is attributed to the fact that she had always remained a 'pale alien'

(*Leaf*, p. 61), and is only waiting to be drawn into the community of her 'real' parents. Zorayda's position is similar to Quashia's. Both are lost children, and have been brought up as aliens in the enemy camp. The lost Black man and the lost white woman are juxtaposed. Despite this similarity, their positions are not comparable. The lost site – the 'original' homeland – remains accessible to the white child, as the Angrian community draws her within its boundaries. But Quashia is truly homeless. His country is lost, and the only position he can occupy is that of the envious and desiring Other subject of colonialism. Even while the theme of adoption and search for 'true' homes draws a comparison between the Black man and the white woman, it does not create speaking positions for the Black woman, whose voice remains unheard. Seemingly Black women, like Lady Zelzia in *Albion and Marina* are presented instead. The only 'real' African women presented are Quashia's dead mother (*African Queen's Lament*) and Zamorna's dead African wife (*Leaf from an Unopened Volume*). Both are dead; and the image of the Black woman is invoked only to evoke a memory of a lost past kingdom. The Family Romance acquires a racial dimension in these stories. The white child, when reunited with the parents, is easily accepted, and inherits its rightful position within European society. No such inheritance is available to the Black child, who has been ejected from his home irrevocably and is, at the same time, violently denied any position within the coloniser's world.

The other child of uncertain parentage in *A Leaf from an Unopened Volume* is not the paragon of beauty that Zorayda is, but a dwarf, a 'misshapen abortion' who has been, as Adrian says, haunting 'my steps and my dwelling for seven years'. A result of miscegenation, he is displaced not only from his present abode, but cannot refer to any one site as the place of origin. Misshapen and grotesque, he stands as a warning against the sexual transgression of racial boundaries. He is held a prisoner in the dungeons of Sulyman Palace, on charges of conspiring to kill the King. The lost child is always presented in a violent posture and as a potential murderer of the King (the father of the kingdom); in the case of the dwarf, his own father. Thus, the lost child is a dangerous figure, and must be guarded against, just as Adrian's strong steel corselet had protected him against Zorayda's attack. Similarly, Adrian houses the dwarf in the cavernous chambers of Sulyman palace. The Orientalist overtones of the name

135

of the dark Gothic palace, used as a place of criminal redress and punishment, are significant. The dwarf is kept in the 'entrails' of that prison/palace, the place where traitors and would-be assassins are imprisoned. Adrian personally tortures the dwarf. He is stopped by an involuntary cry: 'Emperor, Emperor, will you torture your own son?' (*Leaf*, p. 62). At this point, the dwarf's Negro companion, cries out in a 'solemn and warning air': 'remember Sofala; Remember the shores of Heimad' (*Leaf*, p. 62). The warning is uttered in vain. Adrian recalls Sofala, his Black wife, recognises the Black man as her brother Shungaron, but that does not prevent him from killing his supposed son, who pays with his life, along with his uncle, for 'Treason and Falsehood' (*Leaf*, p. 63). The Black child is killed, and a homogeneous white community (the coloniser's dream) is established.

The replay of the Family Romance in the Brontë juvenilia adds to the child's search for its parents the element of racial and cultural difference. The hierarchy which is part and parcel of any notion of difference places the white races in a position of dominance over the Black, now subject, races. The discourse of the novel adopts this hierarchisation, and places its own central narrative subject by the operation of this system of differentiation. The juvenilia, by bringing similar forces to play, eradicates and effaces the Black subject from the margins of representation, to portray the establishment and securing of a white colonial state in the land of the African Ashanti.

PROBLEMS OF IDENTITY: THE MINA/MARY DICHOTOMY

The trio of stories examined above were written prior to Charlotte Brontë's second sojourn at Roe Head. *The Roe Head Journal*, fragments of a diary, was written during her stay at Roe Head school as teacher, a period that is often seen as the dividing line between her juvenile and mature work. This diary is not only a personal record of Charlotte Brontë's loneliness at Roe Head, but allies the longing for home (the 'real' Haworth Parsonage) with the fictional land and characters that she and her siblings had created. As such, it is a good example of the fact/fictional blending in writing, not only in writing which is accepted to be fictional, but in a journal which is supposed to contain the 'authentic' voice of the homesick and exiled Charlotte Brontë. As such, the process, can be seen to be similar to Charlotte and Branwell Brontë's 'writing-in' of themselves as characters into their fiction. The role of the lost child, deprived of both the moors and the Angrian world, is now occupied by Charlotte Brontë herself, exiled from Haworth. In the poem, beginning 'We wove a web in childhood' (Christmas, 1835), the separation from the 'reality' of Haworth is coupled with that of the 'imaginary' Angrian world. The nostalgia for home is expressed through descriptions of a lost security and comfort: to the 'sight of the old familiar faces' is added the 'satrap stretched on cushion soft' (*Poems*, p. 187). The prose piece appended to the poem shows the absolute fusing of the factual and fictional worlds: 'Never shall I Charlotte Brontë forget what a voice of wild and wailing music came thrillingly to my mind's almost to my body's ear, nor how distinctly I sitting in my school-room at Roe Head saw the Duke of Zamorna . . . ' (*Poems*, p. 170). The dullness of school life is exacerbated by the inability to write: 'My ideas were too shattered to form any defined picture as they would have done in such circumstances at home' (Bonnel Collection [98{8}] BPM, 11 August 1836). The 'writing' self, one that could form 'defined' pictures, is inaccessible outside Haworth. Haworth and Angria fuse into one. The use of the diary illustrates the 'mixed' nature of writing: fact and fiction blend to mutate the voice of the writer. Diaries and journals are usually read as 'authentic', but the diaries of Charlotte Brontë, far from being about the real conditions of her life, adulterate them with intermixtures from her world of the imagination. The search for autobiographical references from her novels is thus rendered impossible. The diaries, which are even more authentic than the novels, traverse the factual and fictional arenas, and cannot be read as a pure and uncrafted delineation of a life.

This period marks the advent of Charlotte Brontë as 'individual' author as, away from home and Haworth, she develops the Angrian stories on her own. In fact, the introduction of a host of female characters and the concentration on love and sexuality in these later juvenile stories are often looked at (e.g. Ratchford, 1941 and Maynard, 1984), as examples of the themes that acquire mature form in the published novels. However, the themes of adventure and dangerous sexuality are related, and Brontë criticism has sadly overlooked the theme of colonial adventure that lies at the heart of the juvenilia. Again, I would not like to separate the juvenilia into easily recognisable stages or periods, by which colonial adventure can be associated with the earlier stage, and dangerous and exciting sexuality with the later, but to read the theme of colonial exploration and consolidation as the consistent backdrop of the imaginary world created by the Brontë children at play. Delineations of far-off lands and peoples permeate the discourse of the novel. An establishment of European supremacy and the political and cultural assimilation of the Other was conducted through a forceful and violent negation of that Other. The novel, held together by the notion of a central narrator, used that notion of supremacy to construct a terrain in which the difficulties of holding such a notion in place gained prominence. Narrative events echoed the 'difficulty' of the concept, as narrative structures and the creation of narrative suspense centred around it. Stories of travel and settlement in exotic foreign lands brought the Other into the text in racial and cultural terms, and presented that Other subject in positions of abject defeat, as an unregenerate residuum, or as a symbol of threat and danger to the carefully constructed edifices, built to ensure the security of the colonising powers. Fear and anxiety were then invested in the ambiguous figure of the Black wo/man, who, both as savage and colonised native, confused the sexually determined positions of masculinity and femininity. In this process, the positions of the Black man and white woman remain comparable, while the Black woman is totally effaced from the margins of representation. The 'progress' of the novel from *Robinson Crusoe* to *Roxana* records the movement of the narrative focus from the figure of that Black man to white woman. In the difference of narrative positions ascribed to these similar but differing figures can be seen the kind of subject-position that is attributed to either. For example, the narrative centre is never given to the Black man, who always appears as the object of discourse or investigation. Women are given the position of the narrator: in fact, texts are devised and contrived to equal, to stand in, to *be*, their lives. Women are objectified as the text, whereas Black figures appear within texts to disturb the narrative terrain.

The Brontë juvenilia 'kills' the external adversary, Quashia, and transfers the dissensions and dichotomies into the domestic, though still colonial, terrain, shifting its examination to the white settlers within the Angrian kingdom. The 'progress' in the juvenilia is analogous to that of the genre as a whole, where concentration shifts from the Other as racially different to a notion of femininity which takes on that role of anxiety, fear and danger hitherto upheld by the figure of the savage.

During her second sojourn at Roe Head, in 1836, Charlotte Brontë started writing stories which, on the surface, seem to be quite independent of the Glass Town Saga. Sexuality and the expression of female sexual desire are the main themes of these writings. However, the general framework of the Angrian kingdom remains intact, proving that separation from the world of juvenile fantasy and sibling collaboration is never really complete, but continues to influence her writing. Various female figures, especially Mina Laury, have now replaced the figure of Quashia. A variegated terrain of sexual pleasure is created through these contrasting figures. Mina Laury, daughter of a woodsman, is Zamorna's mistress, employed to look after his children from his previous marriage to Marian Hume. Mina's position is ambivalent: she is both lover and servant, equal as a rival and as a recipient of Zamorna's love to Mary Henrietta, his wife. She is at the same time a servant, a person who is paid to look after children, almost a sort of governess.[14] The contrasts between Mary Henrietta and Mina Laury focus on class differences. Mina Laury, daughter of a woodsman, is strong, independent and actively asserts her undying love for Zamorna. Mary Henrietta's love, in contrast, is of the more passive, languishing variety.

In the meantime, the Angrian world has undergone crucial changes. External dangers have been exterminated, only to be replaced by the power struggle between Northangerland and Zamorna. Zamorna, as a result of the war with Northangerland, is in exile in Europe. This concept of European exile is particularly interesting, and the coloniser flits around from one terrain to another never settling anywhere. The notion of home is thus made fluid, and in the image of Zamorna in exile in Europe we can see how territorial boundaries are totally merged as Zamorna (once the Duke of Wellington) is separated from his *African* home. Robinson Crusoe's inexorable wandering is called to mind here, or the final 'settlement' of Moll Flanders in her Virginian plantation. The figure of the Creole, which is to play such a large part in the determination of the status of the Other in *Jane Eyre*, is brought into being by such processes of displacement and movement, where the home of the wandering subject is lost and difficult to identify.

Angrian loyalties, divided between Zamorna and Northangerland, affect Mary's position as she flits between father and husband. The question of Mary's death looms large at this period. She is seen to pass from her father to her husband, and it is in this movement from one man to another that her position and identity are determined. *The Return of Zamorna* uses the notion of the mirror-image to illustrate the problem of identity. Mary, in exile, separated from both father and husband, reminisces to her mother:

> I recall now vividly one of those evenings. I recall the touch of my father's hand on my shoulder, as I sat playing to him hymns and religious chants . . . I remember the full and bell-like sound of my piano, even my own voice, my own figure as I saw it reflected from a mirror above my head. I feel again the delicious consciousness that I was making my father happy.
>
> (*SHCBM*, vol. 2, p. 289)

Recognition of self (image in the mirror) is ratified by the presence of her father, and happiness and joy confirmed when imparted to the father. Zamorna intrudes into this ideal father-daughter relationship. Mary is thrown from father to husband/lover:

> the Duke himself was coming into the room, that he was standing not far off, that he was watching me – gazing at me with love, with pride, with admiration in his eyes. . . . A thousand times have I derived sensations of paradise from watching his simple noble attitude alone.
>
> (*SHCBM*, vol. 2, p. 289)

Her own reflection, joy in herself, is replaced by the image of the Duke, and the pleasure she feels in herself is now reflected to her through his eyes, rather than in the mirror. Mary's image is reflected back from the mirror in which she sees herself, bound in ideal love to her father, to the eyes of Zamorna, which transform her into an object of desire.

The conflict between her father and husband persists, and this, as the unfolding of the narrative will show, jeopardises Mary's identity, and her social, political and personal position. Mary's identity hinges on this ambivalent positioning:

> What am I? . . . I am the only daughter of Percy, who

now troubles Verdopolis and beneath her foundations opens
flood-gates which perhaps some may close. I am the wife
of that military adventurer, that Prince of my native West,
who now heads this young country in its desperate resistance to hold allied nations.

(*SHCBM*, vol. 2, p. 149)

Despite being the 'legitimate' queen, Mary's identity, determined
by her father or husband, is uncertain. This uncertainty is
enhanced with the outbreak of the war between the two, making
her position comparable to that of Zamorna's other (illegitimate)
lovers.

So the position of the woman, either as legitimate queen or
illegitimate lover, is never secure. Mina Laury, Zamorna's most
constant mistress, is, because of her class origins and her liaison
with the Duke, placed on the fringes of Angrian society. She is
described as

a fine girl dressed in rich black satin, with ornaments like
those of a bandit's wife, in which a whole fortune seemed
to have been expended, but no wonder, for they had doubt-
less been the gift of a King!

(*SHCBM*, vol. 2, p. 13)

Mina Laury looks like a 'bandit's wife', dressed in the 'gifts of a
King'. The figure of Mina Laury, the other woman, is decked
with the fruits of plunder, and then presented as the site of a
dangerous and exciting sexuality. Banditry, theft, lawlessness,
marauding bands – the illegal terrain of the novel (as identified
by Davis), and the gifts of a King, the lawful legitimate sovereign,
are juxtaposed in the figure of Mina, creating ambiguity, uncertainty and tension. Her health and strength are described as 'a
model of beautiful vigour and glowing health, a kind of military
erectness in her form, so elegantly built' (*SHCBM*, vol. 2,
p. 133). Her beauty is natural, and distinguishes the mistress from
the wife. This class difference is connected to a naturalness and
lack of sophistication, and Mina Laury's lack of social restraint
brings back the concept of fascinating savagery into the centre of
the text.

She does not look for reward or recompense from Zamorna:
accepting the 'fact' that her 'master' 'has never and can never
appreciate the unusual feelings of subservience, the total

141

self-sacrifice I offer at his shrine' (*SHCBM*, vol. 2, p. 134). Their relationship is portrayed in terms of enslavement and devotion:

> She took it [his embrace] as a Slave ought to take the caress of a sultan, and obeying the gentle effort of his hand, slowly sunk into the sofa by her master's side.
>
> (*SHCBM*, vol. 2, p. 136)

Her feelings are reciprocated in kind by Zamorna. He bids farewell in the following words:

> I give you such true and fond love as a master may give to the fairest and loveliest vassal that ever was bound to him in feudal allegiance.
>
> (*SHCBM*, vol. 2, p. 137)

Sexual enthralment is expressed through the metaphor of a sultan/slave relationship. Sexual submission to a man is compared to the submission of a peasant girl to her master. His power is described as similar to the power an Oriental potentate exercises over his slaves. The Orientalist overtones ally this text to writings like *Roxana*, where the exploration of subjectivity and sexuality seems to be completely dependent on the evocation of rich, luxurious foreign Other lands. This again allies the terrain of sexual pleasure to the processes of expanding trade and geographical exploration. Thus the story of *Mina Laury* (written on 17 January 1838) explicitly deals with the theme of a steadfast and slavelike devotion.

Passing Events (21 April 1836), *Zamorna's Exile* (19 July 1836) and *The Return of Zamorna* (January 1837) deal with the two women as they follow Zamorna to and from exile, and vie for his love. The first piece is written with 'Charles Townshend' as narrator. *Zamorna's Exile* is a poem written in the first-person voice of the hero. The stories record the war between Zamorna and Northangerland and the vicissitudes suffered by Zamorna, Mina and Mary, as they follow him into exile. As mentioned earlier, the place of exile is envisioned as the more familiar European terrain: Marseilles, in *Zamorna's Exile*. Familiarity and strangeness, the known and unknown, are completely intermixed.

The replacing of the savage Other with that of woman as Other has unsettling implications for the status both of the narrating subject and of the Other which it eradicates and removes in the process. As long as that Other had been racially and culturally separate, the only problem had been keeping outside forces at bay. But once the Other is associated with internal factors, specifically, in novelistic representation, with a dangerous and recalcitrant sexuality, the process of obliteration cannot remain so stark. The figure of the woman, called to the service of the concept of the Other as disturbing sexuality, is not so schematically dealt with. In the earlier text, Zorayda, the lost white woman, had been easily incorporated within the Angrian world; these later texts look at the figure of this woman as disturbing, and the stability of the colonial settlement is shaken not only by external savage factors, but by internal elements. Notions of outside and inside are blurred in the process. What is most interesting is the juxtaposition of the Black man and the white woman in positions of disturbance and unease.

Caroline Vernon, perhaps the last 'juvenile' work, written between May and December 1839, introduces Caroline Vernon, illegitimate daughter of Northangerland, as the Other woman. The 'exchange of women' between the two warring generals, is replayed with the entry of Caroline.

The surprising re-entry of the long-dead Quashia brings racial dimensions back into the story. The sexual unsettling is thus again allied with racial difference. The story begins with an insolent letter from Quashia to the Duke of Northangerland, asking for permission to marry Caroline Vernon. The letter claims that Mary (Northangerland's legitimate daughter and Zamorna's wife) had once been in love with Quashia, as is Caroline at the moment. The tenacity of African scenes and themes, despite the gradual Eurocentrism of Angria, connects the concept of sexuality as exciting and dangerous, upheld by the figure of the woman, to the kind of fears and anxieties associated with the figure of the racial Other. Caroline's final seduction is effected, however, not by Quashia, but by Zamorna. A sojourn in corrupt Parisian society awakens her to a knowledge of sexual lust. In the sexual dream that is woven in Caroline's mind, Oriental motifs predominate. Images of power are inter-mixed with her sexual fantasies as she dreams of herself as the 'chief Lady of the [imaginary] Republican principals [*sic*]', and as married to its Caliph: 'and to be called the Sultana Zara-Esmerelda . . . with at least a hundred slaves to do her bidding' (Gerin, *Five Novelettes*, p. 313).

The excess of glory and romance that Caroline longs for can only be expressed in Orientalist terms. This love is finally reciprocated and expressed in similar Orientalist language: 'If I were a bearded Turk, Caroline, I would take you to my Harem,' says the Duke (Gerin, *Five Novelettes*, p. 353). Sexual pleasure is associated with Orientalist excess.

Caroline Vernon replays the story of the lost child, brought up outside its own home, as Quashia had been. As the illegitimate daughter of Northangerland, Caroline becomes Zamorna's mistress, while the socially sanctioned position of wife is reserved for Northangerland's legitimate daughter. Caroline Vernon, as well as Mina Laury, dwells on the fringes of the social world. Homelessness and displacement create uncertain and ambiguous areas of discourse, which are then associated with pleasure and danger. This is the hallmark of the novelistic genre as a whole, which creates narrative suspense by playing around with such factors. Textual disturbance, excitement and danger are now brought home – domesticated – and the colonial adventure is transformed into a family saga, a soap opera, in which fathers and daughters, guardians and husbands, vie for positions of political and sexual supremacy. In the meantime, Quashia, the deposed (supposedly killed), African prince, lurks in the forest – dark, hidden and mysterious – and makes covert entries into this realm.

Research and writing about the Brontë juvenilia concentrate on the archaelogical task of unearthing and deciphering 'hidden' material. The initial interest in the juvenilia was guided by an autobiographical interest in the Brontës, inaugurated by the publication of Elizabeth Gaskell's biography of Charlotte Brontë. All the qualities associated with the novels were available in the picture of the life in Haworth Parsonage, and the strangeness of the lives and deaths of the Brontë children could easily be allied with the stuff that their fictional writing was composed of. This autobiographical interest has led to the formation of the Brontë Society and the establishment of the Brontë Museum. The *Brontë Society Transactions*, the regular journal of the society was first published in 1895. The first collection of Brontë juvenilia, by Symington and Wise, appeared in 1936, and was preceded by a collection of letters in 1933. This again serves to illustrate the close connection that is made between the writing of the juvenilia and its collection and editions and the events of the lives of the Brontës. Similarly, Fannie Ratchford's edited collection of Charlotte Brontë's later juvenilia, entitled *Legends of Angria* (1933) was accompanied by the publication of *The Brontës' Web of Child-*

hood (1941), a biographical account of the period in which the juvenilia was written. The researches of Christine Alexander concentrate on the 'literary' value of these writings, and are interested in them as a ground for discovering 'the development of Charlotte Brontë's technique as a writer' (Christine Alexander, 1981, p. 19). More recently, John Maynard (1984), has read the juvenilia as the uncensored, pure terrain that informs the more self-consciously crafted mature works.

While the value and necessity of such works cannot be denied, their limitations must be acknowledged. The search for more and genuine Brontë documents is guided by a notion of 'authenticity': a notion that in the unsupervised and unguided play of the Brontë children is visible a spontaneity of writing which can then be easily identified with their personal genius and talent. The extrication of Charlotte Brontë's manuscripts from those of her brother also denies the significance of the collaborative nature of the exercise, to concentrate on the growth of an individual writer of genius.

But the most important oversight, to my mind, has been the neglect of the colonial enterprise that binds the juvenile narratives. This is the factor that allies the juvenilia with the novelistic genre as a whole, as well as with Charlotte Brontë's published writings. The resemblance is not only in theme, but refers to the most important formal device that accrues to the novel – the creation of a narrative subject. Presented as homogeneous, the subject is nevertheless constructed in an inextricable, dialectical relationship with an Other. In discourses that recreate the Other in colonial situations, it is the savage, noble or otherwise, who represents the differentiated terrain. The Other is sometimes figured forth in the Black man and at others in the woman. Race and sexuality combine to form that disturbed terrain against which the dominant narrative subject has to find its being.

The feminist celebration of women's novels has placed Charlotte Brontë on a pinnacle, her novels, especially *Jane Eyre*, being seen as the earliest instance of the voice of feminine and feminist desire. Influences on this writing have been sought in the details of her autobiography, while later feminist criticism has brought out the problematics of the voice, as of its celebration. This 'tradition' has not taken the juvenilia into account. The ignoring of the imperialism within the Brontë writings by feminism is indicative of the implicit imperialism within feminist literary tradition. An examination of the juvenilia is imperative in the establishment and understanding of the imperialist motive in the development of the novel, both as a genre, and in the case of individual authorship.

6

THE POLITICS OF LANGUAGE IN *THE PROFESSOR*

The main theme running through Charlotte Brontë's juvenilia had been the establishment and consolidation of an English colony in West Africa. The process of displacement, both of Europeans as they made the journey across to Africa, and of Africans as they were dispossessed from their lands and brought under European domination, allies the juvenilia to the imperialist interests of the English novel. *The Professor* traverses a different world, which is largely European, and where the process of displacement is not accompanied by dispossession. In this novel, English cultural, rather than political, hegemony, is established. The movement from the juvenilia to *The Professor* is comparable to the history of the novel, as it progresses from *Oroonoko* to *Roxana*: even while confined to a European milieu, the later writings contribute to the processes of colonisation, which had been dealt with in a more direct manner in the earlier texts.

Let us have a look at the publishing history of *The Professor*, which can be seen as illustrating the birth of the notion of an individual author. Written in collaboration with Emily and Anne Brontë, a triumvirate of novels under the pens of Currer, Ellis and Acton Bell followed the poems published by them. *The Professor* was rejected by the publishers, which separated the manuscript from the joint publishing venture and gave it a 'life' of its own. The fame that 'Currer Bell' acquired with the publication of *Jane Eyre* brought an end to the collaborative enterprise between the sisters. Subsequent novels, like *Shirley*, were later published and sold as written 'by the author of *Jane Eyre*'. *The Professor* remained unpublished till Charlotte Brontë's death, despite her revisions of the first transcript. Even then, the publishers, John Smith and Arthur Nicolls, waited until after the publication of the *Life* by Mrs Gaskell (25 March 1857) to publish *The Professor* on 6 June of the same year. Thus, *The Professor* underwent a massive transformation from the initial writing within a collaborative enterprise to ultimate publication, when it emerged as the first novel written by Charlotte Brontë, famous woman writer, whose 'life' was now touted as contributory to the nature and genius of her work.

The Professor was now identified as written by Charlotte Brontë, and separated from the partnership venture of Currer, Ellis and Acton Bell. Moreover, the use of the male narrative voice makes it difficult to read the novel as a reflection of the author's life, or of Victorian womanhood. The perfect relationship between author and work cannot be maintained. Instead, *The Professor* witnesses the absolute separation of the two, demonstrating the ways in which the author uses certain novelistic devices to frame and build up a readable narrative. The self-consciousness of this enterprise is amply illustrated within the text itself, which sets out to examine the use of language, which is then made to reflect or form the identity of the user.

The critical responses to *The Professor* reflect its publishing history, with the result that it is a much neglected text, and is usually read as the transition from the juvenile to the mature period. It is also read as Charlotte Brontë's attempt to take Southey's advice to temper the romanticism in her writings. However, *The Professor* does not establish the writer in the sphere of English novel-writing; fame was acquired only with the triumph of *Jane Eyre*. Feminist critics are embarassed by *The Professor*, as the feminine or feminist voice identified with Charlotte Brontë is not easily heard within this novel. Nevertheless, the 'importance' of *The Professor* must be established. We can, in fact, read in it the triumph that is claimed for *Jane Eyre*, a triumph made possible by the use of the male narrative voice, bringing to attention the fact that female-authored novels use both male and female narrative voices. This male voice is that of an Englishman who, in the polyglot and cosmopolitan atmosphere of Belgium, is made to examine the primacy of his mother tongue. Contradictions in the notion of Englishness are thereby highlighted. Cultural superiority and 'civilisation' are associated with an ambiguity similar to the ambiguity that had been attached to the figure of the 'noble savage'. The male protagonist is marginalised and never firmly ensconced within English society. The marginal position of the hero is highlighted with the introduction of the heroine, whose English mother married a Swiss man. The heroine speaks French, and desires to learn English in order to establish a connection with her matrilineal heritage. A knowledge of her mother tongue is imparted by her male tutor, who subsequently becomes her lover and husband. As the title of the novel indicates, the pedagogical enterprise is central. As the professor teaches English to a motley group of Europeans, a notion of Englishness – its importance and superiority – is advocated. The hero finds love and happiness, as well as a firm position in society, in the process. The power relations defining the hierarchies between teacher and students are here translated into sexual terms, as a male professor teaches female student(s).

This chapter will highlight certain features of the novel, with the use of the first person male narrative voice and its relation to a notion of Englishness (represented as 'civilisation') forming the main focus of the examination. *The Professor* is about teaching English, and contains within its pages a detailed discussion of the pedagogical and ideological significance of the teaching of this language. The imperialist impulse is thus contained in the educational exercise in *The Professor*, where the superior status of the English language is used to bolster the superiority of the central narrative voice. The relationship between language and identity is given further treatment with the introduction of Frances Henri, the female subject, who is shown in various positions of ambiguity. Her status in the school where both she and William Crimsworth teach is uncertain: she is sometimes sewing mistress and at others a pupil in Crimsworth's English classes. Her duality of nationality is used to magnify her anomalous nature: the Anglo-Swiss woman belongs to neither nation, linguistically or culturally, and the fluidity of her status is used to establish the triumph and superiority of the central male English narrator, as she is gradually transformed into an Englishwoman.

Englishness, however, is a concept fraught with contradictions. Its cultural 'superiority' is accompanied by refinement of feeling and sentiment. The contemporary cult of the romantic hero draws directly on this concept. Yet this stress on sentimentality and feeling also leads to a celebration of madness, to which the romantic hero is equally susceptible. Insanity came to be defined as an English malaise, the flip side of a civilisation that prided itself on refinement and delicacy. The notion of Englishness, identified with civilisation, will function in this chapter in the way that the concept of savagery was shown to work in Chapter 2. The concept of civilisation or culture is ambiguous, and subjects classified as civilised are vulnerable to the vicissitudes that this position contains. It is because in this novel Englishness is put in an alien, albeit finally dominant, position that it inherits the ambiguities previously associated with the Other, differentiated by class or race.

The use of the first-person male narrative voice obviously poses problems for those feminist critics constrained to find in the writings of Charlotte Brontë the voice of rebellious and dissatisfied Victorian womanhood. Gilbert and Gubar, for instance, note the use of this voice and see it as part of the 'realism' in the novel, which is dependent on a notion of objectivity and narrative distance. Yet at the same time the notion emerges that the use of this male first-person narrative voice helps the author to occupy the desirable and desired male position, and thereby to create and enact fantasies comparable to those of the juvenilia, which also operate through the medium of a male narrator. The author/text identification is made. However, while mentioning its links with the juvenilia, critics like Gilbert and Gubar fail to comment on the fact that the male narrator of *The Professor*, unlike the male narrator(s) in the juvenilia, is the central protagonist. Narrative positioning does not draw author and text together (as in *Oroonoko*). Instead, the narrative voice occupies the position of both protagonist and narrator, and therefore relates the story from the point of view of the main character.

Maynard's reading of *The Professor*, while emphasising its links with the juvenilia, demonstrates the ways in which the male narrative voice is different in the two cases. The use of this voice in *The Professor* is more complex and is related to a notion of subjectivity, as the narrator and the hero coalesce into one in the novel. The shift is from 'external description to a relatively objective narrator . . . to a narration that is decidedly filtered and amplified through the inner sensitivity of an involved character' (Maynard, 1984, p. 73). This is what transforms *The Professor* from 'romance to novel' (ibid., p. 75). Maynard's critique of *The Professor* contains a definition or notion of the novel (differentiated from romance) as a form of writing in which the central subject participates in and forms the narrative, i.e. a form of writing that gives centrality to the narrative voice as subjectivity. The novel is seen as a *Bildungsroman*, the narration of the 'life' of the character who is the narrator, with the narrative voice occupying a complex, not merely dual, arena, which can relate events both from outside (as an objective narrator) and from within (as an involved actant).

While looking at the narrative voice in *The Professor* as that of the involved actant, it is at the same time important to see this voice within the novelistic genre and the kinds of use to which it has been put. The first English novel (so-called), *Robinson Crusoe*, uses this voice very centrally, and represents a subject in conflict with his environs, whose ultimate victory rests on the establishment of a colonial settlement based on commerce and displacement of peoples. Europeans, despite the fact that it is *their* sovereignty that is established through the oppression and suppression (subjection) of savage, Other races, occupy a position as tenuous as that of other subjects whom they control. *Robinson Crusoe* emphasises both internal and external points of conflict. Robinson's diary records his dismay at his surroundings as well as his efforts to control them. The diary also contains cogitations on the efficacy of his native religious and ideological systems. The displaced hero becomes the stock in trade of the novelistic genre. Subsequently, Henry Mackenzie's *The Man of Feeling* (1771) comes to represent the emerging concept of the romantic hero, who is characterised by the oscillation between two selves: an authentic and a social self. The aim is to reconcile these selves, so that the protagonist can find a social position in which his deeper authentic self can be expressed (Morse, 1981, pp. 35–6). The failure to do this is recorded in novels such as Godwin's *Caleb Williams* (1794) or Mary Shelley's *Frankenstein* (1818). *The Professor*, in contrast, records a seeming victory, but this victory is marred and spoilt at the very moments of triumph. Maynard's reading of *The Professor* as a 'model of male initiation into sexual maturity' (1984, p. 75) is simplistic, and ignores the underlying sexuality that disturbs the notion of maturity or fruition that his critique proposes. Maynard does not point to the problems of the power play within this sexual initiation, especially as the narrator/hero 'grows' within the precincts of a girls' school, where he occupies the position of a teacher of English. Language, power and sexuality combine to form the realm where notions of identity and control are played out. William Crimsworth, the narrator, as teacher of English, uses this position to protect himself against hostile forces, represented by the alien and tantalising sexual realm (the temptations held out by foreign women), in the same manner that towers and fortifications had guarded the juvenile Angrian world against the savage forays of Quashia and his band of men.

The first seven chapters establish the motivating factors behind the narrator's departure from England. This departure (displacement) links William Crimsworth with the split and fragmented nature and position of the romantic hero. Industrialisation and its system of wage labour marginalise people like William Crimsworth in the job market, as well as socially. However, lack of work is not the only motive behind his departure. This outward movement was seen as positive in *Robinson Crusoe*, where the exploratory and adventurous spirit helped to spread and strengthen European capitalism and colonialism. Crimsworth's departure can be read in the same light.

Let us look at the processes that displace the hero. First, he leaves England because of a division in the family. This separates him from his brother, who is a member of the newly emerging manufacturing, mercantile class brought into being by commercial colonialism. William Crimsworth's displacement from England reflects various divisions within English society. Family ties have been destroyed by industrialisation, replaced by a more complex set of relations dictated by the forces of manufacture and commerce. Thus, though Crimsworth works in his brother's factory, their relationship is not that of siblings, but of employer and clerk. Just as the encroaching manufacturing industries had created bleak towns like X . . . in . . . shire, eradicating scenes of natural and rustic beauty, so do they destroy the harmonious sense of community and family. Thus X . . . is a 'mushroom place', 'concerning whose inhabitants it was proverbially said, that not one in a thousand knew his own grandfather' (*P*, p. 61). A stable community is replaced by a wider and cosmopolitan world, tied by commercial and trading interests. William Crimsworth has to fit into this world.

The difference between the brothers is hierarchised, at one level simply as that between owner and employee of a manufacturing concern. But this difference cannot be seen as limited to that sphere. The vanishing natural beauty of the surrounding countryside is also allied to the gradual erosion of older aristocratic values. That is why, while Edward Crimsworth may be rich and

powerful, he is inferior to William, whose aristocratic countenance and southern accent reveal a 'natural' superiority. The world
of commerce and manufacture appears in a different light than in
Roxana or *Moll Flanders*. Its harshness and violence are highlighted
and shown as antagonistic to more sensitive people. Again, the
romantic emphasis is obvious: for the man of sensibility, values
other than practical or commercial success are of importance.
Yorke Hunsden embodies the hybrid nature of this new class,
combining the ease of the old established aristocracy and the
cosmopolitanism of the new world of commerce and international
trade. Thus class antagonisms are not easily demarcated. The
alliance between Hunsden (old aristocracy) and the workers functions against Edward Crimsworth, who is shown as a mongrel
product of class alliances, his father having been a manufacturer
while his mother was an aristocrat. As an industrialist and manufacturer, he is representative of a violence that is not only directed
towards the working classes, but is also inimical to the aristocracy. So when Edward Crimsworth is denounced by a 'mob' of
workers, that mob is led by Yorke Hunsden, aristocrat, and the
condemnation of Edward Crimsworth is made by reference to
'monsters without *natural affection*', and by calling him a 'family
despot' (*P*, p. 44). The severance of old ties is condemned for the
creation of a work force alienated from the process of manufacture, as well as for the destruction of family life, which is compared to the disappearing countryside. The difference between
the brothers takes on the dimension of class difference – one takes
after his father to forge ahead as a manufacturer and industrialist,
while the other, more aristocratic, finds no place or occupation
for himself within the shores of England.

Significantly, differences in language usage illustrate this point.
First, the rough tongue of Edward is contrasted with the soft and
pure accents of William: 'and his voice . . . had an abrupt accent,
probably habitual to him, he spoke also with a *guttural northern
tone*, which sounded harsh in my ears, accustomed to the *silvery
utterance of the south*' (*P*, p. 11; emphasis added). Secondly, the
narrator is equipped with a knowledge of various European languages, which enables him to find a job. A knowledge of German
procures him a job in his brother's factory as a translator of
commercial documents. And when forced to leave his position
as his brother's clerk, he goes to Belgium, helped by his knowledge of French and a letter of introduction from his friend, Yorke

Hunsden. England has nothing to offer our hero, who has to find something *outside* her shores. William Crimsworth leaves England, like the protagonists of the other texts we have been looking at, and in the same manner as those other protagonists he has to establish himself in another context. He does this by becoming a teacher of English, language becoming his main tool for self-definition and establishment. Commercial success had befriended Robinson Crusoe and Roxana, territorial expansion had accompanied Arthur Wellesley and the heroes of the juvenilia, but the concentration now is squarely on cultural expansion and domination.

In *The Professor*, narrative disturbance and fluctuation are no longer centred on the figure of the savage, colonial or racial Other, but are concentrated and embodied in the figure of the narrating subject. The use of a male narrator in *The Professor* separates the narrative and textual instability from the notion of a recalcitrant femininity. Instead, the narrative instabilities are associated with the buried, unconscious areas of the psyche, and the realm of dangerous and uncontrolled sexuality. A schematised difference between the Other and the subject cannot be made, as the Other and the narrating *male* subject coalesce.

The 'progress' of William Crimsworth becomes possible only outside the shores of England. The contradictions in the progress of the life and character of the male protagonist can be well illustrated by the contradictory movements that accompany it. He has to be sent *outside* England to reinscribe himself within English society. Ironically, the only saleable commodity he has on foreign shores is his Englishness. Somehow, he is doomed to remain an outsider, whose inscription into his immediate environment is always in jeopardy. His 'triumph' is therefore ambiguous. Thus, when he is assailed by hypochondria at the very moment of sexual and emotional fulfilment, this symbolises the ambiguities with which his position is invested.

Hypochondria was usually classified as 'the male analogue of hysteria'.[1] Attitudes towards hypochondria and hysteria, differed regarding the causes of these conditions. The male disturbance was not considered a *maladie imaginaire*, and contemporary medical science was concerned to establish its physiological origins. Sometimes hypochondria was attributed to a malfunction of the spleen, and at others to over-production of bile. In *The Professor*, the hypochondriac attack is made to contain a sexual undercurrent, bringing to attention the associations between mental disturbance and the notion of a dangerous sexuality. Let us go over the section that describes this sudden attack. William Crimsworth is overjoyed to discover that his love for Frances Henri is mutual. This joy is short-lived, as he is overtaken by unbearable hypochondria for eight days.

> but *now* when my course was widening, my prospect brightening; when my affections had found a rest; when my desires folding wings, weary with long flight, had just alighted on the very lap of Fruition, and nestled there, warm, content, under the caress of a soft hand – why did Hypochondria accost me now?
>
> (*P*, pp. 253–4)

Moreover, the hypochondria is envisaged as a woman – an 'acquaintance', a 'guest' who had befriended him in his boyhood –

> I had her to myself *in secret*; she lay with me, she ate with me, she walked out with me.
>
> (*P*, p. 253)

Portrayed as a secret love, hypochondria appears in the guise of a dangerous, forbidden, but fascinating person – a 'sorceress', a 'concubine':

> I repulsed her as one would a *dreaded and ghastly concubine* coming to embitter a husband's heart toward his young bride.
>
> (*P*, p. 254)

This comparison with a secret, forbidden love juxtaposes madness with a dangerous, exciting terrain of sexuality. Madness is imaged as the other woman, seductive and ever-beckoning towards an unknown territory.[2] Given contemporary notions of madness and its connections with forbidden sexuality, this secret could easily be masturbation. The publication (in 1710) of *Onania* and the identification of masturbation as a 'dangerous' practice ('the development of puberty may indirectly lead to insanity by becoming the occasion of a vicious habit of self-abuse' – Henry Maudsley quoted in Porter, 1987, p. 203), closely linked masturbation and insanity. In *A History of Sexuality*, Foucault's vision of the 'monotonous nights of the Victorian bourgeoisie' sets the monogamous and bourgeois form of sexuality – the married couple – against those who were classified as dangerous and forbidden, among them the hysterical woman and the masturbating child. Images of a tempting sorceress and concubine gesture towards a terrain of forbidden sexual pleasure, associated with childhood and enjoyed in secret, and therefore in contention and contradiction to socially acceptable and expressed forms of sexuality.

Hypochondria, despite the search for its physical causes, manifested itself as a mental disturbance. It appeared as a gap or split in the individual's progress towards human subjectivity (somewhat like the gaps encountered by Locke's child). Hypochondria draws attention to the points of instability in individual human subjectivity and to those uncertain areas of consciousness that evade classification. In *The Professor*, hypochondria is dressed in a strange garb. It is associated with magic ('a sorceress') and with childhood. The unknown, unclassified, disturbing and hidden areas of human consciousness surface into the text, and disrupt the subject as he proceeds to 'nestle' into 'the lap of fruition' that he had been so carefully preparing for himself.

The Professor is about the *harnessing* of reason – of gathering forces against states of mind which are characterised as disease. The primacy of 'nerves' or emotional states as causes of mental disturbance is initially highlighted in the discourse around hysteria – the female malady – which is traced directly to the vicissitudes of female sexuality, and seen to be the result of the female condition.[3] The causes of hypochondria, or other manifestations of male mental disturbance, were originally sought within physiology, but could not be contained there. While the medical discourse on madness could not ignore the 'nervous' emotional condition to which mad people seemed to be susceptible, this very fragility of emotional states was celebrated as a manifestation of a 'superior civilisation'. For example, George Cheyne's *The English Malady* (1773) does not derogate the English for their propensity towards madness, but actually celebrates this tendency as a symptom of cultural refinement. The Enlightenment celebration of rationality teeters into a celebration of the *failure* of that rationality.

Foucault in *Madness and Civilisation* (1977c), traces the changes in the definition and regulation of madness, and describes the ways in which the madman and the criminal were brought, with the changes in penology and the regulation of lunacy, under greater control of state confining agencies, such as the police.

The growing emphasis on the confinement of the madman that characterises the governance of lunacy and insanity between the eighteenth and nineteenth centuries in Europe is analogous to the emphasis on the imprisonment of the criminal. Lennard Davis (1983) traced the 'lowlife' interest in the eighteenth-century novel, replete with stories of thieves, vagabonds and such-like figures, to the subversive nature of the genre. The cult of nineteenth-century romanticism concentrates on the super-sensitive hero, to create subjects who hover on the brink of the unknown, who are transgressive in that they contain the potential of traversing into the irrational, uncharted and unknown states of human subjectivity, belying the notion of sovereignty and control. Such figures are celebrated in the contemporary cult of the Byronic hero, marked by 'neurotic gloom; . . . frustrated and alienated from society' (Butler, 1981, *Romantics, Rebels and Reactionaries*, p. 126). In earlier chapters I have shown the identification of savagery and femininity with irrationality: what makes *The Professor* important is that it presents a text where the unconscious, irrational states of being are invested in the main protagonist, the narrator, the *subject* of the discourse. In later novels, such as *Jane Eyre* and *Villette*, this instability is embodied in the female narrator. The perception of a similar weakness in the male narrative position makes *The Professor* a text in which the Other cannot be differentiated from the subject at all, in terms of either gender or race. The fluctuations, gaps and disturbances are therefore more fundamental, and demonstrate the inextricable bind between the self and the Other sites and subjects through which it is formed.

The notion of a homogeneous subject flounders when it encounters breakdowns and gaps which touch on those factors involved in the construction of the subject as such. Those Other unknown terrains, supposedly *outside* the ambit of the subject under construction, constantly emerge to disrupt and disturb. Moreover, the Lockean subject is placed within faulty and unstable systems of representation, putting the human individual constantly at risk. Theories of human subjectivity are forced to concentrate on the gaps and fissures which, as has been argued, are characteristic of the human condition. In this context, it would be useful to dwell on the psychoanalytic concept of the subject, which also concentrates on the risks that the split in the human psyche involves, as the buried unconscious terrain – the denied Other – constantly pushes into the conscious, rupturing and disturbing symbolic forms and systems. Formulations of the formation of human subjectivity juxtapose self and the Other. This inextricable bind between self and Other is, for Lacanian psychoanalysis, antagonistic and self-defining, which is why the Other can never be eradicated, even when it is repressed, colonised or denied.

Irrationality, categorised as Other, has, at different times, been associated with figures such as the savage, woman or a recalcitrant sexuality. Foucault begins *Madness and Civilisation* (1977) with a description of the madman as a passenger – an eternal traveller to unknown and uncharted territories. Medieval Europe used literally to put its madmen on ships – the Ship of Fools. The image of a ship sailing with its mad crew and passengers to unknown destinations is emblematic of the psychic territories to which madness takes the subject. Colonial journeys into vast unknown territories, where strange encounters await the traveller, can be compared to the psychic journeys undertaken by madmen.

The connections between madness and criminality are visible in the way that society has treated the mad and the criminal. The changes in the regulation of criminality and madness between the seventeenth and nineteenth centuries followed a similar pattern. In the first phase, reform concentrated on the building of asylums, to remove and put away the recalcitrant subject. Psychiatry, as a branch of medical practice, emerged gradually in the nineteenth century, and the confinement of madness was accompanied by a belief in the cure and rehabilitation of mad people. The mad individual was no longer to be ejected from society, but an effort was to be made to rehabilitate and reintegrate the Other into acceptable social norms. The pathologisation of madness, however, does not reverse the repressive effect, as madness is seen and treated as a disease (physiological, social or psychical), and brought under the purview of the medical institution. The practice of psychiatry in eighteenth- and nineteenth-century England was marked by the belief in the 'curability' of madness, and regimes in the newly regulated private asylums, and in newly established state ones, were guided by this belief. The effort was to correct the course of the 'shipwrecked' individual. Typical writings from the period concentrate on the importance of education and the exercise of the will in the treatment of mad individuals.[4]

The incorporation of madness into the social realm, its

'bringing into discourse', revolved around a notion of the 'development' of civilisation, which 'cared' for every member within it. For example Henry Maudsley (*The Pathology of Mind*, 1879, anthologised in Skultans, 1979, p. 64), comments on the absence of madness amongst savages, as reported by travellers. There is a note of self-congratulation, as the author comments on the barbarity of savages who would, he speculates, have let the mad person 'perish'. It is only in 'civilised nations' that 'weak units are carefully tended'. The practice of psychiatry was designed to control and cure insanity. Along with the proliferation of a medical discourse on madness, a celebration of madness for its own sake began to emerge. The mad individual was seen as a rebel, in constant opposition to social injustice. Irrationality, social protest and revolution are brought close together in this view. Marilyn Butler's study of romanticism thus sees the rebel and the revolutionary as occupying an irrational stance, and highlights the romantic celebration of such a posture (Butler, 1981). On the other hand, madness was the repository of authenticity: that original, pristine state from which mankind had been compelled to move away. Despite the similarites of the celebration of madness, childhood and savagery, we must nevertheless carefully distinguish the bases of this celebration. Madness is, crucially, the *English* malady, a point of danger to which only 'civilisation' is vulnerable. The ambiguities pertaining to the concept of madness are similar to the contradictions that beset the concept of the noble savage. The mad individual is representative of a site of authentic origin, yet madness is a measure of 'development', and the presence of a discourse, medical or otherwise, marks the degree of 'civilisation' of a nation or culture.

In Charlotte Bronte's novels, madness functions in different ways. Bertha Mason, the imprisoned mad wife in *Jane Eyre*, is perhaps the best-known mad figure in English fiction. She is usually read as the external manifestation of unbridled female sexuality, which while being harnessed and tamed in the person of Jane Eyre, the chief protagonist, is also a state to which she is constantly vulnerable. To take another example of such an externalisation of madness, let us turn to *Villette*. Lucy Snowe, the female protagonist, is forced to spend the school summer holidays with a deformed and bizarre 'cretin'. Lucy Snowe is nervous and unstable. While the first-person narrator insists on her rationality – 'I, Lucy Snowe, plead guiltless of that curse, an

overheated and discursive imagination' (*V*, p. 69), or 'I, Lucy
Snowe, was calm' (*V*, p. 79) – the breakdowns in this stated
position constantly manifest themselves. Thus:

> About this time I might be a little – a very little, shaken in
> nerves. I grant I was not looking well, but on the contrary,
> thin, haggard, and hollow-eyed; like a sitter-up at night,
> like an over-wrought servant, or a placeless person in debt.
>
> (*V*, p. 103)

The adjectives change from 'calm' to 'shaken in nerves', and the
person who had denied having an 'overheated and discursive'
imaginative faculty now presents herself as an 'over-wrought servant' or a 'placeless person in debt'. The adjectives 'thin, haggard,
and hollow-eyed' point to a breakdown in health. It is during
her solitary confinement during the school summer holidays that
she is confronted with the cretin, who was more like 'some
strange tameless animal, than . . . a human being' (*V*, p. 229).
Thus Lucy Snowe's madness is externalised on to another figure,
and the narrator made to look *from the outside* at this creature to
debate its own human position – is it an animal or a human
being? The Other, in this instance, is separated from the self, and
held up as an object of curiosity, wonder, fear and fascination.
On the other hand, *The Professor* internalises this madness to
associate it with the most intimate and close recesses of the psyche
of the central character.

In the first instance, madness is manifested in the strange hypochondriac attack, which is then represented as a secret boyhood
friend. Childhood, secrecy and the roots of an 'original' self
surface in this description. Near the end of the novel the reader
is presented with the figure of Victor, the child, who is shown
to be subject to strange and sullen moods. The picture of the
idyllic English countryside and the ideal and prosperous couple
is the point of repose – the 'lap of fruition' – to which the
narrative is bound. But the narrative constantly ruptures this,
signalling that something is not quite right with this point of
rest. This rupture is reminiscent of the way in which Grace
Poole's/Bertha Mason's laugh is brought into the auditory terrain
in *Jane Eyre*. It is unexpected, disturbing and harsh: 'I have a
word to say of Victor ere I shut this manuscript in my desk –
but it must be a brief one, for I hear the tinkle of silver on
porcelain' (*P*, p. 286).

It is difficult to locate the point of interruption in this sentence – is the word on Victor kept 'brief' because of the 'tinkle of silver on porcelain' or is the smooth running of family and social life jarred by the presence of Victor? The auditory imagery – 'tinkle' – appears as a warning sound that wakes the subject (and the reader) from the pleasant reverie into which the text had been drawn. We have been drawn into the presence of the Freudian uncanny, as the homely, familiar and cheerful are transformed into the unfamiliar, uncomfortable and strange. Victor is:

> pale and spare, with large eyes . . . I never saw a child smile less than he does, nor one who knits such a formidable brow when sitting over a book that interests him, or while listening to tales of adventure, peril, or wonder, narrated by his mother, Hunsden, or myself. But though still, he is not unhappy – though serious, not morose; he has a suscep-tibility to pleasurable sensations almost too keen, for it amounts to enthusiasm.
>
> (P, p. 286).

This detailed description of the child is similar in tone to the classificatory descriptions that had brought the savage Other into the purview of European discourse. The discourse on the savage Other (of figures such as Oroonoko or Friday), was marked by a concentration on the details of physical appearance. Here the details have shifted to the mental faculties of the child. The con-centration is now on the nuances of feeling – 'still' as opposed to 'unhappy', 'serious' and not 'morose'. A psychological classifi-cation categorises the child as a person with a delicate and fragile mind, part of his *English* heritage, yet points towards the necessity for a careful upbringing and education, echoing contemporary optimism about the efficacy of education, training and guidance. Victor occupies the position of the object of the gaze; he is described with scientific precision, allying him with the Other, which has to be classified and described to be understood and incorporated. The emphasis is on the education of the mind:

> Victor learns fast. . . She [Frances] sees, as I also see, a something in Victor's temper – a kind of electrical ardour and power – which emits, now and then, ominous sparks; Hunsden calls it his spirit, and says it should not be curbed. I call it the leaven of the offending Adam, and consider that

it should be, if not *whipped* out of him, at least soundly disciplined; and that he will be cheap of any amount of either bodily or mental suffering which will ground him radically in the art of self-control. Frances gives this *something* in her son's marked character no name; but when it appears in the grinding of his teeth, in the glittering of his eye, in the fierce revolt of feeling against disappointment, mischance, sudden sorrow, or supposed injustice, she folds him into her breast, or takes him to walk with her alone in the wood; then she reasons with him like any philosopher, . . .

(*P*, pp. 288–9)

This long description of the child's peculiarities contains various and differing attitudes towards madness, reflective of the attitudes expressed in the contemporary discourse. On the one hand, it is seen as a 'spirit' which must be allowed to flourish; on the other it is viewed as the 'leaven of the offending Adam', as part of man's fallen nature, against which the individual and civilisation must constantly be on guard. The violence in the father's attitude ('*whipped* out of him' – underlined in the original), is similar to the violence with which recalcitrant and rebellious Other children had been dealt with in the juvenilia (cf. the Duke of Wellington's punishment of Quashia or of the dwarf). The mother is unable to classify her son's mental features: she merely soothes and comforts the uncannily violent emotional manifestations. She believes that love and reason may 'cure' what is so strangely amiss in the child. The difficulty of classification (the three adults each have a different definition of the child's condition) invests the child with features of the uncanny. Something is wrong, but it is difficult to say precisely what that may be.

William Crimsworth's childhood hypochondria reappears in his child. Thus a feeling of plenitude or a point of rest evade the narrator, whose fantasy of a perfect English idyll is inhabited by a child who suffers from what has been designated an English malaise – morbidity, sensibility, madness. Englishness functions in an ambiguous way, as symbol of civilisation and its strengths, superior and rational, but at the same time full of pitfalls and dangers for the subjects constituted within it.

LANGUAGE AND IMPERIALISM

Englishness is presented as a strength in the English-teaching enterprise in *The Professor*, as William Crimsworth achieves professional success in Belgium through teaching English to foreigners. Ejected from England, where he had been unable to find a suitable occupation, the only marketable commodity he has – the English language – rests on an assumption of English cultural superiority. The imperial motif is thus transferred from the commercial to the cultural realm, and language becomes a ware to be sold on the open market.

Teaching English includes a teaching of literature, but this is reserved for kindred colonised people, who alone are deemed fit to participate in the superior glories of English civilisation and culture. The teaching of English, as both literature and language, has a strong ideological content, reflective of and constructed within social hierarchies and divisions. Within England, class divisions were kept intact by propagating a *correct* use of language, while in the wider colonial enterprise of imparting a knowledge of English, the teaching of literature served a twofold purpose. First, it operated to garb colonial oppression and violence (cf. Viswanathan), and impressed on native cultures the notion of the 'superiority' of European civilisation. Secondly, by imparting to native subjects a knowledge of the language and culture of the colonial power, it created Western-educated natives, who were to collaborate with and act as the agents for the dissemination of colonial power and authority. However, the second objective did not function in quite the straightforward manner in which it was envisaged, as it was the Western-educated native who formed the main basis of resistance and threat to colonial powers.

The teaching exercise in *The Professor* can easily be viewed against the class-bound and colonial tradition that accompanies the teaching of English. As we have seen, the notion of English cultural superiority is fraught with the danger of toppling into areas of irrationality or madness. This *Other* facet of the civilised subject is kept at bay in *The Professor* by an exaggerated xenophobia and misogyny (both of these characteristics are shared by Lucy Snowe, who also teaches English in a foreign school). Thus the Belgian and Flemish schoolboys in *The Professor* are constantly reviled for their 'phlegmatism' and coarseness, and are set apart from their sensitive and 'feeling' English teacher. *The Professor* is unequivocal in its depiction of the superiority of the English language: the teaching of English to foreigners is never made comparable to the acquiring of foreign languages by English people. Crimsworth's knowledge of French and German is his asset: this is used to procure him jobs, not to impress upon him the cultural superiorities of another nation. While Crimsworth's badly pronounced French is forgiven, the failure of the Belgian schoolboys to acquire proficiency in the pronunciation of English marks them as mentally deficient. As they 'splutter, hiss and mumble' (*P*, p. 94) through their English reading lesson, their 'short memories, dense intelligence, feeble reflective powers' (*P*, p. 98) become obvious to the teacher. English is taught merely as language to them, while the teaching of literature is 'saved' for the 'nearly' English (female) subject, who is then drawn in, holding the hands of her male mentor, into the English community.

The first English lesson described in *The Professor* is a reading of *The Vicar of Wakefield*. Goldsmith's depiction of an English rural idyll is taught to the schoolboys because of the 'prime examples of conversational English' (*P*, p. 94) it contains. The schoolboys are not drawn into the literary beauties of the text; instead, it becomes an incomprehensible gibberish in their reading. The English teacher is disgusted by this rendering, and calmly and superciliously rereads the passage to them in 'standard' English. This had the 'effect of taking them down a peg or two in their self-conceit' (*P*, p. 95), enabling the master to go to the next step: 'to raise myself in their estimation' (*P*, p. 64). The power play in this teaching exercise is obvious. The text is the protective citadel within which the new English teacher can hide and draw his strength. The teaching methods portrayed, such as reading and spelling exercises, and the emphasis on pronunciation and spelling were popularly used during the period. Reading, associated with pronunciation, links the English teaching exercise with the promulgation and maintenance of certain class hierarchies, which are then posited as *national* identity. In the account presented by this text, Englishness remains the birthright of middle-class southerners, and the cultural superiority presented outside England obfuscates class and regional divisions within English society, and is not representative of English social and political hierarchies. Imperialism has its domestic cognates in the suppression of regional and class differences.

The xenophobic William Crimsworth moves from the boys' school to the neighbouring girls' seminary. Misogyny is added to the xenophobia with this move, as it is no longer the boorish foreignness of the students that is reviled, but the girls' efforts at sexually attracting their male teacher. The buttresses William Crimsworth erects against the sexual assaults of his female students are highly significant. A detailed examination of his first entry into the girls' school well illustrates this. He is at first dazzled by the sight of the young women – 'girls of fourteen, fifteen, sixteen, some young women from eighteen . . . up to twenty' (*P*, p. 113) – and this shakes his equanimity for an instance: 'I did not bear the first view like a Stoic' (*P*, p. 113). However, he immediately takes hold of himself, and begins to exercise his power as teacher. The classroom layout symbolises these power positions. The teacher is placed on an 'estrade', and raised above his pupils. Thus elevated, he is able to take 'prompt measures' to bring discipline back to the classroom and equanimity to his own ruffled emotions. The 'trois demoiselles du premier banc' (*P*, p. 75) are kept in strict check by unmitigated emphasis on academic achievement. However, despite repulsing their sexual advances, the first-person male narrator takes great care to individualise and name his female pupils. Whereas the boys in Pelet's school had been dismissed by a few adjectives, the girls demand greater attention.

The naming of the girls is important, and brings back to mind the significance that names and the act of naming occupy in novelistic discourse. Besides creating a particularity of subjectivity, the act of naming also places the named person as the object of inquiry and the narrative gaze. Thus the ascription of names to these female pupils helps to exercise power over them. The detailed descriptions of their physical appearance and the fine distinctions drawn between them, along with the narrator's insistence on his successful resistance of their sexual advances, function as narrative pleading. The need for reiteration gestures at the weaknesses in the narrative positioning. So while successfully quelling the coquetry of the pupils, he falls prey to the attentions of Mme Reuter, the female directress – 'By a transition so quiet as to be scarcely perceptible, the Directress's manner changed . . .' (*P*, p. 118). The position of power that Mme Reuter enjoys is ineffective, as she is overtaken by a hopeless passion for her English tutor. This sexual temptation is obviated by a secretly witnessed love scene between Mme Reuter and M. Pelet, enabling Crimsworth to avert the sexual temptation held out to him by Mme Reuter, the more experienced foreign woman.

Thus, the English lessons provide the male narrator with a cultural tool and give him a national identity which, in this instance, is smug and secure in the belief in its superiority. These English lessons ultimately bear fruit with the introduction of Frances Henri. Frances Henri is English, and yet not so. However, her first introduction is via her Englishness: she is *heard*, for the first time, while reading aloud an English lesson. William Crimsworth, perched on his estrade, is shocked into attention by that surprising diction and accent:

> the voice was a voice of pure Albion, the accent was pure and silvery, it only wanted firmness and assurance to be the counterpart of what any well-educated lady in Essex or Middlesex might have enounced . . .
>
> (*P*, p. 154)

The class and regional origins of the enunciation immediately point to the subject as endowed with the desirable quality of Englishness. The auditory impact of this passage is indeed startling. The reader, along with William Crimsworth, is woken up by that 'pure and silvery' accent. The first feature that marks the entry of the woman is her Englishness. Moreover, as a Protestant, Frances Henri does not have any of the despised foreign habits, and her honesty, sensitivity and sincerity indeed make her worthy of inclusion in the English community. Her hesitating and shaky voice will eventually be transformed by her English tutor/lover/ husband.

Language proficiency had provided William Crimsworth with a job, as well as membership of the English cultural club. His economic marginalisation was thus compensated for. But in Frances Henri's case, matters are rather different. Her national origins are divided between Switzerland and England, and she has completely lost touch with her mother tongue. Her male English tutor's role is to recover this lost maternal territory for her, and to re-establish her within the English community. However, before going on to look at the processes that complete Frances Henri's Anglicisation, I would like to bring in the image of a separation from the mother in the person of William Crimsworth himself. This is significant, as Frances Henri is returned to her matrilineal heritage – to her dream of England as Canaan – by a figure who is also severed from maternal ties and engaged in a futile effort to recover that lost territory for himself. The relation between maternity and the idea of lost origins seen in *Roxana* and *Moll Flanders* is reiterated here. Both male and female protagonists are involved in a search for maternal roots, and the identity of both subjects, despite class and gender differences, is located in this fantasised site.

Thus, when William Crimsworth had first met Yorke Hunsden at his brother's birthday party, he had been found gazing at his mother's portrait, which was hanging in his brother's dining-room. It was not a pretty face, but William Crimsworth had discerned in his mother's portrayed features a 'kindred' spirit. He sees himself as united to his mother and as possessing that very sensibility which made him teeter, as he says, on the brink of hypochondria in his childhood. This sensitive maternal strain reappears in his son.

This portrait is returned to William Crimsworth by Yorke Hunsden, who had bought it in a sale at Crimsworth Hall. A brother sells his mother's portrait, which is then returned to the other sibling. Hunsden, ever sardonic and sarcastic, attaches a note to the present:

> There is a sort of stupid pleasure in giving a child sweets, a fool his bells, a dog a bone. . . . In giving William Crimsworth his mother's picture, I give him sweets, bells and bones all in one . . .
>
> (*P*, p. 235)

The idealised union with the mother does not take place; instead his benefactor takes the opportunity to compare him to a child, a fool (a madman) and an animal, divesting him of the rationality and maturity for which he is aiming. William Crimsworth, for the first and only time, smarts under the taunts of his friend, and puts away his mother's portrait.

Frances Henri's separation from her mother not only deprives her of maternal love (as in the case of William Crimsworth), but cuts her off from her matrilineal heritage, culturally and linguistically. Unable to speak English, she idealises England as the mother country. Frances Henri's progress in achieving her ideal is figured forth in little cultural details, such as tea-making, which serve as symbols or measures of her success.

William Crimsworth is the male English agent through whom this recovery is effected. English imperialism is now personalised and sexualised into a little love story. However, the power positions remain unmitigated, and in fact acquire greater strength with the addition of this new perspective. The first conversation between master and pupil does not break out of the pedagogic framework: the male tutor questions, while the female pupil provides hesitant answers. In the first staccato question and answer sequence which characterises the conversations between the two, the man seeks to fix the identity of the woman:

'You have had lessons in English before?' I asked.
'No, Sir.'

(*P*, p. 155)

Or

'You are not a native of Belgium?'
'No.'
'Nor of France.'
'No.'

(*P*, p. 167)

These short stichomythic sentences allow the male teacher to harangue and be peremptory in his address. For example, whenever Frances slips into French, she is admonished:

'Speak English, if you please –'
'Mais –'
'English.'

(*P*, p. 167)

The command 'Now answer me in your mother-tongue' (*P*, p. 167) is bound to be obeyed, as it serves Frances Henri's desire to do so. Female desire and identity are bound to a meek and obedient submission to the English male tutor. The bilingual woman is asked to speak English at vital moments. The phrase, 'Speak English now, Frances' occurs throughout the text, interrupting their bilingual conversation.

Frances Henri's eventual return to her mother tongue and motherland confers on her the status of an Englishwoman. But given the powerful mediation of the male tutor in this process, this movement cannot be viewed as a return to authentic roots. The final English identity acquired by Frances Henri remains replete with the ambiguities and dualities associated with colonial subjects and cultures.

Frances Henri begins her career as a sewing teacher in Mme Reuter's school, and her position is inferior to that of her colleagues. Moreover, she is a Protestant in a Catholic country, and does not participate in the little intrigues and conspiracies, which she scornfully disdains. Frances Henri is therefore marginalised in the school, just as William Crimsworth had felt marginalised in his brother's factory. But while Crimsworth had depended on his own intellectual and linguistic tools to pull himself out of that situation, the woman has only her male tutor and husband to depend on. Thus Frances Henri blooms under William Crimsworth's attentions, as she becomes more assertive as a teacher and more attractive as a woman. Crimsworth shows a proprietorial interest in the change, watching it as a 'gardener watches the growth of a precious plant' (*P*, p. 176).

Frances Henri is subjected, at first, to spelling and dictation exercises. Composition acquires a special place in this teaching enterprise, and is used by the teacher to look into the pupil's mind and to enhance the interrogative process in which the woman is placed.

Literature teaching enters at this point, as the relationship between teacher and pupil is sexualised. Literary texts are introduced as a *private* lesson for Frances Henri, who then proves her capacity and worthiness. As Frances Henri is introduced to the secret and valuable recesses of English culture, her tutor congratulates himself and the pupil falls in love with him against the backdrop of the poems and ballads of Scott and Wordsworth. Love and teaching go hand in hand, as the woman is drawn into the fold of English culture.

Frances Henri, however, is not shown merely as a passive receptor in this exercise. She blossoms into a writer, imitating the poems of English romanticism. We are being presented with the picture of an emerging woman writer. While this emerging writer is replaced in the novel by the schoolmistress, the connection between a woman writer, male tutelage and a mother tongue is laid down as the prerequisite for successful female authorship. There is a hint that the conditions necessary for female authorship consist of the establishment of a full identity for the writer, a stable position in society and a fulfilling marital/sexual union. The publishing history of *The Professor* provides, in a way, a record of the emergence of the female writer. The novel, once refused, was published only after the author's recognition by the contemporary literary world. Recognition and success had given 'life' to this text, while the text itself explores the prerequisites for a successful writing practice.

The colonisation of Frances Henri does not work merely to establish the superiority of the male tutor. Female subservience does not prevent her from voicing independent, even feminist demands. She expresses her desire to continue teaching after marriage, and constantly reiterates the necessity of financial independence from her husband. The duality of language and nationality, which had initially separated her from her English origin, is kept within the textual terrain to form a playful and linguistically ambiguous arena of sexual pleasure. Frances Henri is flirtatious, as 'she teases me in French or entreated me in English' (P, p. 276). The woman teases the man, tries his patience and subverts his authority, just as naughty colonial subjects had 'mocked' the colonial overlords (see Homi Bhabha).

While a politics of language marks the sexual power relations in the text, feminism, in the demand for financial and professional independence, remains an important aspect in the portrayal of the marriage. Duality of nationality and tongues is accompanied by a duality of roles. As William Crimsworth narrates:

> So different was she under different circumstances, I seemed to possess two wives. . . . In the daytime my house and establishment were conducted by Madame the directress . . . silence, industry, observance, attending on her presence . . .
>
> (P, pp. 273, 274)

and in the evening

> as I entered our private sitting-room, the lady directress vanished before my eyes, and Frances Henri, my own little lace-mender, was magically restored to my arms . . .
>
> (P, p. 276)

The sexual and professional identities of Frances Henri are kept separate, allowing her to occupy different positions. These different spheres enable oscillation between the consciously held 'feminist' position in the text, expressed in the demand for independence, and the femininity, tantamount to subservience, that characterises the sexual play. Interestingly, the subordinate sexual position does not place the woman completely under the man's power and tutelage, but works (albeit flirtatiously and playfully) to subvert that power. Moreover, the ambiguities in the male position itself help to create ruptures within patriarchal structures.

The Professor, as a novel, plays around with the notions of Englishness and civilisation. At one level, things English are identified with cultural supremacy and development, at another, this very notion of civilisation is shown to be fraught with dangers and obstacles. Englishness is embodied in the figure of the male narrator, and a notion of cultural superiority helps him to re-inscribe himself as a member of a glorious civilisation. While the horrors of England ('Birmingham and Manchester . . . St. Giles in London' [*P*, p. 260]) are repudiated, civilisation itself is seen as fraught with contradictions. The civilised subject is the coloniser at the same time as he comes to play a role similar to that of the noble savage. Despite this comparison, the difference in the narrative positions keeps the noble savage and the civilised subject in a differentiated space, and this difference must always be kept in mind. The noble savage is brought into view as an object of inquiry, as he is made into the object of the Western gaze. In discourses that look at civilisation (and its discontents), the narrative position is occupied by the subject in person. Points of ambiguity, hitherto objectified or externalised in other figures (the lunatic or the criminal), are thus internalised in this text.

The Professor uses a first-person male narrative voice to effect a first-hand rendition of the life and progress of an Englishman. However, William Crimsworth's narrative does not remain confined to the delineation of the events of his own life. It soon becomes engaged in another project: that of showing the gradual Anglicisation of Frances Henri. Patriarchal and colonial motifs rise to the surface as an Englishman narrates the story of the incorporation of a woman into English cultural forms.

What is interesting is that no firm position of power or weakness is ascribed to one or the other – ambiguity remains the final word.

7

REREADING FEMINISM'S TEXTS
Jane Eyre and *Shirley*

The readings of the Brontë juvenilia and *The Professor* can be seen as 'discovery', as an unearthing of buried material, making possible a rereading and a reinterpretation of those writings that have given Charlotte Brontë a position in the annals of English literature. Women – feminists and non-feminists alike – have read and reread *Jane Eyre* to celebrate it as a text where the female author, the female protagonist and the female reader are joined together in sisterly harmony and recognition.

Jane Eyre is perhaps the most celebrated female *Bildungsroman* in English literature. The eighteenth-century notion of a homogeneity of subjectivity has been seen to be fraught and flawed. Other sites of subjectivity, denied and ignored in the conception of the rational Enlightenment subject, were, instead, transferred to categories that stubbornly remained outside this desired formulation: sexuality, childhood, madness and savagery. These Other sites were in turn (over)invested and seen to be both fascinating and fearful. The novel as a literary form develops around the notion of that subject, while at the same time recording a split in subjectivity between the self and an Other. The novel, formally about a consistent, narrating subject, is also about the relationship between that subject and its Other(s). In the writings by Charlotte Brontë so far examined, the Quashia figure in the juvenilia provides an instance of a meeting between the subject and the colonial Other, whereas in *The Professor* the subject and the Other merge, as the central male narrator and protagonist is brought face to face with the gaps and chinks in his own subjectivity.

The position of *Shirley* is equally well established within the feminist canon, especially if we remember that the *Feminist Review* was inaugurated (in 1979) with Helen Taylor's article on the novel. *Shirley*'s differences from *Jane Eyre* make it a text with a different significance for feminism, providing an example of the way in which a third-person narration can be used to examine questions of femininity and women's position. *Shirley* is a novel about industrialisation, and an uneasy comparison between women and the working class is made within its pages. The similarities and differences between women as capitalism's Other and the position of workers has made *Shirley* a text where questions of the relation between Marxism and feminism directly raise their head, as the critical history of the novel illustrates. Also, going back to the notion of the novel as a realist genre, *Shirley* can perhaps be seen to be the most 'realist' of Charlotte Brontë's novels – social division, difference and relations being the main focus of the narrative.

This chapter is a rereading of Charlotte Brontë's major works, and the effort is to see how the imperialism of the earlier texts survives and is decipherable from within mainstream nineteenth-century women's texts. Though my reading is limited to the works of one author, it can nevertheless be extended to the nineteenth-century novel as a whole. The history that I have traced so far looks at the processes through which the notion of the central narrative voice of the novel came into being. Again, I would like to reiterate that early feminism, in its enthusiasm, overlooked the complicity between the female or feminist voice and imperial processes and motifs in the novel, as well as the difficulties of keeping this female voice in its position of centrality, since it came into being from within a discourse that had placed and construed it as the colonial Other. We have seen (in *The Professor*) how the Other and the self merge even within the pages of a novel spun by a male narrative voice, making it difficult to identify the position of the male as sovereign and stable. This problem is even more marked in a woman's text, and the following readings of *Jane Eyre* and *Shirley* will concentrate on the fluidity of subject-positions within narratives.

Jane Eyre, written in the first-person female voice, records the growth and development of a female character. A *Bildungsroman*, it is based on the notion of consistency of growth and development. The publishing and critical history of *Jane Eyre* demonstrates, even more than *The Professor*, the problem of fictional utterance in the novel, as in this text the narrative seems to thematise the question of the emergence of language.

Let us begin by looking at the publishing history of the novel. *Jane Eyre*'s links with autobiography are crucial in this context. As we saw earlier, the eighteenth-century novel was usually published as an autobiographical document, 'discovered' and 'edited' by the author, and its claims to verisimilitude were based on this convention. Similarly, *Jane Eyre*, published in 1847, was subtitled: 'an autobiography edited by Currer Bell'. Far from being a perfect and authentic blending of female author, female subject and female condition, the text was presented as somebody else's document, over which the author (the fictional Currer Bell), had only editorial control. The editorial fiction was discarded in the second edition, when *Jane Eyre* appeared only with its title and as written by Currer Bell. Despite this, it is not easy to dismiss its original stance as autobiography, since references within the text signal and maintain that status: 'But this is not to be a regular autobiography: I am only bound to invoke memory where I know her responses will possess some degree of interest' (*JE*, p. 115). Raymond Williams, in his essay, 'Novels of the 1840s' (in Barker, *et al.*, 1986, *Literature, Politics and Theory: Papers from the Essex Conference*), has also pointed out the significance of the dropping of the autobiographical fiction, which has been primarily responsible for the reading of *Jane Eyre* as a realist novel. The gradual stripping of the various fictions regarding the authorship of *Jane Eyre* – first, its editorial nature, and second, the emergence of Charlotte Brontë, female author, from behind the androgynous pseudonym Currer Bell – has led to the creation of the other fiction: a reading of the novel as a narration that is true to life; the creation of an autonomous and authentic female subject and her incorporation into a steady and stable community.

As autobiography and *Bildungsroman*, *Jane Eyre* traces the development of the central narrator from childhood to young womanhood. The main theme is thus the development of a central narrative voice, as the character, Jane Eyre, 'learns' a use of language, while spinning the tale of her life and locating her identity and subjectivity within that narrative. The central identity is posited in the text, most crucially, in conjunction with an Other figure, that of Bertha Mason. The following reading of *Jane Eyre* will be divided into two broad parts: the first will look at the various externalised manifestations of Other female subjects – Other women – who form the colonial motif and through whom the central subject tries to define and place herself. The second part will look at the difficulties *Jane Eyre* presents for any account which tries to read the text in terms of the 'growth' of Jane Eyre, highlighting the difficulties of keeping the notion of a consistently developing narrative subject in place, specifically in relation to the text's internal representation of the problem of language and self-expression. The use of a female narrator brings to the forefront the problems associated with notions of femininity and female sexuality.

THE OTHER WOMAN AS MIRROR-IMAGE

Bertha Mason is introduced into the text by a 'low, slow ha! ha!'. The sound of this laughter reverberates through feminist literary history. Variously read as dangerous (Woolf), as denied passion (Showalter, Gilbert and Gubar), as protest (Kaplan), as imperialist oppression (Rhys, Spivak), Bertha Mason occupies the position of the obliterated and repressed Other, necessary for the emergence of the central coherent and unified female subject and the narrative of her development and growth. This laugh is first heard as a rude interruption to Jane's soliloquy on the rooftops of Thornfield Manor. That famous passage begins on a note of narrative pleading – 'Who blames me? Many no doubt; and I shall be called discontented' (*JE*, p. 128). The reverie on the roof records a longing for 'incident, life, fire, feeling', and extends the heroine's personal suffering to include all womankind and, more significantly, all other oppressed sections of humanity. 'Women are supposed to be very calm generally: but women feel just as men feel'; they are like the 'Millions [who] are condemned to a stiller doom . . . in silent revolt against their lot' (*JE*, p. 141). This soliloquy is interrupted by 'Grace Poole's' laugh:

> When thus alone, I not unfrequently heard Grace Poole's laugh: the same peal, the same low, slow ha! ha! which, when first heard, had thrilled me: I heard, too, her eccentric murmurs, stranger than her laugh.
>
> (*JE*, p. 129)

The passage – the reverie and the interruption – has been read over and over by feminist critics. Virginia Woolf's comments on it (published in the *Times Literary Supplement* in April 1916) are perhaps the best known. She sees this abrupt interruption of the reverie as an example of uncontrolled, impassioned and angry writing, which detracts from the quality of the prose. Recently, Cora Kaplan (1986) has drawn attention to the connection between women's demands and those of the condemned 'millions' in the reverie. The comparison between Jane Eyre's personal situation and the oppression suffered by other groups brings out the revolutionary potential in the text. The laughter is not merely an interruption, a rude jerk, that brings the text back to its narrative functions, but connects the reverie – the 'tale my imagination created' (*JE*, p. 141) – to the figure of the Other woman, the real source of the laugh, against whom, and in relation to whom, the central subject in the narrative is to form itself, and to progress on what has been regarded as a triumphant march.

Bertha Mason and Jane Eyre first meet through a mirror, as Jane looks into the mirror to see Bertha's image reflected back to her. This incident is portrayed in a relation of events to Rochester, so that the man remains the mediator between the two women: 'oh, sir, I never saw a face like it! It was a discoloured face – it was a savage face' (*JE*, p. 311).

The mirror-image in which Bertha Mason is first met is an echo of another mirror-image, when the little Jane saw her own image reflected to herself and recognised herself as a 'heterogeneous' thing. The opening passage of *Jane Eyre* serves to illustrate the heterogeneity of the position of the female narrator. Jane's position behind the curtains on the window-seat emblematises her separation from the members of the Reed family. The subject forms a notion of its self through images which pose and expose the narrator's identity. The image in the mirror reflects little Jane's understanding of her social and subject-position:

Returning, I had to cross before the looking-glass; my fascinated glance involuntarily explored the depths it revealed. All looked colder and darker in that visionary hollow than in reality, and the strange little figure there gazing at me with a white face and arms specking the gloom, and glittering eyes of fear moving where all was still, had the effect of a real spirit: I thought it like one of the tiny phantoms, half fairy, half imp, Bessie's evening stories represented as coming out of lone, ferny dells in moors, and appearing before the eyes of belated travellers.

(*JE*, p. 46)

The 'heterogeneous thing' beheld in the mirror has to be gradually homogenised and made to represent a fully articulated and articulating, 'free' and autonomous, female subject. One of the ways that this is done is through the inheritance of her Uncle Reed's Madeira vineyards, which provides Jane with a competency and frees her from dependence on the circumscribed employment opportunities available to the impoverished genteel Victorian woman. Colonial possession and wealth restore her to the family of origin (her Uncle Eyre/her *father's* brother). Social identity and security, even a notion of roots, are transferred to another spot – another island, Madeira. Colonial possessions and wealth, Creolise, as it were, the central figure, whose inscription within English society remains heterogeneous. The conclusion of *Jane Eyre*, often read as a reinscription of the female subject into the European world, is problematic, because the final point of rest cannot be separated from the processes through which it is achieved. Gayatri Spivak's reading (*Critical Inquiry*, 1985), of the last chapters shows how Jane had always remained within the boundaries of the English family and home. Spivak reads the final pages of the novel as a bringing back of the female protagonist into the fold, as a de-marginalisation which places her firmly as a homogeneous and autonomous subject. This interpretation ignores the processes of displacement that this placing is dependent on. As in *The Professor*, this process of stability is aided by, and dependent on, displacement from England, and subjects so formed occupy very tenuous positions.

The insistence on the 'integrative' qualities of the text echoes biographical readings (by Maurianne Adams, for instance) which see the process of writing *Jane Eyre* itself as an effort to re-establish contact with the family network, that had, in childhood, fostered the writing and creative abilities of the Brontë children. In the face of the collapse of that collaborative enterprise and family disintegration (Mr Brontë's illness and Branwell's growing degeneration), Adams argues, the writing of *Jane Eyre* brought into operation Charlotte's latent talents and capacities, and also prepared her for the greater world outside (see Adams, 'Family Disintegration and Creative Reintegration: The Case of Charlotte Brontë and *Jane Eyre*' in Wohl, 1978, *The Victorian Family: Structures and Stresses*, p. 176).

The success of *Jane Eyre* provides a short-lived haven before other processes of disintegration begin to disturb the peace of the Brontë family. The writing of the text is seen as a reflection of the way in which a marginalised and homeless woman is provided with a home and family. This home is finally located in a dark Gothic haunt – Ferndean manor – and the stabilising marriage is with a lame and blind Rochester. This makes it difficult to attribute to the last scene of the novel an unequivocal sense of ease. Instead, it offers an uncomfortable and unsure placement within society.

The relationship between Jane Eyre and Bertha Mason is resonant of the discourses on the status of the Other, sometimes as savage, sometimes as an uncontrolled realm of sexuality, and sometimes as the irrational states of human consciousness. Moreover, this relationship is always mediated by the figure of Rochester, white, English and male. The women, for example, are contrasted by him through a series of epithets: 'Compare those clear eyes with the red balls yonder – this face with that mask – this form with that bulk' (*JE*, p. 322). The difference between the two women is highlighted in terms of their *physical*, facial features. Jane, the protagonist, is given human characteristics – a face, a form and 'clear eyes', whilst the other woman is not recognisable as human – the words 'balls', 'mask' and 'bulk' dehumanise Bertha. Despite this, the two figures have often been seen as different manifestations of the same subject, and the madness, savagery and animality of the one woman only the external manifestation of the uncontrolled rage and passion of the other. Jane Eyre adopts Rochester's description to muse on the apparition:

> What it was, whether beast or human being, one could not, at first sight, tell: it grovelled, seemingly, on all fours; it snatched and growled like some strange wild animal.
>
> (*JE*, p. 321)

The meeting between the two women is presented as a colonial encounter, highlighting and dramatising questions regarding human subjectivity, rationality and civilisation.

Savagery, madness and sexuality, defined as Other, merge in the figure of Bertha Mason. Jane Eyre in confrontation with Bertha Mason faces, in a mirror, the 'dark' Other side of her own psyche. A mimetic relationship is set up between the two women. This process of mimesis is as much doubling as opposition and serves to destabilise, as well as to secure, Jane's identity. If Bertha Mason is Jane's antithesis, the distinction between them can only be secured by a type of initiation or rite of passage in which, momentarily, they are the *same*.

At other points in the text Jane's status as human is questioned in a manner similar to Bertha Mason's. The most striking instance of this is found in the scenes following Jane's departure from Thornfield Hall. Lost, homeless and penniless, Jane wanders into the surrounding countryside, little knowing where her journey will take her. Will, conscience and consciousness desert her at this point:

> As to my own will or conscience, impassioned grief had trampled one and stifled the other. I was weeping wildly as I walked along my solitary way: fast, fast I went like one delirious.
>
> (*JE*, p. 348)

The delirium is both physical and mental, as control of 'will and conscience' and limbs is lost. It is also akin to madness, a relinquishment of all rational faculties, echoing the madness of Bertha Mason ('crawling forward on my hands and knees').

It is at this point of breakdown that the image of the mother enters. The barely human Jane Eyre turns to 'nature' for maternal comfort and succour:

> Nature seemed to me benign and good; I thought she loved me, outcast as I was; and I, who from man could anticipate only mistrust, rejection, insult, clung to her with filial fondness. Tonight, at least, I would be her guest – as I was her child: my mother would lodge me without money and without price.
>
> (*JE*, p. 350)

Jane Eyre had left Thornfield Hall in response to a call from an imaginary mother – 'a white human form . . . [who] gazed and gazed on me' (*JE*, p. 346). Mother, nature, mother nature are evoked as a magical site, going beyond and lying prior to the social – a refuge and haven to turn to when rejected by human society. It is the savage, mad and animal Jane who turns to this image. The mother/daughter dyad reappears. Presented as desirable – the endless gaze – a return to that moment is effected by nearly losing all human qualities, and the subject-under-construction is merged into its Other through this gaze. The progress of the *Bildungsroman* is dependent on the obliteration of

179

these positions. Moments in which the subject's progress is disrupted and questioned bring into focus the problems associated with a notion of consistency of subjective development and progress.

The contrast between Bertha Mason and Jane Eyre is extended to the creation of images of other women in the text, bringing back into focus the processes of obliteration and domination on which the sovereignty of the narrating subject rests. As Gayatri Spivak points out, nineteenth-century British literature cannot be read 'without remembering that imperialism, understood as England's social mission, was a crucial part of the cultural representation of England to the English' (Spivak, 1985, p. 243). Her criticism of *Jane Eyre* as the 'cult text of feminism' (ibid. p. 244) rests on the neglect, by feminist readers, of the broader issues of colonisation, the exercise of imperial power and its control over women as it is represented within this text. It is impossible to ignore the mad and inhuman figure of Bertha Mason, who lies behind the text's struggle towards the creation of an independent and autonomous subject-position for a woman, and who also stands witness to the processes that obliterate any such possibility. The 'axiomatics of imperialism' through which such a figure is represented and brought into being is not confined to the figure of Bertha Mason, but occurs in more diffuse forms in other instances, suffusing the text with imperial motifs.

Jane Eyre, the central figure, contrasts herself (in the same manner in which she is contrasted to Bertha Mason) to other women whose subject-position can be seen to have been determined by the processes of imperialism. The pedagogical system designed to construct Jane Eyre as a rational and independent subject acquires significance, as it is now extended to make a comparison between Jane Eyre and these other women. For example, on the eve of her marriage to Rochester, Jane is shown desperately holding on to the image of herself as a plain governess. While Rochester contrasts her with 'other' women and describes her as different from and better than his various European mistresses as well as 'the Grand Turk's whole seraglio – gazelle-eyes, houri's form, and all!' (*JE*, p. 297), Jane protests against this 'Eastern' allusion and the comparison with women who are bought and sold as commodities in an 'Eastern' bazaar. Jane places herself in the role of educator and reformer: 'I'll be preparing myself to go out as a missionary to preach liberty to them that are enslaved – your harem inmates amongst the rest' (*JE*, p. 297).

Jane, in the imperialist role of educator, carefully marks the *differences* between the European woman and Eastern harem inmates. The text thus picks up the 'harem' motif which had been so preponderant in contemporary women's writing. Mary Wollstonecraft had used the comparison with a Turkish seraglio to differentiate between the desired feminist subject and the dependent female subjects created within contemporary society. The image of the Oriental woman as sexually oppressed, but at the same time fascinating, recurs in this novel, and is used as a contrast to the main character.

Jane emerges in the role of educator at several points. St John Rivers's proposal of marriage is accompanied by an offer to work as a 'conductor of Indian schools, and a helper amongst Indian women' (*JE*, p. 429). However, the opportunity to be 'grilled alive in Calcutta' is refused. In this proposal, the role of the European as missionary and teacher, bringing education, knowledge and an awareness of human status to the Eastern woman, is graphically represented.[1] *Jane Eyre* envisages the spread of a certain kind of education and training not only to the colonies, but to other communities within Britain. The imperial cultural enterprise aimed to spread its influence into all sections of the indigenous British population. This is embodied in the text in the school set up by St John and run by Jane to cater to the educational needs of the daughters of the British peasantry. The peasantry are shown to respond favourably to Jane, who sees her teaching as a 'duty': 'to develop these germs [of gentility]: surely I shall find some happiness in discharging that office' (*JE*, p. 385). It is this same team, St John and Jane, who intend to spread their teaching to include the daughters of the Indians (peasantry? middle classes?), designing a pedagogical system aimed towards creating subjects in their own image – that is, in the mould in which Jane herself had been formed and trained. Jane's comments on the advantages derived from the Lowood education are significant in this context:

> I had the means of an excellent education placed within my
> reach: a fondness for some of my studies, and a desire to
> excel in all, together with great delight in pleasing my

181

teachers, especially such as I loved, urged me on. I availed myself freely of the advantages offered me.

(*JE*, p. 115)

Jane's education makes of her a person who can pride herself on her 'harmonious thoughts', 'better regulated feelings' and 'disciplined and subdued character' (*JE*, p. 116). The second stage in her progress is to inject a similar training into other women, bringing them into the familiar world of 'civilised', middle-class, European norms.

The scope of proposed educational systems can be seen as an ever-expanding process: Rousseau's plans for Emile had excluded Sophie; Astell and Wollstonecraft had tried to extend the system to include the middle-class Englishwoman; the Brontës, in their own lives, had grappled with many a scheme to set up a girls' school and questioned and proposed curricula,[2] while *Jane Eyre* proposes the inclusion of other women – Turkish harem inmates, ignorant Indian daughters and daughters of the British peasantry – within this scheme. Jane's protest at Rochester's comparison of herself with Turkish harem inmates, pointing to a hesitant and diffident recognition of the sexual oppression of *all* women and of the need for protest against such oppression, nonetheless places the educated Englishwoman in a position superior to her more unfortunate sisters, who are seen to need her guidance and to be infused with *her* recognition of human status.

The figure of Bertha Mason is significant, as she represents the failure of the pedagogical, colonising enterprise. Recalcitrant and uneducable, she escapes the dominating and hegemonising imperialist and educational processes. As a Creole, she is differentiated from the 'authentic' native, and represents multiple points of dislocation that the colonising venture had brought in its wake. The figure of the Creole had been brought into being solely by colonial/imperialist ventures. The Creole is sometimes a white person born in the colonies – of European origin, not born in their own country. Crucially, as a white European, the Creole is different from natives (Aboriginals), as also from Negroes, who had been brought to the islands as slaves. However, a person of mixed European and Indian – native – or Black descent would also be classifed as a Creole. The racial classification is based not on colour alone but on displacement from the place of origin. The Creole is geographically displaced – s/he is born in the

West Indies, and, because of the possibility of racial intermixture, cultural and racial displacement also become important. The category Creole is applicable only to European settlers and their descendants (of mixed race or otherwise). It denotes an access to colonial power and wealth. However, racial intermixture shakes the seat of this power. This meeting – of peoples, of cultures – was negotiated and guided by colonial and commercial interests, and did not result in an amalgamation of races and cultures, but used class and racial differences to extend and strengthen colonial edifices. Bertha Mason, in *Jane Eyre*, is a Creole, constructed and formed under these conditions.[3] Her racial origins remain vague. Her Blackness, to which her madness is attributed, must be seen along with her possession of colonial wealth and fortunes, which enabled her to marry a white Englishman. Neither white nor Black, Bertha Mason provides the site for the colonial encounter in the text, and is connected to the other racially ambivalent female figures that we have been looking at. In this instance, the savage Other is represented by a Creole, a figure brought into being by the hierarchising and dominating processes of commercial colonisation. *Wide Sargasso Sea* (Jean Rhys, 1966), written as a correction of *Jane Eyre* and as an effort to bring the discourse of the Other woman to the forefront, best shows how the Other is mediated and created by the processes of colonisation, and does not represent an 'essential' or original moment. Crucially, in *Wide Sargasso Sea* it is a *white* Creole woman who represents the figure of the colonised double.[4]

THE UNCANNY, THE GOTHIC AND THE ROMANTIC

The process of doubling involves a distortion of images. The colonised subject, created by and within the processes of colonisation, alters, while imitating, the image of the coloniser. The psychoanalytical origins of the notion of doubling can be traced to Freud's essay on 'The Uncanny' (1919).[5] The word uncanny (*unheimlich*) in German, can be understood only in its relation to its opposite (*heimlich*). As Rosemary Jackson puts it:

> *Das Heimlich* also means that which is concealed from others: all that is hidden, secreted, obscured. Its negation, *das*

unheimlich, then functions to dis-cover, reveal and expose areas normally kept out of sight.

(Jackson, 1981, *Fantasy: The Literature of Subversion*, p. 65)

The process by which the familiar becomes unfamiliar, the homely and comfortable strange and alien, involves a doubling, which may take the shape of a reflection (as in a mirror), the creation of images (shadows) or repetition, replay.

Freud carefully distinguishes between the presence of the uncanny in life and its creation in works of fiction. The distinction he makes between magical and strange effects in fairy tales and in works which allude to reality divides the 'history' of the novel into categories similar to those used by Robert. The history of the novel proceeds from fairy stories which have no reference to or basis in reality to the novel proper, where realistic and fantastic elements merge to create the heterogeneous novelistic terrain. The heterogeneity of the novel form has also been pointed out by Lennard Davis, whose very different methodology reveals a discourse divided in its reference to its sources in fact or fiction. The novel is marked by this ambiguity and heterogeneity. The instability of its representation leads to the creation of uncanny effects.

The emergence of the Gothic novel in the eighteenth century is perhaps the most striking example of a discourse centred on the creation of the uncanny. The stock theme of the late eighteenth-century Gothic novel is that of endangered femininity, which in turn, is associated with dominant notions of female passivity. Female subjectivity and sexuality are presented as vulnerable, and narrative excitement and tension centre around the ways in which this female subject can overcome the dangers that beset her. While female sexuality is portrayed as vulnerable, it is only through a recognition and establishment of 'true' romantic love that the conflicts within the text are resolved.

The 'rise' of the novel saw the combination of various forms of writing, amalgamating the real with the imaginary – stories of adventure and exploration, tales of sentiment and romance – taking the terrain/subject of the narrative to unknown, frightening and dangerous areas. As has been seen, Watt's initial thesis, emphasising realism, has been reworked, and the unknowable, unknown areas that the novel deals with, highlighted. The recognition of the Gothic as part of the 'originating' moment of the genre has usually marked the novel as a domain where women writers predominate, examining questions of femininity and female desire. Moreover, the emphasis on the Gothic diverts attention from a linear progression, both as regards the narrative terrain of the novel (so that a novel can no longer be read as a straightforward delineation of the 'rise' and 'growth' of a subject), and as regards the 'history' of the novel (which can no longer be read as a progress towards greater/better social mirroring). It points out, in a dramatic manner, the splits in both processes, and a simple narrative of growth and development is radically altered. Terry Lovell continues from Watt's thesis, to show that the novel is related to capitalist ideology as a 'Janus-faced' form – advocating, on the one hand, growth and development, a step-by-step process leading to stability and prosperity – and on the other appealing to the capitalist subject as consumer, where the 'fantastic' quality of the commodity carries the subject *away* from the mundane realities of a bourgeois existence. The division between leisure and work is reflected in the novel, and the novel, seen as leisure-time activity, is associated with women, who in this dichotomous scheme have often been associated with leisure and pleasure.

Despite this identification as a woman's genre, the preponderance of the male narrative voice in the Gothic novel is worthy of note. The Gothic combines the novel of sentiment, the novel of adventure and the Oriental tale to create a form where the dangers of and a notion of dangerous sexuality become its main focus. William Beckford's *Vathek* (1786), which brings together the Gothic and the Oriental tale, is a good example of this genre. Significantly, the atmosphere of strange and disturbing sexuality drawn in this novel is connected with Beckford's mode of life: Beckford himself had been accused of homosexuality and pederasty. This notion of a dangerous sexuality differs from that in *Moll Flanders* or *Roxana*. In Defoe's texts sex was presented as adventure, comparable to colonial adventures, and promiscuous sexual behaviour was used by the female protagonists for their rise in the emerging capitalist world. In the romantic, Gothic concept of dangerous sexuality this danger inheres in its transgressive predilections, where, along with the disturbance of social order, the subject as desiring or as object of desire transgresses, and moves into areas where its status as rational human being is put in question. Sexuality is associated with madness, which is at times construed as disease or aberration, and at others celebrated for its transgressive and revolutionary potential.

Jane Eyre, in the figure of Bertha Mason, represents the madness of sexual excess as frightening. But, in so far as this image is also made to embody and contain the elements associated with the savage in colonial encounters, it is difficult to read it as merely frightening. The image of sexual excess in *Jane Eyre* inherits at once the Gothic underside of transgressive sexuality *and* the danger of the colonial Other. As such it is a condensation – threatening, but also something desired. Remember how the picture of the savage had merged into a description of Jane, and how, in that savage-like state, Jane had desired a return to the lap of mother nature. The narrative is thus destabilised by the blending of the concepts of savagery and madness. It combines, especially in the figure of Bertha Mason, the dangers evoked by the savage, colonial Other, with the dangers of a transgressive sexuality. Both sites destabilise, representing a fearful desire.

Again, it is *Vathek*, written in 1786, which is seen as recording the 'swing over from classicism to romanticism'.[6] This swing is the change from a reading of the text as a collation of fabulous and fantastic events such as those that constituted the eighteenth-century Oriental tale, to a reading that associates the strangeness of the tale with the life of the author. This connection is extended, critically, to establish the notion of the 'realism' of a novel and this changed reading refers to a particular mode of composition. For example, the 'dangers' of *Vathek* are traced to the short, inspired spurt in which it was written. 'The fit I laboured under when I wrote *Vathek* lasted two days and a night,' writes Beckford (1970, *Vathek*, p. xiii).

It will be useful to look at Mary Shelley's preface to *Frankenstein* in this context. This tells the story of the *mode* of writing the novel and was written at the request of Mary Shelley's publishers. It was welcomed as an opportunity of revealing the background to this unusual novel:

> I am the more willing to comply because I shall thus give a general answer to the question so very frequently asked me – how I, then a young girl, came to think of and to dilate upon so very hideous an idea.
>
> (1968, *Frankenstein*, p. 5)

The biographical interest is visible here – the preface tries to unravel the mystery of the writing – of the relationship between a 'young girl' and the 'hideous' story. The author herself can be seen as a Gothic heroine. However, the curiosity of the readers was not limited to the person of the author, but concerned itself with the charmed coterie in which she lived – 'the daughter of two persons of distinguished literary celebrity' as well as being Shelley's wife. Mary Shelley wrote the story during a romantic journey in the Swiss Alps in the company of the two most famous poets of the day – Shelley and Byron. The Gothic romantic excess in the novel, the use of a male narrative voice, as well as the creation of a male hero, preclude the identification of the narrative with life or reality. However, the addition of the preface performs that autobiographical function: the little historical details relate Mary Shelley's novel to contemporary romanticism, and *Frankenstein* itself becomes part of the romantic project.

Accounts of literary composition contained in prefaces, autobiographies and anecdotal references describe the process of writing as inspired and sporadic – as a manifestation of heightened and abnormal mental states, sometimes drug-inspired. Coleridge's interrupted poem 'Kubla Khan' is perhaps the best-known example of this mode of writing. Inspired and visionary, such moments are easily lost, resulting in fragmented pieces of writing.

Let us pause to go over the shifts in the concept of the author/text identification. In relation to most eighteenth-century novels this concept refers to a thematic congruence of the events of the narrative and the life of the narrator, who is often differentiated from the author. In female first-person narratives, written by a female author, as in the novels of Manley, this identification had been used to draw readers voyeuristically into the author's life.

In the contemporary Gothic novel, represented by writings such as *Vathek* (1786), *The Monk* (1786) or *Frankenstein* (1818), the bizarre and unusual events in the narrative can be traced, by means of prefaces and references to autobiography, to events in the author's life. Sexual irregularity is highlighted in these novels. Sexual transgression, as both narrative and autobiographical event, gains prominence in the equation that is made here between author and text. The author/text identification can be seen to result in the cult of the romantic author, according to which the process of literary composition is inspired and visionary. This notion of literary composition as inspired, in turn, hints at a breakdown of reason. Literary composition is seen as a manifestation of a special moment, of a unique access to states of consciousness not normally within human reach. Coleridge's 'Kubla Khan', both in its portrayal of the mad poet and in its much-vaunted interruption, sees the nature of literary and poetic writing, as well as the personality of the poet, as fragmentary and disconnected. Coleridge's writing, in 'Kubla Khan' and the interrupted chapter of the *Biographia Literaria*, highlights the disconnectedness, the breakdown and the fragmentation of poetic imagination and expression.

A fragmented mode of writing is also visible in the composition of the Brontë juvenilia. Charlotte Brontë's comments on the trance-like states of literary inspiration are important in this context. *Jane Eyre*, however, is not a fragmentary piece, but an autobiography, tracing the growth of subjectivity. Here we see that the Lockean formula of gradual development is back in operation. Moreover, the writing of autobiography can also be seen as a romantic exercise – as witnessed in Rousseau's *Confessions* or Wordsworth's *Prelude*. The tracing of a linear growth of subjectivity was also an established Romantic practice. Diaries, journals and confessions are significant in the construction of the life of the writer/poet – a life that is then read to illustrate the poetry and other writing. Despite its insistence on the fragmentariness of literary inspiration, the connection that is made between the writer's life and works somehow still draws on a notion of consistency and coherence, and a linear connection between reality and the text.

The concentration on disconnectedness does not abandon the connection between author and audience/readership. It is a politics of language that is deployed to draw the reader into the author's world. Wordsworth's *Preface to the Lyrical Ballads* (1798), highlights the inspired and emotionally heightened content of poetry (the 'spontaneous overflow of powerful feelings').[7] Further, the *Preface* draws the poet/writer into a community with the readers; the poet is a 'man speaking to men' (Wordsworth, 1966, p. 48). A direct connection is drawn between the language of the poet and that of the audience. The concept of fragmented and spontaneous writing keeps the links between author and text intact, so that the notion of correspondence between reality and the representational form is strengthened. The linear connections between the author and the text, and between the text and its audience, remain in this formulation, which, along with the stress on poetic inspiration and spontaneity, records a contradictory attitude towards literary composition. The tension in the account of writing which sees it as inspiration or excess in the writing subject yet also as expressing development and growth creates the tensions visible in a text like *Jane Eyre*.

As autobiography, *Jane Eyre* concentrates (as it must) on the growth of its central character. The motif it uses to record this growth is a use of language, as Jane learns to tell the story of her life. The text, therefore, becomes a form of commentary on the production of the expressive or writing subject. *Jane Eyre's* project is, at one level, to put the interrupted reverie on the rooftop of Thornfield into a coherent and consistent form, and at another, to celebrate this sporadic, jerky expression as spontaneous and inspired.

NARRATIVITY AND SUBJECTIVITY

The recognition of Jane Eyre in the mirror as a heterogeneous being and the description of her crawling on all fours focus on the instabilities of the narrator's position. The figure of the Other woman – as Bertha Mason, as Turkish and Indian women, or as English peasant women – functioned as external manifestations of the Other, creating colonial situations in the text. A more fundamental disruption takes place with the internalisation of disturbing factors and their inclusion within a European reality. *The Professor* presented a first-person male narrative, where the position of the narrator was disturbed and disrupted by a strange and inexplicable hypochondria. *Jane Eyre*, at one level, transfers that hypochondriac state into another subject, and embodies it as the dark passion of Bertha Mason. But, at another level, and in so far as it is structured like an autobiography, its other task is to trace the growth of its protagonist. In its concern with the portrayal of the development of a rational and unified female subject, *Jane Eyre* constantly stumbles across problems in the notion of linear growth and development of subjectivity and narrativity.

Let us examine the 'development' of the narrative voice by focusing on the instances when Jane Eyre speaks directly in the text. The first 'speech' by Jane Eyre is a protest against the injustices she suffers. She is struggling to speak – to put thoughts into words. This struggle results in the utterance of a piercing scream, which is described as 'involuntary', when she must have been 'out of herself' (*JE*, p. 44). Instead of an easy congruence and commerce between the mind, the tongue and the sentence uttered, Jane's efforts to tell her story are jerky and clumsy: 'my tongue pronounced words without my will consenting to their utterance' (*JE*, p. 60). The involuntary expression – its spontaneity and lack of control – is also a protest. The utterance is dangerous, both as regards its source, springing from the depths of being – without the 'consent' of the 'will' – and in its content, in the protest of the little child against injustices perceived. At this stage the inarticulateness is attributed to her juvenile status and the inability of children to analyse and express. The Lockean notion of the child as someone who has to 'learn', gradually, a use of language, is contained in the desire to establish a perfect correspondence between thoughts, emotions and words. Jane is to progress towards more coherent forms of expression.

A perfectibility of narration seems to be the point to which the narrative of *Jane Eyre* is travelling. Perfect speech is seen as a liberation, by means of which the enunciating subject could break his/her shackles and emerge into full autonomous subjectivity. The difficulties in this progress towards 'mastery', and the ensuing liberation from masters, are highlighted in the earlier parts of the narrative. Little Jane's second involuntary outburst occurs in an impassioned encounter with her Aunt Reed. However, the sense of victory after the outburst is short-lived, as the child begins to dread the punishment that she is sure will ensue. Fluency of speech, in this instance, does not liberate, but highlights power positions.

The first ten chapters centre around this notion of a perfect and liberating speech and the efficacy and effects of spontaneous and controlled expression. In Lowood, Jane first tells her story to Helen Burns, to 'whom I spoke as I felt' (*JE*, p. 90). However, this perfect correspondence between feelings and expression is not subsequently held as an ideal. Subsequent narrations of Jane's life story are celebrated for their exercise of control and are consciously edited, as, for example, when the story is told to Miss Temple – 'Thus restrained and simplified, it sounded more credible: I felt as I went on that Miss Temple fully believed me' (JE, p. 103). The emphasis in this version of the narration has shifted from freedom of expression to the notion of attracting and involving the listener: the story must be made 'credible'. Restraint is the keyword in this narrative, and a concept that the text constantly invokes.

If we look at *Jane Eyre* in this way we can see how the question of self-representation and articulation is repeatedly foregrounded and problematised. Jane's struggle towards perfect speech is accompanied by her growth as an artist. *The Professor* had given the readers a picture of the growth of a female writer: here, art serves the function that writing had in the previous novel. The relationship between the mind and identity of the painter and the paintings is differently articulated in these instances. In the first place, an exploratory trip is undertaken by Rochester into the recesses and mysteries of Jane's mind, thus setting the theme of the romance; in the second, a conscious effort to halt the veering between imagination and reality and to fix the subject in a position of rationality and clarity is made, echoing the romance/reality oscillation; whilst in the third, subjectivity and sexuality merge as the desiring female subject spontaneously and unconsciously draws the portrait of Rochester, creating that area of ideal union to which the text aspires. These three instances act as illustrations of the creation of the central subject in *Jane Eyre* as it veers between various positions, making the text a means of questioning the status of its own narration. Again, romantic and sexual union is posed as that ideal site, but, given the operation of sexual difference, such a site remains out of reach.

Let us examine each of these paintings as they occur in the text. First, paintings are used (like the compositions in *The Professor*) to provide the hero with a glimpse of Jane's mind. Rochester seeks to know Jane through her paintings. He notices an 'elfishness' of mind at work: 'but I dare say you did exist in a kind of artist's dream-land while you blent and arranged these strange tints' (*JE*, p. 158). The artist's world of the imagination is portrayed as a visionary and unreal dreamland. The failure of the paintings is attributed not only to lack of skill and training, but to the nature of the artistic inspiration itself. It can only be seen as sporadic, unsustained and unreachable, and the artistic expression 'but a pale portrait of the thing I had conceived' (*JE*, p. 157). The revelation of Jane's mind, whether through her narration, her speech or paintings, is concerned to give a picture of a being struggling to bridge gaps between concepts (emotions and thoughts) and speech or representational form. At times an 'unconscious' realm is hinted at, where the expression, though incomplete and unsatisfactory, nevertheless emanates from a 'pure' source; at other times, controlled rational expression is recommended. The progress is always towards a perfect blend, where expression and concepts mix completely. The romance in *Jane Eyre* is used to provide this site of perfect speech, but, given the power positions in the romance – its Gothic undertones, its evocation of the Other – the autonomy of the female subject is constantly jeopardised. The contradictions in Jane's position are therefore contained not only in the instabilities of the narration, but also in the notion of progress which it carries, in those sites and moments when language, expression, desire and the character of the speaker/artist are, or are seen to be, perfectly united. The identification of the text with the narrator (at one level the narrative as autobiography of Jane Eyre, edited by Currer Bell, and at another as the expression of the female author's, Charlotte Brontë's, perfect understanding of the female condition) ignores the way the text itself comments on the problematic relationship between representation and the subject. Unrepresentability is the text's main motif, which, like romantic composition, is marked by momentary and evanescent expression. The logical progression that is part of an autobiographical project cannot be followed through, as the text constantly reiterates the impossibility of linear progress, of mastery over words and of homogeneous narration to highlight and celebrate, instead, those short sporadic moments of inspired utterance.

The second instance of Jane as artist is provided when she tries to discipline her mind and to force it into a recognition of her 'real' position. Faced with the imminent visit of the beautiful Blanche Ingram, Rochester's bride-elect, Jane tries to 'bring back with a strict hand such [emotions] as had been straying through imagination's boundless and tractless waste, into the safe fold of common sense' (*JE*, p. 190). Reason is now brought forward, and made to tell, in 'her own quiet way, a plain, unvarnished tale, showing how I had rejected the real, and rapidly devoured the ideal' (*JE*, p. 190). The painting exercise becomes a means of self-discipline, and a way of representing social hierarchical position through the creation of concrete images. Jane paints two portraits, one of herself, sketched in two hours and entitled 'Portrait of a Governess, disconnected, poor and plain'. To offset this, an imaginary portrait of Blanche Ingram is made, requiring a fortnight's work, with raven ringlets and Oriental eyes. The contrast between the real and the ideal is imaged and put forth to keep in mind the distance between desire and reality. Here Jane paints out of her mind's eye, not in order to indulge her imagination, but to control and direct it.

Art, in this description, is seen as a conscious means of self-control, through which the straying imagination is made to recognise the limitations of subject-positions. The emphasis is on rationality and control. Art becomes a form of chastisement, highlighting the educational purposes of the text. The narrator/artist is to prune and fashion herself according to her social circumstances.

Jane's later portrait of Rochester is in sharp contrast to these paintings. This 'speaking likeness' (*JE*, p. 262) of Rochester is involuntarily made and, in fact, helps to close the gap between the mind and the representational object: spontaneity, imagination, sexuality and sexual desire combine to produce a portrait that faithfully represents the painter's state of mind.

This painting should be read in conjunction with the scene in the garden, where the restraints on Jane's speech were similarly broken down. The painting of Rochester's portrait presents the love story as the point at which the gap between representation and emotion closes, and the subject emerges into an arena of perfect expression. The spontaneous declaration of love –

> I am not talking to you now through the medium of custom, conventionalities, nor even of mortal flesh; it is my spirit that addresses your spirit; just as if both had passed through the grave, and we stood at God's feet, equal – as we are!
>
> (*JE*, p. 281)

– envisages a realm beyond the social, where the divisive forces that have constructed the two subjects can be ignored. Like the reverie on the roof, it expresses a desire for a site of equality, where difference, sexual and economic, would be obliterated. This moment, which marks the ultimate triumph of the female subject, is interrupted: first by Rochester's proposal, and secondly by the sudden burst of lightning and thunder which drives the lovers indoors. The proposal of marriage to Jane is abrupt and commanding: 'But, Jane, I summon you as my wife . . .' (*JE*, p. 282). Immediately the demand and declaration of perfect unity is sundered, as the sexually differentiated positions of power within the institution of marriage are reiterated. Finally, the splitting of the great horse-chestnut tree by lightning also serves to symbolise the separation and difference – the impossibility of unity – in the positions of Jane Eyre and Rochester.

This famous scene in the garden is preceded by other scenes where the hero seeks to probe into Jane's mind, and where unity turns into linguistic direction and control and spontaneous self-discovery and discovery of the Other are revealed in terms of differentiated access to, and mastery over, speech. The conversations between Jane Eyre and Rochester echo the roles of the confessor and the confessing subject, with the woman in the confessing position. The confessor remains male. Short stichomythic sentences characterise the dialogue (as in *The Professor*):

'You have been resident in my house three months?'
'Yes, sir.'
'And you come from?'
'From Lowood school, in ————shire.'

(*JE*, p. 153)

The conversation continues:

'Miss Eyre, have you ever lived in a town?'
'No, sir.'
'Have you seen much society?'
'None but the pupils and teachers of Lowood; and now the inmates of Thornfield.'

(*JE*, p. 154)

The woman is interrogated; information is elicited from her. She is also cast in the role of auditor, listening to a narration of the events of Rochester's life. The discourse is controlled by the male questioner, who determines what it is he would like to know, and who draws his own conclusions from the responses. The power relation in the confessional rests on the authority invested in the person of the confessor, according to Foucault (1977). In the circumstances, Jane's declaration of equality and independence is a form of protest against a discourse in which she is controlled and guided by her male master and lover. Her declaration is a desperate effort to establish her own voice within the story that is being written. In such instances, Jane as narrative voice (teller of the story) and Jane (the character whose story is told), are separated, and the narrator has occasionally to step outside, and in the voice of 'special pleading', to establish her autonomy and strength. Sentences like '*I* care for myself' (*JE*, p. 344) forcefully express the desired position of strength.

The spontaneous drawing of Rochester's portrait is thus related to the spontaneity of the declaration of love and equality that is made in the garden scene. Similarly, the painting of the portrait also points to the control on female expression, whereby perfection of expression marks a moment of relinquishment of will on the part of the female artist. The portrait reflects Jane's enthralment, her subjection, her captivity and the complete relinquishment of her autonomy, her*self*, to the image of Rochester. The spontaneity of drawing does not portray an autonomy of subjectivity, but a surrender to the older patriarch. The painting as an expression of sexual desire shows the female artist as enthralled and captured. The Gothic associations become obvious in the picture of the woman imprisoned by a sexual desire, which, in so far as it is inimical to the autonomy of the subject, is dangerous. By allying the spontaneity of artistic expression with sexuality and sexual desire, the passage presents this spontaneity, not as securing the self-expression of the subject, but as something that puts her at risk. If artistic expression is transgressive, the spontaneous expression of Jane's sexual desire signals danger. Jane's progress is marked, and marred, by her status as sexual subject. Again, the textual contradiction between a steady notion of growth and the celebration of spontaneous expression emerges to jeopardise the *Bildungsroman*: the text constantly betrays its own project as the narrative of the growth of an individual subject and slips into the celebration of sporadic and inspired artistic and romantic moments.

The last scene is usually read as a triumph of the struggling subject. As Showalter (1977) points out, the maimed Rochester and the curbed Jane Eyre have both come to grips with the limits of their own situation and are therefore able to lead fulfilled and harmonious lives. Jane's dark passion and Rochester's overweening masculine pride are curbed, enabling them to live happily ever after. Gayatri Spivak (1985) also reads this last scene as one of eternal happiness, and sees Ferndean Manor, the home that Jane Eyre finally lives in, as a fulfilment of the desires expressed in the first scene, where, despite the obvious marginalisation, the subject had remained within the precincts of the English country home. The last scene merely establishes her more firmly within it.

However, the last scene of the novel is as disturbing as the last scene of *The Professor*. First the setting is Gothic: 'deep buried in a wood' (*JE*, p. 455). Ferndean Manor is situated deep inside a forest – 'There was a grass-grown track descending the forest aisle, between hoar and knotty shafts and under branched arches' (*JE*, p. 455). It is a lifeless place. Rochester, its master and main inhabitant, is blind, upsetting the image of a complete and homogeneous human subject in the place of the patriarch himself. Rochester's blindness is not to be equated with what has happened to Jane's passion. Whereas her passion, compared to madness, is pruned and brought under control to allow the emergence of the female subject and to place her in a position of greater stability, Rochester, as a blind man, is rendered helpless. Completely in Jane's power, he symbolises the dangers and points of dislocation to which the autonomy and sovereignty of the male subject are vulnerable. His blindness focuses on physical disability as a destabilising factor. The final perfect union is not between two autonomous individuals, since the powerful male is subject to stressful imaginings, and his body is maimed.

The final inscription of Jane Eyre into middle-class England is as wife to a blind man. The famous sentence, 'Reader, I married him' (*JE*, p. 474), remains the ultimate instance of narrative pleading, a recognition of the gaps between the longings that the text had expressed and the final point of rest at which it arrives.

Jane Eyre is a text where the female subject under construction is forced to encounter its Other. While the externalised Other is 'killed', the positions then made available to this more controlled subject are replete with factors inimical to a notion of harmony and peace. The death of Bertha Mason has been seen as symbolising the curbing of uncontrolled passion (as female sexuality and female anger), and has usually been read as establishing the central narrator's triumph and success.

Feminist literary criticism has always looked on the voice of *Jane Eyre* as triumphant. Initially, it had celebrated this, and more recently a recognition of the cost of the triumph has led to a critical revaluation of that celebratory tendency. However, both readings ignore the fluctuations and difficulties involved in the final position of rest that the text achieves. Feminist discourse, informed by colonial history, has, in its concentration on *Jane*

Eyre as an imperialist text, overlooked the difficulties in being Jane Eyre, that is, the difficulties of a sovereign femininity placed within a system of patriarchy, which seeks to control and guide it.

SHIRLEY OR THE DOMESTICATION OF THE THEME

Published in 1849, *Shirley* gives up the first-person narrative voice used in *The Professor* and *Jane Eyre*. The narrative perspective is now hidden under an omniscient and objective third-person narrative voice, and has to be deciphered and discovered. This novel, about industrial strife, merges class and gender issues as its main focal points and the colonial position veers between the image of the striking worker and a concept of autonomous and rebellious femininity.

I will read *Shirley* to bring out the fluctuations in its dominant subject-position, as well as its delineation of the problems of femininity and female identity. Both women, Caroline and Shirley, are involved in a search for their mother, and discovery of maternal identity is associated with the formation of subjectivity itself. Caroline's meeting with the 'real' mother determines her identity and brings her back to health and happiness. Shirley's quest is expressed through her essay on Eve, recording a search for origins. This essay, crucially, is evaluated by Louis Moore, the male tutor, who subsequently becomes Shirley's lover and husband. The mediation of a sexualised pedagogical practice is thus given a central position in this search for a mother and a matrilineal heritage.

Shirley's essay interrupts the text: it is inserted into it as a separate narrative. In a manner similar to the narrative address to the reader, the text calls attention to itself. This interpolation can be seen as a formalist device, similar to the 'violations' Victor Shlovsky sees in Sterne's *Tristam Shandy*: 'By violating the form, he forces us to attend to it' (Shlovsky, 1965, p. 30). Louis Moore's diary is similarly inserted into the text. The similarities between Shirley's essay and that diary are limited to their function as narrative interpolation. Their differences, of mode and address, are more fundamental. Shirley's essay was 'written in the schoolroom', under Moore's tutelage and for his perusal and assessment. Moore's diary is private, meant for no other eyes but his.

Crucially, this personal diary is *about* Shirley, so its insertion punctures and disrupts the narrative vantage-point enjoyed by the women. Shirley, the powerful woman, is now seen through the eyes of Louis Moore, and rendered into the object of *his* narrative. The class–differentiated power positions which define the relationship between the middle class, the gentry and the emerging working class delineate *one* relationship of difference, which is defined and observed through a female vantage-point. The dominant femininity envisaged, then, is in turn delineated in sexual terms, and a gendered hierarchy made to disrupt and denigrate this dominant position. In the terms I have been using and establishing so far, it is when Other positions are no longer externalised, but are included in the subjective narrative position, that narrative disruption and instability become an intrinsic part of the textual utterance.

A COLONIAL ENCOUNTER: THE ATTACK ON THE MILL

Shirley is a novel about industrial strife: the conflict between the commercialism of the newly established mill-owners and manufacturers and a wider, national 'English' interest. Thus, industrial conflict does not just divide mill-owner from mill-worker, but also differentiates the interests of the new industrial classes from those of the older aristocracy. Social divisions, used to describe sibling rivalry in *The Professor*, are now made to delineate a national division, as the older aristocracy are shown to maintain and conserve a way of life that is identified as patriotic and English, while the commercial interests of mill-owners are regarded as crass and insensitive to English values. Robert Moore, mill-owner, is foreign, part Belgian and only part English, and emblematic of the alien nature of the new order brought in by industrialisation which is contrasted to older, more established notions of Englishness.[8]

Despite this, Moore's foreign status does not prevent his eventual incorporation into English society. He is drawn in, first, through a literature lesson. Shakespeare's *Coriolanus*, taught to Robert Moore by Caroline Helstone (who is the eighteen-year-old niece of the parson, and in love with Robert Moore), does not function merely as a salutary lesson to his pride, but evokes an adequately appreciative response from him: 'and still as he

198

read he warmed' (*S*, p. 116). His final incorporation into the fold of Yorkshire society is through marriage with his 'literature teacher'. His mark – the mark of industrialisation – on the Yorkshire scenery is unmistakable and indelible – 'the cinder-black highway, the cottages, and the cottage gardens; . . . a mighty mill, and a chimney, ambitious as the tower of Babel' (*S*, p. 599). The conflict between the industrialists and the aristocracy can be seen to represent the conflict between different notions of Englishness, and does not take on the proportions of an insurmountable confrontation between English and Other or foreign interests. The semi-English, commercially identified Robert Moore can be drawn into the English fold, and the joint marriages with which the novel ends mark the celebration of the union of English commerce with the old aristocracy and the newly emerging professional middle class, thereby defining a new social configuration in England.

Shirley locates its Other positions in two sites: in the strife between the workers and the mill-owners, and in the problems of female identity and subjectivity. Let us consider the delineation of working-class strife and the textual devices which portray the striking workers in a manner similar to the savage or colonial Other. The scene of the attack on the mill is crucial as it locates the Other in the image of the striking worker. A 'crash – smash – shiver' is followed by a yell:

> A yell followed this demonstration – a rioters' yell – a North-of-England – a Yorkshire – a West-Riding – a West-Riding-clothing-district-of-Yorkshire rioters' yell.
>
> (*S*, p. 386)

The auditory impact of this passage is comparable to the way in which both *The Professor* and *Jane Eyre* had introduced their readers to the presence of the Other, signalling the entry of disturbing and disruptive elements in the text. The reader is directly addressed in this passage: 'You never heard that *sound*, perhaps, reader?' (*S*, p. 335). Attention is drawn to the yell and the incomprehensibility of the sound, introducing the rioting workers as an alien factor – something *else*, something other, obviating rationally held positions and views. The rioters' yell is an irrational and incomprehensible sound and can only evoke similar responses: 'It is difficult to be tolerant – difficult to be just – in such moments' (*S*, p. 335). The detailed, graded description – 'rioters', 'North-of-England' and so on – locates the yell in a separate area – externalised and alienated. This detailed classification expresses a need to comprehend, analyse and *place* the Other.

This scene has been read by Terry Eagleton as an example of the way in which the novel, about industrial strife, marginalises and effaces working-class positions to become a text that can only be read as a discourse about middle-class women:

> It would be truer to say that the event is at once structurally central and curiously empty – empty because the major protagonist, the working class, is distinguished primarily by its absence. . . . It [the attack] is seen from the vantage-point of Caroline and Shirley.
>
> (Eagleton, 1988, pp. 47–8)

Helen Taylor has extended this notion of an absent protagonist to include the women in the scene, who are, in her reading, seen to be absent as well, so that *Shirley* betrays both its feminism and its sympathy for working-class struggle (see Taylor, 'Class and Gender in Charlotte Brontë's *Shirley*').

I would like to keep the main points that Terry Eagleton identifies in this scene – its hidden nature, its auditory impact, and its feminine vantage-point – to delineate its ideological and narrative positioning. These elements can easily be transposed to enable a reading of the scene as an example of a colonial encounter in which the subject meets the Other to which its identity is bound, and in whose reflection it is to recognise its own image. The darkness, covertness and the *mystery* of the scene ally this meeting to other colonial encounters. The Other, in such descriptions, remains hidden in darkness, its presence felt but not fully perceived. The effort at exact definition acts as a covering up of this incomprehensibility. Rationality, control, order are seen to be slipping away at such moments, and the narrative address becomes pleading, asking for sympathy, directly addressing the reader. The language is emotive and allegorical:

> Wrath wakens to the cry of Hate: the Lion shakes his mane, and rises to the howl of the Hyaena: Caste stands up, ireful, against Caste; and the indignant, wronged spirit of the Middle Rank bears down in zeal and scorn on the famished and furious mass of the Operative Class.
>
> (*S*, p. 386)

The women's voyeuristic position both excludes them and places them in the powerful position. The covertness of the scene does not merely remove the rioting workers from the direct line of the reader's vision, but is described by an audience who are themselves hidden and deprived of direct participation in the action. The violent attack by the workers on the mill is indeed the central scene in the novel. The female vantage-point marks out the workers as the disturbing and unknowable Other element. However, at the same time the women themselves are hidden in darkness, unseen by the men with whom they identify, and their position is similarly determined by their marginalisation. This colonial encounter is rendered in a manner that does not put the female protagonists in a position of dominance, as the dominant vantage-point enjoyed here is broken at other places in the text, where the women themselves are portrayed as subordinate. The tensions of *Shirley* can be located in the oscillation of its narrative position and theme, by which femininity is portrayed as both dominant and subservient.

The paternalist response that had been invoked by the suffering of the workers is now abandoned as working-class men are compared to howling wild hyenas, against whom the majestic lion has to protect itself. The 'famished and furious' operatives have to be trampled on and completely annihilated. Just as concepts of justice and fair play were overlooked in the face of colonial rebellion, so they are not invoked at this instance where class interests have to be maintained.

Violence and justice are very fluid terms in the textual delineation of working-class demands and action. Stories of attacks on other mills keep the antagonism between the mill-owners and workers at the centre of the text, and work up fear about the maintenance of social order and harmony. Growing unemployment is blamed for working-class despair. Desperate, dangerous men roam the countryside. The portraits of men such as Moses Barraclough or the near-crazed Michael Hartley detract from the political dimensions of the workers' struggle and show them as somehow inhuman or savage. The magical quality of the yell has the same effect.

This is one response to the workers' plight. The other is to appeal to human sympathy, and to evoke a paternalistic response from the readers. For example, when the Farrens household is described, images of hunger and poverty predominate – the distress of the parents is described in a sympathetic tone, evoking a similar response from the reader (see *S*, p. 158).

Even when drawn in this humanitarian manner, the workers remain in the position of the Other. Pity and sympathy may be invoked, but they are still alienated and are not given full human status. Whether delineated in a sympathetic manner or otherwise, the workers are kept in the position of the Other in *Shirley*, where narrative and ideological positions merge to forge an examination of middle-class femininity in Victorian England. The ultimate response to the working-class situation and the identification of class interest is made by Shirley, in conversation with Caroline. There is no hesitation about where her interests lie:

> If once the poor rise to gather and rise in the form of the mob, I shall turn against them as an aristocrat: if they bully me, I must defy; if they attack, I must resist, and I will.
>
> (*S*, p. 268)

The radical split between the two classes is graphically represented here. The women, excluded from the scene of the attack on the mill, are nevertheless still identified with the dominant narrative position. Gender and class divisions intersect to create the divided social terrain in the text. But despite mutual subordination to the patriarchal interests of the middle class, gender and class interests do not merge: both thematically and formally, they are kept apart.

THE SEARCH FOR FEMALE IDENTITY

The attack on the mill fixes ideological perspectives to a limited extent only. In that description, subject and object of discourse are differentiated, and the middle-class Victorian woman's point of view is dominant. The identification of the third-person impersonal narration with the author's (Charlotte Brontë's) gender and class position perhaps rests on the recognition of such scenes in the text, where the sharp differentiation of subject and object places the women in the subjective, narrating position. However, if *Shirley* is to be viewed as a text in which women occupy the main narrative position, we have to note not only the places at which the feminine vantage-point is dominant, but also the way that the text problematises the story of the women and of female positioning.

Shirley is not a *Bildungsroman*, unlike *Jane Eyre* in which the problems of female enunciation and narration are traced through the development of an individual character. *Shirley* divides its search for female identity between two characters, Shirley Keeldar and Caroline Helstone. The motif of the Family Romance is very strong in this quest. Both women are motherless (indeed parentless), and their search for a mother is allied to the search for roots. A mother–daughter reunion emerges again as a fantasised site of fulfilment, towards which both women are bound and through which they expect to find a firmer establishment within the social milieu.

Let us first look at the figure of Caroline Helstone. Eighteen years old, she is engrossed in a hopeful dream of glorious romance. However, this dream is dangerous as love, dreamt of as fulfilment and happiness, is beset with hidden dangers. The following diatribe on love emphasises its dangers:

> Love, when he comes wandering like a lost angel to our door, is at once admitted, welcomed, embraced: his quiver is not seen; if his arrows penetrate, their wound is like a thrill of new life: there are no fears of poison, none of the barb which no leech's hand can extract: that perilous passion . . .
>
> (*S*, p. 121)

The passage is written in the third person, but at a crucial moment it shifts: love comes wandering to *our* door. Author, narrative subject and reader are drawn together in this first-person plural, and identified as female. This identity is endangered by its vulnerability to strange wandering *men*, who are associated with love. Love is thus personified as male in the above extract, unknown (a wanderer), deceiving (disguised as an angel), uncanny, as the pleasure of his piercing arrows is transformed into a pain that may last throughout life. Nevertheless, the paradox for women remains, as the harmony in the last scene is a result of successful sexual union. In the novel, Caroline is shown to be lovesick, as love is withheld from her, and as she grows nervous at the prospect of the idleness and uselessness of an unmarried middle-class Victorian woman's life. The text takes this opportunity to delineate the lives of such women (the chapter on 'Old Maids') and to give an account of the limitations of employment opportunities for the genteel, single impoverished woman, especially in Caroline's desperate bid to become a governess.

Caroline's illness is of nervous origin: no physical cause can be ascribed to it. Its associations with hysteria are obvious in the way it is manifested as well as in its treatment. While other characters are unaware of the romantic origins of this depression, the reader is included in Caroline's secret, so that when a sudden illness overtakes her, its emotional causes are known. Caroline herself is, at first, shown to be surprised at the onset of the fever: 'Am I ill?' (S, p. 399). She gazes at herself in the mirror, and sees not a languishing face but a flushed one:

> Her eyes were bright, their pupils dilated, her cheeks seemed rosier and fuller than usual. . . . She felt a pulse beat fast in her temples: she felt, too, her brain in a strange activity: her spirits were raised; hundreds of busy and broken, but brilliant thoughts engaged her mind: a glow rested on them, such as tinged her complexion.
>
> (S, p. 399)

The image that the mirror throws back is of an exhilarated, sexualised, half-crazed person. Objectively, even scientifically, the narrative voice describes Caroline's physical features and their relation to her mental state. No sudden eruption of the first-person pronoun occurs to draw the reader into the text. The image is presented as something to be gazed at and objectively analysed: 'Her eyes', 'her cheeks', 'her spirits'. Caroline is turned into the object of discourse, and made to occupy the Other position. Ill, excited, nervous, the female subject – with whom the narrator had seemed momentarily to identify in the passage on love and who had in other instances occupied the dominant narrative position through which a dangerous Other position had been revealed (in the scene of the attack on the mill) – is now turned into the Other herself. The illness is portrayed in terms of a nervous excitement: the beating pulse, the teeming brain, the raised spirit, the brilliant, but *broken*, thoughts. The eighteen-year-old Caroline stands on the threshold of life. But this threshold seems to lead to madness, which is associated with her romantic predilections. Crucially, the text occupies different enunciatory positions – identification *with*, and judgement at a distance *of* the sexuality of the female protagonist, as if it did not know how or where to situate itself.

The recovery from this love-sickness is effected with the discovery of the identity of her mother. Cause and cure of illness are not related. The text, instead, brings in the motif of maternal identity as determining feminine identity. Earlier, in *The Professor* we saw how Frances Henri's mother's English origins had helped to re-establish her within the English leisured classes. Later, in *Jane Eyre*, the image of the mother appeared in dreams and visions, helping the protagonist at moments of crisis. The re-creation of the mother/child dyad in Charlotte Brontë's writings can be seen as evocative of the originary pre-Oedipal moment, and to delineate a site which lies prior to and beyond the social. The fantasy of origins is related to a site of perfect union and love, and is replayed here to make Caroline recover from her mental illness, and to denote a return to human subject status. By positing the mother/child dyad as central, the replay of the Family Romance in this instance ignores the difficulties of this journey backwards. However, the vicissitudes of the journey cannot be ignored. Caroline's illness entails a toppling into an irrational, inhuman state, which then appears as a prerequisite for such a journey. The recovery is effected in a miraculous manner, for which no scientific or physical causes can be discerned. The reunion of mother and daughter remains magical and miraculous, as if it could somehow evade a strong placement within the social symbolic realm which the text constructs.

Shirley, however, is different from Caroline. As squire and mill-owner, she combines in her person the conflicting interests of the landed gentry and the manufacturing classes. As an independent woman she evades many of the constraints that define her sisters. The special position she occupies is made clear in a speech to Caroline and Mr Helstone:

> Shirley Keeldar, Esquire, ought to be my style and title. They gave me a man's name; I hold a man's position: it is enough to inspire me with a touch of manhood, . . .
>
> (S, p. 213)

However, the masculine position enjoyed by Shirley does not preclude her from being placed within situations that echo Caroline's. Stripped of the social constraints on Victorian femininity, the figure of Shirley becomes an even more potent site through which the problems of female identity can be addressed.

A hysterical illness is again portrayed, as even Shirley, the strong woman, falls ill and 'wastes away' for no ostensible reason. Her illness is based on an unfounded fear of having contracted rabies. A psychosomatic illness is used to highlight the vicissitudes to which subjectivity is vulnerable. The fear is ungrounded, and it is only through a confessional encounter with Louis Moore (male tutor/lover/husband) that Shirley's fears are dispelled and her drooping spirits brought back to health and energy. This illness weakens and renders vulnerable the image of a dominant and strong female character, who is shown to be in need of male care, protection and ministration. Moreover, she is in love, and the sovereignty and independence of her situation is weakened and indeed shown to be lost in this instance. As Caroline reports to Robert Moore: 'Shirley is a bondswoman. Lioness! she has found her captor' (*S*, p. 562).

Robert Moore marvels at the captivity of such a woman, and exults in the image of this 'fair and imperial' slave. Love again enters to enslave, weaken, endanger and to render vulnerable female strength. That the text then uses this love in the marriage of Louis Moore and Shirley Keeldar to bring about the harmony of the last scene demonstrates the weaknesses inherent in the female position. Three of Charlotte Brontë's major novels – *The Professor*, *Jane Eyre* and *Shirley* – end on a note of marital and social harmony. But in each of these novels the dangers of sexuality for the narrating subject are highlighted. The point of rest in the happy endings, in each case, rests on harmonious sexual union, so the social harmony envisaged can only be seen as tenuous and liable to change. *Shirley*, written from women's point of view, constantly returns to the difficulties of the limitations of femininity. Although in the first instance the women were differentiated from the working-class Other, this difference is often muddled to make femininity the disturbing and disruptive Other in the text.

Shirley's essay on Eve, the universal mother, harks back to a matriarchal past when women occupied positions of power and freedom. The essay, which punctuates the third-person narration, occurs as a 'real' instance of one of those *devoirs*/essays/paintings which were used by other heroes to delve into the minds of their lovers/pupils.[9] Written by the female pupil for the male tutor, its inclusion in the text is made possible only through *his* careful retention of it and through the value expressed by this gesture.

Let us go over the essay in some detail, as it remarkably repeats and condenses the themes of exoticism and human subjective development which I have argued are key constituents in the history of the formation of the novel. Eve is seen wandering in an Edenic world, like the wandering savages in Rousseau's description. Her innocence is broken when the male Lord descends to endow the imaginary Eve with the faculty of Genius. Indeed, the descent works like the moment of rupture, separating the pre-Oedipal child from the mother and propels Eve on her journey towards human subjectivity. The essay can be read as a search for the lost mother and as a fantasised picture of a site of dominant and powerful femininity. Its emphasis on remoteness, both in time and space, takes on romantic overtones, as a harmonious existence of nature and human beings is delineated. Fertility and natural abundance are ascribed to this site. Exotic magicality is brought to Europe, and a picture of a fantasised forest, analogous to the island paradise which was such a favourite site for colonial adventures, is then drawn:

> A forest valley, with rocky sides and brown profundity of shade, formed by tree crowding on tree, descends deep before me.
>
> (S, p. 456)

It is a picture of a tropical island paradise. The forest-dwellers are savages, human only in so far as they have human emotions, but they do not possess the power of thought or 'genius'. Eve is the parentless and lonely child of this Edenic place. Again, the constituents of human subjectivity are put into question:

> You see in the desolate young savage nothing vicious or vacant; she haunts the wood harmless and thoughtful: though of what one so untaught can think, it is not easy to divine.
>
> (S, p. 457)

Knowledge descends on her as she sits longingly in the forest – the lord of the night appears to the 'Daughter of Man' and everything changes, as he bestows on the female the capacity to think. The Lord cries out to her:

> I take from thy vision, darkness: I loosen from thy faculties, fetters: I level in thy path, obstacles: I, with my presence,

fill vacancy: I claim as mine the lost atom of life: I take to myself the spark of soul – burning, heretofore, forgotten!

(*S*, p. 459)

The story of Genesis is reworked to portray a powerful and ascendant Eve who is blessed in the 'bridal-hour of Genius and Humanity' (*S*, p. 459). This moment is marked by her recognition of the lord, who is male. Humanity – knowledge and creativity – are seen to spring out of the pairing of the female with the dominant male principle. The recreation of the mother/daughter dyad as the moment of origin is shattered with the entry of the third factor, the Law or Name of the Father. The moment and site of human origins is ascribed not to the purity of the pre-Oedipal state, but to the Oedipal moment, when the child, brought to recognise the phallus as the symbol of human difference and division, is propelled on its hazardous, but exciting, journey, into human subjectivity.

Shirley's comment on her essay of an imagined site of female power echoes the significance of that vision:

'I never could correct that composition'. . . . 'Your censor-pencil scored it with condemnatory lines, whose signification I strove vainly to fathom.'

(*S*, p. 460)

Louis Moore's (the male tutor's) approval and ratification are necessary. This essay, in its contents, envisaged a female origin for humankind. It is also an instance of a female enunciation. This enunciation has to be authorised by the male who, despite social inferiority, wields power. The male tutor/female tutee motif enters strongly as the search for female identity and roots is ratified by the male tutor. Despite this, there seems to be a resistance in the pupil, in her inability to 'correct that composition'. However, the resistance is not strong enough to permit Shirley to completely ignore her tutor's comments, and the essay about matrilineal heritage has still to be condoned by the male tutor. The essay tries to construct a story about matrilineality, through which an ancient lineage could be drawn for the female squire, Shirley Keeldar, and her position as an independent property and mill-owner in contemporary Victorian society justified. The plea for female emancipation and education is transferred into a plea for the right of female property ownership, and the demand for the rights of woman is expressed as a charter for the rights and privileges of bourgeois women. The interruption of this dream of a powerful mother functions as censorship, guided by the male, whose position, despite economic subordination, remains powerful.

LOUIS MOORE'S DIARY

The interruptions of the third-person narration in *Shirley* function in different ways. At times interruption ushers in a more self-conscious authorial voice, which, in turn, functions to draw the reader and subject into a harmonious community. At others, it is punctuated to let in other representational forms, as in the inclusion of Shirley's essay on Eve. Louis Moore's diary is included in a similar manner. The use of a male diary is significant, as it brings a first-person male narrative voice into the text. Thus Shirley, despite the paternalist male position that she enjoys, is rendered subject to the gaze and pen of Louis Moore.

Before going on to look at the diary, let us consider the ways in which the relationship between Louis Moore and Shirley is described. As with the other social relations in the text, Shirley Keeldar and Louis Moore are drawn together by contradictory and ambiguous ties. Louis, as Shirley's ex-tutor, had once been her paid employee or servant. The position of the male tutor is anomalous and not fully analogous to that of a female governess. To the genteel poverty that characterised both female governess and male tutor was added, in the case of the woman, the fact of sexual 'redundancy'. To a subordinate social and economic position was added sexual vulnerability. The male tutor, on the other hand, is a romantic figure, invested with a sensitivity and a sensibility that keeps him away from the crassness and commercialism of the society around him and associates him with the deeper 'English' values that the text is trying to establish. The power invested in the pedagogical process is mediated by factors other than the educational – sexual, economic and cultural – and cannot be seen to rest simply with the teacher or the imparter of knowledge. The sexualisation of the power relationship between a male teacher and female student(s) is illustrated in the reverberations of the phrase 'my master', when uttered by women characters in Charlotte Brontë's novels.

The first lesson described in Shirley was a literature lesson.

Shakespeare's *Coriolanus* had been used by Caroline to draw the foreigner Robert Moore into the glories of English culture and society. When Englishwoman taught foreign man the economic power relations had remained intact, and the text, instead of being made an emblem of English cultural superiority, had used the figure of Coriolanus to draw a comparison between Robert Moore and a noble patrician figure.

The female teacher and the male student do not mirror the relationship between a male teacher and a female pupil. Similarly, the male diary is crucially different from Shirley's essay. The private diary, meant for no other eyes, is the result of a secret mode of composition: the writing is Louis Moore's 'evening's comfort' (*S*, p. 487). Elaborate arrangements have to be made to enable this writing process: the fire has to be replenished, candles have to be lit, chairs have to be put in the right position, while a secret pocketbook emerges, waiting to be written on. The sudden address to the reader includes and introduces the secret of the diary:

> Come near, by all means, reader: do not be shy: stoop over his shoulder fearlessly, and read as he scribbles.
>
> (*S*, p. 487)

A conspiratorial collusiveness is demanded of the reader. The diary, secret and private, is a record of sexual desire and conquest.

Recounting a secret passion and love, it has a generic resemblance to the host of male diaries that record sexual adventures and conquest. These also portray sex as dangerous, something that has to be locked up and hidden. The best-known in this genre, Walter's *My Secret Life* (written between the years 1851 and the 1890s)[10] is presented as a mammoth record of the pseudonymous writer's sexual adventures and peccadilloes. The writing of this diary conjures up a similar image: a man, sitting covertly at his desk, and assiduously recalling and creating the narrative of his sexual life. The secret, therefore, seems to refer to the writing of this diary. The recorded sexual adventures, whether referring to 'real' or imaginary events, are fantasised, in so far as they are recalled, and recreated for narrative purposes. The secret, the pleasure, the secret pleasure are contained in the process of writing. The publication of this secret diary, this secret life, draws the reader into this private domain, and extends that pleasure into the perusal of the text. Thus both writing and reading a secret diary are pleasurable acts, and drawing the reader into the process communalises the private arena of sexual fantasy. This mid- to late-Victorian text locates sexual pleasure, desire and adventure outside the bounds of legally sanctioned marriage; it locates it in working-class women, servants or prostitutes. The illicit pleasure that emanates from the text is allied to a notion of sexual transgression of social boundaries.[11]

Louis Moore's diary is, on the surface, of a different kind. It is about 'real' and 'true' love, which is hardly comparable to the sexual licentiousness expressed by Walter. But, in its obsession with class positions and in its need to divest Shirley of her cultural accoutrements and social position, it expresses a desire for mastery that presupposes the servility and social degradation of women:

> If I were a gentleman, and she waited on me as a servant, I could not help liking that Shirley . . . I should wish to stay an hour: I should linger to talk with that rustic. I should not feel as I now do: I should find in her nothing divine; but whenever I met the young peasant, it would be with pleasure – whenever I left her, it would be with regret.
>
> (S, p. 488)

Shirley has to be impoverished, 'de'-civilised', for Louis Moore to approach her. The sexual excitement envisaged is with a rustic, a savage, a servant.

The diary shows these motifs of female sexuality and bondage in operation in the wooing scene between Shirley Keeldar and Louis Moore. While she mocks him for his 'tutor'-like disposition and position, and compares him to her dog (ambiguously, as recipient of love and also for dog-like, slavish devotion), he teases her with the image of a young orphan-girl as his prospective bride. He turns to Shirley to provide him with this fantasised power, and miraculously enough, she responds to her 'master'. However, Shirley continues to be playfully teasing, and the relinquishment of her property and position to Louis Moore, though sure, is slow.

Shirley's unsettling of the narrative vantage-point makes it difficult to decipher the main narrative stance, or to keep it in its position of centrality. Working-class strife and demands appear in the garb of the dangers once embodied in the savage and colonial Other. The two central women characters, potentially identified with this Other, are nonetheless given a position of

211

distance from this socially disruptive space and control over it. Yet the narrative position does not rest squarely on the shoulders of the women. The crucial differences of class between them are mitigated by the way in which the subject-positions of both are destabilised. Thus Caroline sits on the edge of hysteria, and slides into an asocial space of maternal recovery, while Shirley produces a counter-discourse of female emancipation as writer only to be drawn into the tutelage and sexual fantasy (also written) of the male. Femininity, both as social and subject-position, is seen to be tenuous, and therefore not just the affirmation of the women's text, but the place where the text seems to confront its own instability of writing, the impossibility – against the grain of the final subjugation of Shirley herself – of securing a singular (feminine) place.

Both heroines, young, unmarried and motherless, are shown to be embroiled in a search for identity, in which romantic and sexual love is seen as the site of perfect placement. But, in the manner of Gothic and romantic novels, this love also represents the sites of disjuncture and danger for the subject concerned. The dangers of love have to be domesticated and tamed for social and sexual harmony to reign. But, given the vicissitudes in the love story, the final resting-place does not totally convince.

Even within this very English novel, where the foreign motif (specially as travel) enters only partially as the patrician foreigner and is then contained and domesticated in the image of the working class, the inherent instability in relation to enunciation, particularly in the realm of sexuality, surfaces again. Crucially, the woman is moved backwards to a point of origin at the same time as the text polarises around class and gender positions which both reinforce and undermine each other. It is in the production of texts within texts that *Shirley* runs back to the origins of writing, as well as forwards to the containment of all writing (by women) in a voyeuristic masculine prerogative and control.

Women's writing, its connections with social realities, the novel as a form where women emerged to create a woman-to-woman discourse, or even the status of the novel as a form which questions and disrupts the narrative terrain within a fact/fantasy oscillation – are questions and issues that have been thoroughly examined within novel criticism. However, if a historical dimension is added to this examination (and by history I mean the history of the form itself, as well as the historical moment of the creation of texts, along with a history of its reception), the complexities of the genre will be highlighted, and the need for constant re-examination and perusal felt. *Jane Eyre* and *Shirley* have been read with the intention of such a re-examination, and to extract from these very popular novels meanings that relate to women's lives, not as a simple straightforward address but as revealing of the complexities of the subject-positions in which they are placed.

LANGUAGE, SUBJECTIVITY AND LITERATURE
An afterword

The task of the literary critic, both as teacher of literary texts and as writer about them, is difficult to define. The difficulties of this definition spring from and add to the difficulty of defining the term literature itself.

The most contentious aspect about what has been delineated as literature is its relationship to history. The bond between literature and history is both inextricable and problematic, and – from Sir Philip Sidney's differentiation between the probable truth of 'poesy' and the particular truth of history to Fredric Jameson's edict, 'Always historicise!' – forms a part of the critical discourse of literature. Literature, at one level, can be seen as history, as the fictions it creates reflect and express the stories and myths through which a nation and a culture choose to express themselves. The study of literature as history also involves a study of the history of literature and of the ways in which literature is defined and the sites and modes of its dissemination.

The intervention of feminism into the field of modern-day literary criticism has been the most significant development in the field in recent times. Feminist literary criticism starts from the premise that literary texts are gender differentiated, both in the way that literature is defined and disseminated, and in the contents of the discourse. The recent emphasis on gender hierarchies in literary texts and history has brought into focus the relationship between fictional and poetic writing and political, historical reality.

The realist school saw this relationship as a connection between literary discourse and a material, 'objective' reality. Initially, feminism adopted realist critical modes to formulate its gender-differentiated analysis. The history of literature was used by feminism, in its initial moment of content analysis, to examine the *contents* of the stories that cultures have devised for themselves. Lately feminism has had to extend the notion of gender differentiation to include other fragmenting categories that cross over and augment the gender hierarchies to which its initial concern had been limited.

In this context, the incorporation of the history of colonialism and imperialism into the field of literary criticism has been crucial, as it has been instrumental in relating literature (as writing, teaching and criticism), to a worldwide historical process. The most valuable aspect of this new intervention has been the demonstration of the way in which a practice of literature is translated to reflect political and economic hierarchies.

This book began with an examination of the eighteenth-century concept of 'man' – of the structures that form human subjectivity. It began with a textual examination of a seventeenth-century novel. The effort is not to trace the 'origins' of a notion of literature to the eighteenth century, but to use the contemporary discourse on human subjectivity and its relation to language to form an idea of the subject of literature. The book is centred on the novel as a discourse of that unified and coherent subject. Importantly, the political manifestations of this philosophical and literary concept can be seen in the inauguration of the bourgeois democratic order, based on the notion of the rights and sovereignty of the human individual. The new system of political government ushered in by the French Revolution sanctified the status and rights of the human individual as the citizen-subject of the emerging nation state. The slogans of human equality and liberty led to the formation of a discourse on the nature of the liberties and the rights of the citizen-subject. National sovereignty and individual rights are defined in relation to and for each other, as the identity of the nation state is defined by its citizens. Philosophical debate on the status of the individual showed the relationship between the individual subject and language. The most influential account of the development of human subjectivity equated it with the development of use of language, as Locke's child had learnt to give thoughts and feelings verbal shape and expression. This description of the individual was followed by narratives recording the development of civilisations and cultures, as in the writings of Rousseau and Condillac, a development associated with, and represented in terms similar to, the growth of the individual. The sovereignty and identity of the nation were seen as the conglomerate of the individual subjects that formed its citizenry. The newly emerging nation state was thus to be 'manned' by citizens educated and imbued with the concepts of democracy: above all, with subjects *schooled* in the exercise of reason.

The democratic influences of the French Revolution are visible in the discourse on language, its relationship to the individual, and in the community, society or culture to which the individual belongs. Wordsworth's image of the brotherhood between the poet and his readers – 'a man speaking to men' (Wordsworth, 1966, 'Preface to the Lyrical Ballads', p. 48) – reflects the democratic ideal of the French revolutionaries. The community the poet addresses is composed of 'ordinary' men, and poetry is democratised to include all men within its address. The romantic notion of unadorned expression is encapsulated in Wordsworth's recommendation of the use of the 'real language of men' (Wordsworth, 1966, p. 58).

This same appeal to plainness and directness of speech is made by Mary Wollstonecraft:

> I shall disdain to cull my phrases or polish my style. I aim at being useful, and sincerity will render me unaffected; . . . I shall not waste my time in rounding periods, or in fabricating the turgid bombast of artificial feelings . . .
>
> (Wollstonecraft, 1978, p. 82)

Wollstonecraft allies directness of expression to the enunciating or writing subject, whose plain style reflects and reinforces an honesty and straightforwardness of character, which is extended to include a concept of personal dignity and pride. Wollstonecraft's plain-speaking and plain-writing woman seeks to re-place women within language and society. For Wollstonecraft, women were relegated, on the one hand, to the domestic sphere, and on the other, to the sphere of deceptive, sexual pleasure. Remember how Locke had compared the powers of eloquence or a false and hyperbolic use of language to the pleasures of deception and the 'fair sex'. It is against this dual positioning that Wollstonecraft insists on a clear style of expression in order to undo and reconstruct women as educated, democratic and autonomous subjects, and therefore as part of the citizenry of the bourgeois nation state. The use of a certain kind of language is advocated, defining the 'free' subject within a rightful place in a democratic society. This notion of the sovereignty of the individual rests on possession of language and mode of expression. The freedom to use this language – the much-vaunted democratic right of the freedom of speech – while it presupposes a 'mastery' of the language, adds the notion of responsibility, directs and censors the use of language and delineates the *limits* of expression. So the quest for a perfect language and the perfect correspondence between objects, thoughts and expression constantly stumbles across the inability of words to perform this function. This happens, for example, even in Locke's formulation, so that he feels constrained to include a chapter on the 'abuse' of words. Similarly, the notion of a perfectly coherent subject was seen to flounder every time gaps in this envisaged subjectivity were encountered. The constitution of a state or republic forming a political entity, based on this notion of coherence, was bound to encounter points of dislocation.

★

The eighteenth-century concept of the citizen-subject related the individual to the emerging nation state by the formulation of a set of rights that defined the status of each individual. Both women and Black subjects were excluded from this formulation. Moreover, certain states of being, such as madness, disease and criminality, formed categories that were at once the effect of, and evaded, a definite exclusion or inscription. These excluded categories, despite rigorous control and governance, could not be ignored. Instead, the historical process of dealing with these Other sites shows the ways in which these same categories push against and seek to transform the notion of democracy, of rights, of the nation and its subjects.

'To speak a language is to take on a world, a culture': this quote from Franz Fanon shows dramatically the links between language and culture. It also points to the differentiated and hierarchised linguistic arena in which subjects are addressed and constructed, and grapples with the ways in which, by 'taking on' the coloniser's language, the colonised can deal with that language, even from positions of subservience. Wollstonecraft recognised the differentiated and hierarchised nature of the address, and protested against the way women had been relegated within language to a 'false' and 'deceptive' area; she appealed to women

217

to break out of this mould and, through a reformed language, to take their rightful place within society and culture. The address to the colonised subject places him/her even further down the hierarchy and within irreconcilable positions of Otherness, making entry into the centre of the discourse more difficult. The colonised subject has always to negotiate his/her relation to the coloniser's language. This negotiation is even more complex than the one recommended by Wollstonecraft, as it has to take on the different cultural worlds that access to different languages has opened up, and place itself as subject within different and differentiated systems. The most simple (yet still difficult) strategy is to deny the languages of imperialism and to go back to a use of the mother tongue, and to establish the notion of the national language. Examples of such a strategy abound, from the status that national language and literature are given in struggles for national liberation (see Benedict Anderson) to the sense of national pride with which Third World writers seek to enrich the mother tongue.

The most dramatic and well-known example of such a gesture in recent times has been made by the Kenyan writer Ngugi, who after having been acclaimed as a novelist in English, decided to give up writing in English in favour of his native Gikuyu. He defines his decision as a political one, tied to notions of national identity:

> I believe that my writing in Gikuyu language, a Kenyan language, an African language, is part and parcel of the anti-imperialist struggles of Kenyan and African peoples.
>
> (Ngugi, 1988, *Decolonising the Mind*, p. 28)

This statement succinctly spells out the relation between nation, a nationalist spirit and language, as well as the task/responsibility of the writer. The Third World post-colonial writer turns to the mother tongue, not merely in a search for origins – a sense of identity – but in a spirit of democracy and community, even of nation-building. Wordsworth had described the poet as a man amongst men, and had seen this community as drawn together by a common use of language. The post-colonial writer seeks his/her audience in the once-colonised nation, and seeks to construct a form of address that transcends the lessons and languages learnt from the coloniser. A nationalistic reading celebrates these gestures of renunciation of the imperial tongue and equates the reversion to indigenous, national tongues with the processes of decol-onisation.

Simple celebration of the return to the mother tongue, how-ever, tends to romanticise this movement as a healing of linguistic divisions, which helps to draw the people of the nation together into an undifferentiated terrain (the national culture), defined and constructed by the national language. It ignores the ruptures that the processes of colonisation had created, and concentrates on the task of re-excavating the original terrain of pre-colonial forms and structures. The difficulty – nay, impossibility – of this task is well illustrated within these very efforts. Ngugi's sojourn in Gikuyu has to take cognisance of the pedagogical practices preva-lent in East Africa, and to make his experiment relevant outside the literary/dramatic community he sets up in his native village. Indeed, in *Decolonising the Mind* he constantly debates issues of language and the apt medium of writing for the African writer, as well as the relationship between the African languages and the languages of imperialism. The post-colonial subject/nation/community arises *out* of and refers to the subject formed within colonial systems/discourses, making it necessary to look *again* at the colonial world and the divisions that it brought about.

The advent/introduction of the coloniser's tongue – English, in our case – split the colonial terrain, and created various divisions within that society and culture. Ngugi traces the roots of these divisions to the educational system designed by the colonisers. Schooling, from kindergarten through to university level, cuts the subject off, severing him/her from the community/culture of childhood, as well as from the 'real' community of the people. The educational system exiles the child, and while s/he learns to 'master' the other tongue, and to live through the narratives and stories of the imperial masters, the feeling of homesickness – of severance from one's own stories or one's 'real' home – creates a radical split within the child's psyche. The child has to deal not just with two *forms*, but with two languages of address – and the division between the home and school becomes sharpened.

The advent of English education thus added a pedagogical and linguistic dimension to the split terrain in which the colonial subject was to have its existence. While Ngugi has beautifully delineated the psychic and subjective splits that a linguistically divided system brings in its wake, the tracing of a *history* of that education will show how it both created and helped to keep in place class and social divisions. To come back to the lessons to be learned from Indian history: the class-based purposes of English education had already been formally spelt out in Macaulay's 1835 minute. In the twofold purpose he had designed for English education the reference had been specifically to the upper classes of Indians as the apt subjects for an English education; if sufficiently impressed with English culture, this would be the class most likely to collaborate with British administrative and commercial interests. If we look at the various colleges (seats of higher learning) in Calcutta in the middle of the nineteenth century (the Hindu College, Sanskrit College, Fort William College), we will see how these institutions kept native caste structures intact, while creating a new class division, based on access to and mastery over English language and literature.

The use of different languages at school and at home splits the world of the child into that of the private, domestic sphere and the public world of the school and formal systems of education. This split echoes the private/public divide, and can in turn be related to the way in which the 'darknesses' of superstitious religious beliefs were relegated to indigenous systems of learning, and modern, rational scientific knowledge seen as the property of the Western coloniser (see Chapter 1). Partha Chatterjee (1989) has shown how the late nineteenth-century Indian nationalist movement ascribed a more positive dimension (as far as the Indian side was concerned) to this division, using it to form concepts of the inner and outer – the inner self being associated with a spiritually elevated sphere, while the outer was identified with the world of Western science and rationalism. This division has its domestic cognates in the ordering/dividing of the world into the public (school, work, government, administration) and the private (home, childhood, family). This division thus takes on a gendered dimension, in which the 'essential' self is associated with the inner world of the home, and the public world is seen as male, European, scientific and modern. The inner world also becomes the place of repose – a site for healing those wounds that the colonised subject has necessarily to suffer in forays into the outer world.

What is the place of literature in this split linguistic domain? At one level literature is the most public form of writing, literary writing forming the main pillar of national identity. At another level it is the most private of all discourse, recounting dreams, desires and feelings that the public world has no space for. Literary language is twofold – a special language, deceptive and playful, imaginative; and literature as reflective of social reality, with the value of literature inhering in its realism, its capacity to render social truths in a fictionalised manner.

It is this twofold nature of literary writing that makes the task of the post-colonial literature teacher complex and difficult to evaluate. Leaving aside the debate regarding the language of literature – English literature vs. our own literature – the study of literature itself has to take on board the *history* of its formulation as an academic subject. I have argued that like English, which had been introduced as a colonial tool, the histories of native literatures (in the 'mother' tongue) cannot remain completely innocent of the imperial venture, and neither do they rest in an arena outside that venture. This does not, in any way, justify or explain away the function and purpose of English teaching in our countries – instead, it is an effort to place the teaching of English, to relate it to our social and political realities and to recognise its historical task and position.

English in India was designed to create a class of Western-educated natives. In the post-colonial situation, this particular address of the subject continues unabated – the value of a knowledge of English in the job market is witness to the class prerogative that English continues to enjoy. What has changed dramatically, as pointed out by Loomba (1989) is the sheer number of students studying English and the texts of English literature. This dramatic proliferation also indicates the entry of a large number of women students, as English occupies an equally preferred position in the marriage market as it does in the job market. My study of the novels of Charlotte Brontë has been guided by these considerations. As more women enter the subject, literature's special address to women needs to be further highlighted. Women scholars have made a significant contribution in the field of post-colonial literary criticism, have shown how literature can be read in a differentiated manner and have demonstrated how the different addresses have to be honed and focused.

The novels of Charlotte Brontë provide a rich example of this collusion, in relation to their content as well as their history within feminist criticism. However, the problems of teaching the literature of imperialism have not been solved by feminism's 'Other' reading. Instead, this reading points to the need for new, yet 'Other' readings – for a re-examination of the text that will further bring out its relation with the Other subjects of the Western Enlightenment.

NOTES

1 THE SUBJECT/S OF THE NOVEL

1 Partha Chatterjee analyses Bankim Chatterjee's (the 'first' Bengali novelist) essays to show the split Indian/Bengali subject who was emerging from within the nineteenth-century British educational and administrative systems. A very interesting study of the period is found in Benoy Ghose's biography of Vidyasagar, *Vidyasagar o Bangalee Samaj*, whose 'Notes on the Sanskrit College' outlines the way that an education for Indians/Bengalis should combine elements of both English and indigenous educational systems.

2 See Aarsleff, 1982, *From Locke to Saussure: Essays on the Study of Language and Intellectual History*.

3 Ian Michael, 1987, *The Teaching of English: From the Sixteenth Century to 1870*, traces the history of English teaching methods, emphasising the step-by-step hierarchised process. English lessons began with spelling (emphasis on syllables), reading (stressing pronunciation), dictation (providing a sense of meaning or of words in their context), and composition (through which the student was to display proficiency in the language by writing essays her/himself.

4 Angela Davis's *Women, Race and Class* (1982) combines racism with sexism to look at how Black women are differentiated within Western systems of discourse. Black women in the West are struggling to establish their points of difference from the mainstream 'white' women's movement, and in their concentration on racial difference, are chalking out a separate arena of discourse for themselves, where their 'realities' will have space for expression. However, the dangers of a belief in authentic expression need to be pointed out yet again, and as Trinh-T Minha points out in her *Feminist Review* article (1987), feminism needs to constantly re-examine its notion of difference, if it is to survive as a dynamic and meaningful movement.

5 The novels examined are E. M. Forster's *A Passage to India* (1924), Edward Thompson's *An Indian Day* (1927), Joseph Conrad's *Lord Jim* (1900) and Graham Greene's *The Quiet American* (1955).

6 The article looks at Phuong, the Oriental woman in *The Quiet American*, and relates the image of feminine passivity to the demands that

modern-day Indian society makes on its women, stressing concepts of female virginity, chastity and passivity. The text is read to bring out images that pertain directly to the life-experiences of its Indian female readers.

7 The Indian school of historians, known as the Subaltern Studies School, has identified women as subaltern, and placed the history of their revolts, rebellions and protests alongside those of peasants, tribals and people of lower castes, whose discourse has been erased from dominant historiography, be it from within the liberal historical or the Marxist project. The difficulties of bringing back to light the stories of these movements have been pointed out by Spivak (1987, 'Subaltern Studies; Deconstructing Historiography', in *In Other Worlds: Essays in Cultural Politics*). The collusion between the British imperial power and men of the native elite had resulted in the celebrated reform movement in the nineteenth century in Bengal, and both Spivak (1984, 'The Rani of Sirmur' in *Europe and Its Others*, ed. Barker) and Mani (1989, 'Contentious Traditions: The Debate on *Sati* in Colonial India' in *Recasting Women* ed. Sangari and Vaid), show how the abolition of *suttee*, celebrated as the most progressive of all these reforms, had little reference to the women that this reform most directly addressed.

2 SLAVERY AND SEXUALITY IN *OROONOKO*

1 Cf. Arsleff, 1982, pp. 284–5 for a fuller analysis of this.

2 See B. Grove (1961, *The Imaginary Voyage in Prose Fiction*) who lists 215 'Imaginary Voyages' in 'Prose Fiction' from 1700 to 1800 in English, French and German, thus pointing out the preponderance of the theme.

3 See Peter Hulme (1986, *Colonial Encounters: Europe and the Native Caribbean*), on how the violent practices of colonialism matched those of cannibalism, so that the horror expressed and felt in these encounters is evinced not only by the savage barbaric practices of the colonial Other, but rebounds on to colonial methods and practices themselves. Of course, Joseph Conrad's *Heart of Darkness* provides the most famous example of colonial horror, where European trading practices and African tribal customs are completely intermixed to create the textual terrain in the novel (cf. Patrick Brantlinger, 1988, *Rule of Darkness: British Literature and Imperialism, 1830–1914*).

4 See Fairchild (1961, *The Noble Savage: A Study in Romantic Naturalism*) and Hulme (1986) for the way that the concept of the savage as noble and fearful permeates the Western encounter with other cultures.

5 See Defoe, *A New Voyage around the World* (1726), for a fictional account of the purpose and manner of the representation of these voyages. Margaret T. Hodgen, in *Early Anthropology in the Sixteenth and Seventeenth Centuries* (1964), points out the various stages through which the European encounter with the so-called savage was negotiated.

6 A recent book, Moira Ferguson's *Subject to Others: British Women Writers and Colonial Slavery 1670–1834*, (1992, London, Routledge), provides a much more satisfactory reading of the novel. Ferguson points out how the polemics of the anti-slavery debate are related to women's protests against their own situation, and she sees in *Oroonoko* a text where the writer has transferred many of her personal grievances on to the figure of the slave. Thus the collusion between the author and Oroonoko is given a different reading, and the figure of the slave provides the author with a site on to which her protests against the feminine condition can be deflected.

7 All biographers have had to struggle with the difficulty of obtaining information about her life: cf. Woodcock, 1948, *The Incomparable Aphra*; Duffy, 1977, *The Passionate Shepherdess*; and Goreau, 1980, *Reconstructing Aphra: A Social Biography of Aphra Behn*.

8 'Native informant' is a term borrowed from anthropology, where the anthropologist (mainly Western, and therefore unacquainted with local mores, customs and most crucially language) uses a research assistant (normally local, young and an aspiring anthropologist) to interpret the society and mores under investigation. Spivak (1987) explains clearly the problems associated with material that is gleaned or acquired in this manner.

9 See David Dabydeen (1985b, *The Black Presence in English Literature*) for a description of the effects of geographical exploration on Renaissance literature.

10 Laura Mulvey's explanation of the cult of the female star shows how the fascination with the woman rests on the very anxieties that the image of the castrated woman engenders. One of the ways out of this anxiety is by over-valuation, by a 'complete disavowal of castration by the substitution of a fetish object or by turning the represented figure itself into a fetish so that it becomes reassuring rather than dangerous' (Mulvey, 1975, 'Visual Pleasure and Narrative Cinema', *Screen*, pp. 13–14). The pleasure associated with the figure of the woman on the screen revolves around this fear/desire axis. The feminisation of Oroonoko can be seen to operate in a similar manner: the fear of the Other (as potentially subversive or disorderly) is harnessed into a picture of desire and fetishised into a beautiful object. The Black man thus becomes the object of the white gaze.

11 See McCullough (1962, *The Negro in English Literature: A Critical Introduction*) for an account of the physical characteristics of the Black man in English literature, and Ruth Cowhig ('Blacks in English Renaissance Drama and the Role of Shakespeare's *Othello*') for the way in which Othello's part has historically been allocated to white actors who need to 'blacken' themselves, in preference to Black actors; the 'fact' that Othello is a Moor is emphasised in order to enable this.

12 Whether the readership of the novel is predominantly male or female is uncertain, as it is not known whether the growing female readership of the novel, as identified by Watt, had already come into being in the seventeenth century. It is difficult to determine exactly

who read this novel. The popularity of *Oroonoko*, however, can be gleaned from the fact that it was made into a play for the Restoration stage by Thomas Southerne in 1695. '*Oroonoko* was among the nine most read novels of the eighteenth century in France', reports Wylie Sypher in *Guinea's Captive Kings: British Anti-Slavery Literature of the Eighteenth Century*, (1969, p. 99), and Duffy comments that 'It's a measure of the book's currency that Oroonoko became a slang term for a smoker, since it's by concentrating on his pipe that Oroonoko himself endures his last torments' (Duffy, 1977, p. 270).

13 Basil Willey characterises the seventeenth century as the age that marks the 'scientific movement' in England, leading to the establishment of the various Royal Societies (see Willey, 1965, *The Eighteenth Century Background: Studies on the Idea of Nature in the Thought of the Period*, London, p. 3).

14 See Spender (1986, *Mothers of the Novel: 100 Good Women Writers before Jane Austen*) for an account of the way in which the literary establishment has systematically repressed and misrepresented women's writing. The Pandora Press project entitled 'Mothers of the Novel' (of which Spender's book forms a part) has undertaken the task of unearthing women's writing, and extending a gynocritical history and reading of the novelistic genre.

15 The differences between Behn's novel and Southerne's play are often commented on (Cowhig, 1983, 1985). The most important difference is that the nature of the representation is completely changed and that Oroonoko from being the object of a narrative voice/gaze is put on centre-stage to become the object of the gaze of an audience.

16 The Family Romance theme is visible here: as Oroonoko (the heir to the throne) and his grandfather (the King) struggle for the same woman. As it turns out, Oroonoko wins the woman, but relinquishes the throne.

17 Aphra Behn, spy for the Royalist cause, took part in the court intrigues that characterised seventeenth-century English politics (see Duffy, 1977, p. 273, for resemblances between the events in the novel and English court intrigues).

18 Shakespeare's *Antony and Cleopatra* contains the most well-known portrait of a 'love-sick slave'. Antony, the Roman general, the conqueror, is conquered by Cleopatra, so that the conqueror/conquered role is completely confused. The text sees this as a process of emasculation, as a symbolic impotence. Thus Scarus reports to Enobarbus: 'I never saw an action of such shame:/ Experience, manhood, honour, ne'er before/ Did violate so itself' (Shakespeare, *Antony and Cleopatra*, Act III, scene x, line 1).

19 This calls to mind E. M. Forster's *A Passage to India* (1924), where the dangers of trusting a native guide are brought home, as indeed are the dangers, on the part of the native guide, in allowing himself to accompany European women unattended by the rules of the British administrators.

3 DANGEROUS IDENTITY: THE MANY DISGUISES OF ROXANA

1 It is interesting to note how Karl Marx makes a similar comparison in *The German Ideology* (1845–6);

> With the division of labour, in which all these contradictions are implicit, and which in its turn is based on the natural division of labour in the family and on the separation of society into individual families opposed to one another, is given simultaneously the distribution, and indeed the unequal (both quantitative and qualitative) distribution, of labour and its products: hence property, the nucleus, the first form of which lies in the family, where wife and children are the slaves of the husband. This latent slavery in the family, though still very crude, is the first property, but even at this early stage it corresponds perfectly to the definition of modern economists who call it the power of disposing of the labour-power of others.
> (Marx, *The German Ideology*, 1939, ed. R. Pascal, New York, pp. 21–2)

2 See Alice Browne, 1987, *The Eighteenth Century Feminist Mind*, for an analysis of the notion of 'instrumental feminism'.

3 If Mary Astell can be seen to inaugurate the issue in the last few years of the seventeenth century (1697) other English (male) writers were not far behind. Even Daniel Defoe in his *Essay upon Projects* (1697) was arguing for equal education for women. Wollstonecraft's list of contemporary writings on the subject is highly illuminating – besides Rousseau's *Emile* (1762) the most celebrated of the lot, she mentions James Fordyce's *Sermons to Young Women* (1765) and *The Character and Conduct of the Female Sex* (1776). Amongst Wollstonecraft's female contemporaries Hannah More's *Strictures on the Modern System of Female Education* (1799) and Catherine Macaulay's *Letters on Education* (1790) are worth mentioning.

4 The Kristevan concept of the semiotic is comparable to the Lacanian Imaginary, in the sense that it represents the 'before' of human subjectivity, the stage prior to recognition of difference.

5 These are some of the categories identified by Gayatri Spivak (1987, p. 46).

6 Psychoanalytical thought itself has posed other ways of looking at motherhood, in which motherhood's aspect of caring and upbringing totally focuses on the child's educational processes. D. W. Winnicott's notion of a 'good-enough' mother (*Playing and Reality*, 1971), takes the emphasis away from the pre-Oedipal mother to the role of mothering and its significance in the growth and development of the child's mind. Building on that theory, Nancy Chodorow's book *The Reproduction of Mothering* (1978) argues for the centrality of the mother in a child's life, and sees how the mother in turn affects the daughter in her future role as mother.

7 Mary Jacobus's article, 'The Third Stroke: Reading Woolf with Freud', in Susan Sheridan (ed.) (1988) *Grafts: Feminist Cultural Criticism* reads Woolf's *Beyond the Lighthouse* to see the significance of maternal (pre-Oedipal) memory for the female artist/writer. The arti-

cle, most interestingly, connects the feminist project of 'thinking through our mothers' – the search for a female tradition – to the nostalgia for the ideal mother/child dyad, as a desire for a return to origins or roots.

8 Fidelis Morgan reads *The Adventures of Rivella* as autobiography – a 'fictionalised tale' which 'contains incidents in her life' (Morgan, 1987, *A Woman of No Character: An Autobiography of Mrs Manley*, p. 20). She uses the *Adventures of Rivella* and excerpts from Manley's other novels to recreate Manley's biography.

9 It is this appeal to reality that brings the novel under criticism and Gildon's attack is based on the so-called factuality of *Robinson Crusoe*.

10 See Chapter 2 for the power relations involved in the process of naming. Also, cf. Peter Hulme (1986) for the significance of the naming process in *Robinson Crusoe*.

11 See Rachel Bowlby (1985, *Just Looking: Consumer Culture in Dreiser, Gissing and Zola*) and Elizabeth Wilson (1985, *Adorned in Dreams: Fashion and Modernity*), for the way that the woman as capitalist consumer is then transformed into merchandise herself. Sombart in *Luxury and Capitalism* defines luxury as 'any expenditure in excess of the necessary' (1967, p. 59). The concept of necessity is a fluid one, and likely to be attenuated according to circumstances. Sombart, however, looks at the concept in relation to capitalism, and the development of cities as well as trade. An interesting aspect of his analysis is the association he makes with the rise of capitalism and 'illicit love'. The figure of the courtesan, in this formulation, occupies that area of 'excess', of luxury, of a good created by superfluous wealth.

12 The accidental utterance functions like a classical example of a Freudian slip of tongue. 'In other, far more significant, cases it is self-criticism, internal opposition to one's own utterance, that obliges one to make a slip of the tongue and even to substitute the opposite of what one had intended' (Freud, 1966, *The Psychopathology of Everyday Life*, p. 86). The text utters, enunciates, that which is absolutely forbidden, and the multiple layers of disguise covering the identity of the protagonist are, at this point, in imminent danger of being stripped apart.

4 CHARLOTTE BRONTË/CURRER BELL: SEXUALITY, THE TEXT AND THE WOMAN NOVELIST

1 Lukács's celebration of nineteenth-century realism as a 'true' mirror of social and economic relationships is, of course, open to criticism. The debate around the Lukácsian concept of realism is best illustrated in Brecht's essay 'Against Georg Lukács' anthologised in the collection of essays, *Aesthetics and Politics*, edited by Fredric Jameson (1977).

2 See Alice R. Kaminsky, 1968, *George Henry Lewes as Literary Critic*, Syracuse University Press, Syracuse.

3 Robert Southey, in his first letter to Charlotte Brontë, dated March 1837, advises her to refrain from writing, writing not being a fit

vocation for a woman. Charlotte Brontë acknowledged this advice. Pleased with her humility, he wrote her another letter, advising her to 'Take care of over-excitement, and endeavour to keep a quiet mind' (Clement Shorter, 1908, p. 130). The recommended tranquillity would lead to repose and stillness and thereby to a delineation of 'objective' social relations, as G. H. Lewes pointed out to Charlotte Brontë while recommending Jane Austen's *Pride and Prejudice* as the ideal woman's novel. But she rejected this advice and recommendation, finding the 'elegant but confined' air of *Pride and Prejudice* inimical to her way of writing (ibid., p. 387).

4 The educational project occupies a central position in Charlotte Brontë's writings. Her heroines are envisaged as students or teachers and a debate about the desired educational system for women can be discerned within the pages of *Villette*. In a way, this can be read as an extension of the educational concerns that were so central to the feminist polemical writings examined in Chapter 3.

5 Mary Jacobus, 'The Buried Letter', in *Reading Woman: Essays in Feminist Criticism* (1986).

6 *Oroonoko*, female-authored and abolitionist, was read as a problematic text. Similarly, *Uncle Tom's Cabin*, the life-story of a Black slave authored by a white woman, recreates some of the problems and contradictions evinced by the middle-class white leaders of the anti-slavery movement in America and England.

5 THE BRONTË CHILDREN AT PLAY

1 Henry Mayhew wrote in the *Morning Chronicle* from October 1849 to December 1850 and compiled from his interviews a series of investigative reports entitled *London Labour and the London Poor*. His work forms an impressive survey of labour and poverty in the mid-nineteenth century. The interview with the needlewomen was undertaken to discover their actual wages and whether low rates of remuneration led to clandestine prostitution. The interview was conducted in a most unusual manner: the atmosphere was staged – the room was dimly lighted and the women were made to sit behind a screen, creating greater anonymity. In these artificial surroundings, confessions and declarations seemed to well out of the assembled women. The only men present were Mayhew and his friend, who were the male auditors for these women's stories.

2 Christine Alexander, 1983, *The Early Writings of Charlotte Brontë*, traces the amalgamation of these various strands in great detail.

3 See ibid. for a detailed description and analysis of the magazines.

4 R. and H. Bellour, 1969, 'Le Jeu des jeunes hommes', *Revue d'Esthetique*, no. 4, p. 343.

5 See Peter Hulme, 1986, *Colonial Encounters* for the significance of a notion of cannibalism in the colonial venture.

6 Charlotte Brontë describes the trance-like states she used to go into while she was writing. Reminiscences of her schoolmates, Ellen

Nussey and Mary Taylor (*SHLL*, vol. 1) also report the somnambulist and ecstatic states that Charlotte experienced during the recounting of these stories.

7 See W. Sypher, 1969, pp. 143–4 for an account of the Quashy legend.

8 The school of Indian historians known as the Subaltern Studies School have identified women as subaltern, along with all those classes of people, defined by gender, class or caste (or in any other way) who have been read out of 'elite' history, both from liberal and Marxist schools. Spivak's critique of the concept of subalternity rests on the difficulties, if not the impossibility, of recreating a subaltern consciousness (cf. Spivak, 1987, 'Subaltern Studies: Deconstructing Historiography', in *In Other Worlds: Essays in Cultural Politics*, p. 199). Other readers of Indian history, Benita Parry for example, find Spivak's strictures too harsh. Her own search for the original native or Indian woman leads her to look at women as 'healers, ascetics, singers of sacred songs, artisans and artists' (Parry, 1987, 'Problems in Current Theories', *OLR*, p. 35). The occupations wherein the real women can be found can only be seen as traditional, and keep women confined to positions which hold only anthropological interest, where they can serve the role of cultural curios for the modern or Westernised observer.

9 See Reza Hammami and Martina Reiker, 'Feminist Orientalism and Oriental Marxism', *New Left Review* 170 (July/August 1988) for the necessity of placing the figure of the Arab woman into her specific historical and social conditions. The effort is not to recover the lost woman, but to see how the historical conjuncture in which she is placed may be made to operate to put her into positions other than that of passive muteness, as is represented by the figure of the veiled Algerian revolutionary.

10 Moira Ferguson (1992) deals in detail with Mary Prince's account. Rather than reading the narrative as a simple instance of the self-expression of the slave woman, she emphasises the mediations that Mary Prince's narrative undergoes, as it is told to her 'friend', Miss S–, who transcribes her story for the anti-slavery lobby. Thus, far from being a 'genuine' utterance, Mary Prince's 'History' has been formulated and tailored to suit the purposes of the anti-slavery lobby.

11 Perhaps the most powerful adumbration of this theme is to be found in Emily Brontë's *Wuthering Heights*, where the adopted foundling Heathcliff (crucially of uncertain racial origin) wreaks havoc on the community by coveting and acquiring the property, daughter and power of his adoptive home. Thematic resemblances between Charlotte Brontë's juvenilia and her sister's only published novel do not necessarily signify a secret, or undiscovered collaboration (as in the mysterious bed plays), but do suggest a fluidity of authorial collaboration which contradicts the static pairing according to contiguity in age upheld by most Brontë biographers.

12 For example, *The Foundling* (31 May–27 June 1833) is concerned with the origins of its main character, Ned Percy, who is literally a foundling, found at the doorstep of his adopted parents. Percy, after the

death of his adopted parents, sails for Africa, in search of fame and fortune. While in Africa, he falls in love with Julia, who, however, cannot marry him, because of the uncertainty of his origins. Love, fame and fortune become entangled with the unravelling of Percy's identity. He turns out to be Edward, Duke of York, and son of Frederick, the Duke's brother, and the first ruler of these lands, according to the history traced by Branwell. This story, which, as its outline shows, follows the Family Romance pattern, forms a blueprint for many of Charlotte Brontë's love stories, i.e., the achievement of love, glory and a greater inclusion within the social framework on the unravelling of true identity and the discovery of real parents.

13 Branwell Brontë's *Letters from an Englishman*, however, treats the war in greater detail.

14 In *Jane Eyre* the story of a servant marrying her master achieves its most well-known delineation, and as the reviews examined in Chapter 4 show, this formed the basis for many of the objections brought against the novel.

6 THE POLITICS OF LANGUAGE IN *THE PROFESSOR*

1 In Roy Porter (1987), *Mind-Forged Manacles: A History of Madness in England from the Restoration to the Regency*, p. 49.

2 The following chapter on *Jane Eyre* will examine more closely the concept of the 'Other' woman and the ways in which female sexuality is made to operate to create categories of women who are kept in a position of jealous antagonism to each other.

3 Cf. Elaine Showalter, 1985, *The Female Malady: Women, Madness and English Culture, 1830–1890*.

4 See Castel (1988, *The Regulation of Madness: The Origins of Incarceration in France*), Porter (1987, *Mind-Forged Manacles*) and Scull (1981, *Madhouses, Mad-Doctors and Madmen: The Social History of Psychiatry in the Victorian Era*) for a historical account of the changes in the regulation in asylums in eighteenth- and nineteenth-century France and England.

Vieda Skultans's excerpts from different writings on madness in the nineteenth century are typically entitled 'Improvement of Education' (an excerpt from William Pickering, London, 1843: *Man's Power over Himself to Prevent and Control Insanity*) or, 'The Importance of Energetically Exercising the Will' or 'The Supremacy of the Will' (excerpts from, respectively, John Churchill, London, 1853: *Elements of Psychological Medicine* and John Charles Bucknill, London, 1854: *Unsoundness of Mind in Relation to Criminal Insanity*). See Skultans's anthology of English psychiatric documents, 1979, *English Madness: Ideas on Insanity 1580–1890*.

7 REREADING FEMINISM'S TEXTS: *JANE EYRE* AND *SHIRLEY*

1 Lata Mani and Gayatri Spivak (1984, in F. Barker, *et al.*, *Europe and its Others*) try to unearth the discourses that marked the British reform of the practice of suttee. Again, the figure of the woman provides the central site for colonial 'reform'. Suttee was gradually banned in India by a collusion between British administrators (men), Anglicised natives (men) and Brahmin pundits (again men). The figure of the woman, thrown from one patriarchal discourse to another, provided a site of contestation resulting in colonial legislative reform.

2 The closest that the Brontë sisters had come to realising their plans for setting up their own school had been in 1844 when they had actually sent out a circular advertising their intended school in Haworth. The curriculum for 'young ladies' included 'Writing, Arithmetic, History, Grammar, Geography and Needlework' with a choice of French, German, Latin, Music and Drawing'. It is unfortunate that in the subsequent letters with Ellen Nussey (in 1846) when Charlotte discusses her friend's plans for a school for girls, the emphasis is on economic and practical considerations, rather than on the curriculum and intended pedagogical practices. However, none of these school projects materialised, so biographical evidence cannot be added to the debate about female education that is carried on in the pages of *Jane Eyre*.

3 Helen Taylor, 1979b, in her introduction to *Portraits*, a collection of short stories by Kate Chopin, also comments on the racial heterogeneity in Louisiana, inhabited as it is by Creoles (mainly white) the Cajuns (of French descent) and the Negroes (freeholding sharecroppers). An interesting connection is drawn in this introduction between the 'local colour' movement and the women's novel, writings by women being seen as the ones in which the local community, with its racial and social divisions, is vividly reflected. *Wide Sargasso Sea*, besides being a rejoinder to *Jane Eyre*, can also be read as a 'local colour' novel. Read in this context, the connection between colonial locales and the coloniser's discourse becomes even clearer.

4 The Spivak/Parry debate over the status of the other woman in *Wide Sargasso Sea* centres around the two figures of Christophine, the 'blue-black' *obeah* woman and the racially mixed Antoinette Crossway/ Bertha Mason. Spivak's critique sees the figure of Christophine, the 'authentic' Black woman, as being tangential to the narrative (Spivak, 1985, p. 253). While Spivak is insistent on the absolute impossibility of recovering the essential original Other self from colonial and imperial systems, Parry sees Spivak's reading of *Wide Sargasso Sea* and of the figure of Christophine within it as guided by mistaken assumptions (Parry, 1987, p. 38). Benita Parry's reading of *Wide Sargasso Sea* tries to shift attention away from the Creole woman to the 'real' Black woman. The text of *Wide Sargasso Sea*, however, locates the Other subject in colonial and patriarchal structures, which do not serve to recover native subjects, but recreate these subjects in

NOTES

the image of the coloniser. The native subject, in Western discourse, can only be a colonised subject, and the search for the authentic, original Other is bound to be futile.

5 In Strachey, 1953, *The Standard Edition of the Psychological Works of Sigmund Freud, vol. 9.*

6 In Mahmoud, 1972, *William Beckford of Fonthill 1760–1844 Bicentenary Essays*, p. 90.

7 See Wordsworth, 1966, 'Preface to The Lyrical Ballads with Pastoral and Other Poems, 1802', in Zall, *Literary Criticism of William Wordsworth*, p. 42.

8 See Terry Eagleton, 1988, *Myths of Power: A Marxist Study of the Brontës*, for an analysis of the social divisions in contemporary England.

9 The fictional representations of this process, seen in *The Professor* and *Jane Eyre*, have a real-life correspondence in M. Heger's comments and corrections of Charlotte Brontë's French exercises.

10 Steven Marcus (1966, *The Other Victorians: A Study of Sexuality and Pornography in Mid-Nineteenth-Century England*), uses internal textual evidence to ascribe this span of time to the writing of *My Secret Life*.

11 To take another example of a mid-Victorian sexual diary: *The Diaries of Hannah Culwick: Victorian Maidservant* (ed. L. Stanley, 1984), are unique in that the illicit sexual relationship that they describe extends to an illicit marriage. The diary is written under the tutelage and for the perusal of her master/husband, who, in the meantime, writes his own diary. The sexual relationship therefore also becomes a pedagogical one, and the pedagogical exercise is based on the relation, the narration, indeed the *composition*, of sexual events. Crucially, the man writes for himself, while the woman writes for *him*, under his direction and for his perusal. Shirley's essay can be read in this light.

BIBLIOGRAPHY

WRITINGS BY CHARLOTTE BRONTË

Alexander, C. (1987), *An Edition of the Early Writings of Charlotte Brontë: 1826–1832*, Oxford, Shakespeare Head Press, Basil Blackwell.

Brontë, C. (11 August 1836), 'Roe Head Journal', Bonnell Collection, [98 {8}], Brontë Parsonage Museum.

—— (1977), *Jane Eyre*, Harmondsworth, Penguin.

—— (1980), *The Professor*, Harmondsworth, Penguin.

—— (1981), *Villette*, Harmondsworth, Penguin.

—— (1986), *A Leaf from an Unopened Volume*, ed. C. Lemon, Haworth, The Brontë Society.

—— (1988), *Shirley*, Harmondsworth, Penguin.

Gerin, W. (ed.) (1971), *Charlotte Brontë: Five Novelettes*, London, The Folio Press.

Ratchford, F. (ed.) (1973), *Charlotte Brontë: Legends of Angria* (1933), New York, Kennikat Press.

Shorter, C. (ed.) (1908), *The Brontës: Life and Letters*, 2 vols, London, Hodder & Stoughton.

Winnifrith, T. (ed.) (1984), *The Poems of Charlotte Brontë*, Oxford, Shakespeare Head Press, Basil Blackwell.

Wise, T. J. and Symington, J. A. (eds) (1933), *The Brontës: Their Lives, Friendships, and Correspondence in Four Volumes*, Oxford, Shakespeare Head Press, Basil Blackwell.

—— (eds) (1936), *The Miscellaneous and Unpublished Writings of Charlotte and Patrick Branwell Brontë*, Oxford, Shakespeare Head Press, Basil Blackwell.

OTHER PRIMARY SOURCES

Astell, M. in B. Hill (ed.) (1986), *The First English Feminist: 'Reflections Upon Marriage' and Other Writings by Mary Astell*, London, Gower/ Maurice Temple Smith.

Beckford, W. (1970) *Vathek*, London, Oxford University Press.

BIBLIOGRAPHY

Behn, A. (1952), *Oroonoko*, in P. Henderson, (ed.), *Shorter Novels: Seventeenth Century*, London, Dent.

—— (1987), *Love Letters Between a Nobleman and his Sister*, London, Virago.

Brontë, E. (1968), *Wuthering Heights*, Harmondsworth, Penguin.

Coleridge, S. T. (1907), *Biographia Literaria*, 2 vols, Oxford, Clarendon Press.

—— (1912), *The Complete Poetic Works*, ed. E. H. Coleridge, 2 vols, Oxford, Clarendon Press.

Condillac, E. (1974), *An Essay on the Origin of Human Knowledge*, New York, AMS Press.

Defoe, D. (1895), *A New Voyage around the World* (1726), London, Dent.

—— (1964), *Roxana*, London, Oxford University Press.

—— (1972), *Moll Flanders*, London, The Zodiac Press.

—— (1975), *Robinson Crusoe and The Further Adventures of Robinson Crusoe*, London and Glasgow, Collins.

Diderot, D. (1976), *Diderot's Selected Writings*, trans. D. Coltman, London, Macmillan.

Forster, E. M. (1977), *A Passage To India*, Harmondsworth, Penguin.

Godwin, W. (1970), *Caleb Williams*, London, Oxford University Press.

Hobbes, T. (1987), *Leviathan*, Harmondsworth, Penguin.

Hume, D. (1874), *A Treatise on Human Nature and Dialogues Concerning Natural Religion*, 2 vols, London, Longman.

Lewes, M. G. (1973), *The Monk*, London, Oxford University Press.

Locke, J. (1952), *An Essay Concerning Civil Government*, in R. M. Hutchins (ed.), *Great Books of the Western World*, vol. 35, London, Encyclopaedia Brittanica Inc.

—— (1961), *An Essay Concerning Human Understanding*, vols 1 and 2, London, Dent.

Mackenzie, H. (1967), *The Man of Feeling* (1771), London, Oxford University Press.

Manley, M. D. (1971) in P. Koster (ed.), *The Novels of Mary Delariviere Manley*, Gainsville, Florida, Scholars' Facsimiles and Reprints.

de Montaigne, M. (1948) *The Essays of Michael Lord of Montaigne*, trans. J. Florio, London, Grant Richards.

More, H. (1987), *Strictures on the Modern System of Female Education* (1799), 2 vols, in A. Browne, *The Eighteenth Century Feminist Mind*, Brighton, The Harvester Press.

Neville, H. (1952), *Isle of Pines* (1668), in P. Henderson (ed.), *Shorter Novels: Seventeenth Century*, London, Dent.

Radcliffe, A. (1980), *The Mysteries of Udolpho*, London, Oxford University Press.

Raleigh, W. (1981), 'Discovery of Guiana, 1595', in (sel.) R. David, *Hakluyt's Voyages*, London, Chatto & Windus.

Rhys, J. (1966), *Wide Sargasso Sea*, London, André Deutsch.

Richardson, S. (1971), *Clarissa*, Cambridge, Mass., Houghton–Mifflin.

Rousseau, J. J. (1953), *The Confessions*, trans. J. M. Cohen, Harmondsworth, Penguin.

———— (1964), *The First and Second Discourses*, ed. and trans. R. and J. Master, New York, St Martin's Press.

Scott, W. (1895), *Old Mortality* in *Waverley Novels*, vol. 10, London, Constable.

Shakespeare, W. (1977), *Antony and Cleopatra*, The Arden Shakespeare, London, Methuen.

Shelley, M. (1968), *Frankenstein or the Modern Prometheus*, London, Minster Classics.

Smith, C. (1969) *The Old Manor House*, London, Oxford University Press.

Southerne, T. (1967), *Oroonoko*, London, Arnold.

Stowe, H. B. (1975), *Uncle Tom's Cabin and A Key to Uncle Tom's Cabin*, New York, George Olms.

Sidney, P. (1968), *The Defence of Poesie*, Menston, Yorkshire, The Scholars' Press.

Wollstonecraft, M. (1978), *A Vindication of the Rights of Woman*, Harmondsworth, Penguin.

Wordsworth, W. (1966), 'Preface to Lyrical Ballads with Pastoral and Other Poems, 1802', in P. M. Zall (ed.), *Literary Criticism of William Wordsworth*, Lincoln, University of Nebraska Press.

CRITICAL, HISTORICAL AND THEORETICAL WRITINGS

Aarsleff, H. (1982), *From Locke to Saussure: Essays on the Study of Language and Intellectual History*, London, The Athlone Press.

Adams, M. (1978), 'Family Disintegration and Creative Reintegration: The Case of Charlotte Brontë and *Jane Eyre*', in A. Wohl (ed.), *The Victorian Family: Structures and Stresses*, London, Croom Helm.

Alexander, C. (1981), 'Recent Researches on Charlotte Brontë's Juvenilia', *Brontë Society Transactions*, vol. 1, no. 18.

———— (1983), *The Early Writings of Charlotte Brontë*, Oxford, Basil Blackwell.

Allott, M. (1974), *The Brontës: The Critical Heritage*, London, Routledge & Kegan Paul.

Anderson, B. (1983), *Imagined Communities: Reflections on the Origins and Spread of Nationalism*, London, Verso.

Baldick, C. (1983), *The Social Mission of English Criticism, 1848–1932*, Oxford, Clarendon Press.

Barker, F. (ed.) (1984), *Europe and its Others*, Essex, Proceedings of the Conference on the Sociology of Literature.

Barrell, J. (1983), *English Literature in History, 1730–80: An Equal, Wide Survey*, London, Hutchinson.

Barthes, R. (1975), *S/Z*, trans. R. Miller, London, Jonathan Cape.

Basch, F. (1974), *Relative Creatures: Victorian Women in Society and the Novel, 1837–67*, London, Allen Lane.

Bellour, R. and H. (1969), 'Le Jeu des jeunes hommes: Introduction a l'analyse comparée des écrits de jeunesse de Charlotte et Branwell Brontë', *Revue d'Esthetique*, no. 4, pp. 337–62.

Bhabha, H. (1983), 'Difference, Discrimination and the Discourse of Colonialism', in F. Barker (ed.), *The Politics of Theory*, Colchester, University of Essex.

—— (1986a), Foreword to F. Fanon, *Black Skin, White Masks*, London, Pluto Press.

—— (1986b), 'Signs Taken for Wonders: Questions of Ambivalence and Authority under a Tree outside Delhi, May 1817', in H. L. Gates (ed.), *Race, Writing and Difference*, Chicago, University of Chicago Press.

—— (ed.) (1990), *Nation and Narration*, Routledge, London.

Blackwood's Edinburgh Magazine, June 1826, no. 112, vol. 19; September 1829, no. 156, vol. 26 and November 1831, no. 187, vol. 30.

Bouce, P. G. (ed.) (1982), *Sexuality in Eighteenth-Century Britain*, Manchester, Manchester University Press.

Bowlby, R. (1985), *Just Looking: Consumer Culture in Dreiser, Gissing and Zola*, New York, Methuen.

—— (1990), 'Breakfast in America – *Uncle Tom's* Cultural Histories', in H. K. Bhaba (ed.), *Nation and Narration*, London, Routledge.

Brantlinger, P. (1977), *The Spirit of Reform: British Literature and Politics, 1832–1867*, Cambridge, Mass., Harvard University Press.

—— (1988), *Rule of Darkness: British Literature and Imperialism, 1830–1914*, Ithaca, Cornell University Press.

Browne, A. (1987), *The Eighteenth-Century Feminist Mind*, Brighton, The Harvester Press.

Butler, M. (1981), *Romantics, Rebels and Reactionaries: English Literature and its Background 1760–1830*, Oxford, Oxford University Press.

Castel, R. (1988), *The Regulation of Madness: The Origins of Incarceration in France*, (trans.) W. D. Halls, Cambridge, Polity Press.

Chatterjee, L. (ed.) (1986), *Woman, Image, Text: Feminist Readings of Literary Texts*, New Delhi, Trianka.

Chatterjee, P. (1986), *Nationalist Thought and the Colonial World: A Derivative Discourse?*, Zed Books, London.

—— (1989), 'The Nationalist Resolution of the Women's Question', in K. Sangari and S. Vaid (eds), *Recasting Women: Essays in Colonial History*, New Delhi, Kali for Women.

Chodorow, N. (1978), *The Reproduction of Mothering: Psychoanalysis and the Sociology of Gender*, Los Angeles, University of California Press.

Clayton, Sue (1983), 'Teaching Film', *Feminist Review*, no. 14 (January), pp. 84–97.

Clifford, J. and Marcus G. (eds), *Writing Culture: The Poetics and Politics of Ethnography*, Los Angeles, University of California Press.

Cohen, M. (1977), *Sensible Words: Linguistic Practice in England, 1640–1785*, Baltimore, Johns Hopkins University Press.

de Condillac, E. B. (1974), *An Essay on the Origin of Human Knowledge, Being a Supplement to Mr Locke's Essay on the Human Understanding*, (trans. Nugent, London, 1756) with an introduction by J. H. Staur, New York, AMS Press.

Cowhig, R. (1983), 'Attitudes to Blacks in Eighteenth-Century Literature: English Writers and the Abolition Movement', in B. Moore-Gilbert (ed.), *Literature and Imperialism*, London, Conference Papers of Roehampton Institute of Higher Education.

—— (1985), 'Blacks in English Renaissance Drama and the Role of Shakespeare's *Othello*', in D. Dabydeen (ed.), *The Black Presence in English Literature*, Manchester, Manchester University Press.

Dabydeen, D. (1985a), *Hogarth's Blacks: Images of Blacks in Eighteenth-Century English Art*, Denmark, Dangaroo P. Mundelstrop.

—— (ed.) (1985b), *The Black Presence in English Literature*, Manchester, Manchester University Press.

David, R. (ed. and sel.) (1981), *Hakluyt's Voyages*, London, Chatto & Windus.

Davis, A. (1982), *Women, Race and Class*, London, The Women's Press.

Davis, L. (1983), *Factual Fictions: The Origins of the English Novel*, New York, Columbia University Press.

Derrida, J. (1976), *Of Grammatology*, trans. G. C. Spivak, Baltimore, Johns Hopkins University Press.

Duffy, M. (1977), *The Passionate Shepherdess: Aphra Behn, 1640–89*, London, Jonathan Cape.

Eagleton, T. (1983), *Literary Theory: An Introduction*, Oxford, Basil Blackwell.

—— (1988), *Myths of Power: A Marxist Study of the Brontës* (1975), London, Macmillan.

Fairchild, H. N. (1961), *The Noble Savage: A Study in Romantic Naturalism*, London, Russell.

Fanon, F. (1967), *Black Skin, White Masks*, New York, Grove Press.

—— (1986), *Black Skin, White Masks*, London, Pluto Press.

Feminist Review, June 1983, no. 14; August 1984, no. 17 and March 1987, no. 23.

Ferguson, M. (1992), *Subject to Others: British Women Writers and Colonial Slavery, 1670–1834*, London, Routledge.

Foucault, M. (1972a), *The Archaeology of Knowledge*, trans. A. M. S. Smith, London, Tavistock Publications.

—— (1972b), *The Order of Things*, ed. R. D. Laing, London, Tavistock Publications.

—— (1977a), *A History of Sexuality*, vol. 1 trans. R. Hurley, Harmondsworth, Penguin.

—— (1977b), *Discipline and Punish: The Birth of the Prison*, trans. A. Sheridan, London, Allen Lane.

—— (1977c), *Madness and Civilisation: A History of Insanity in the Age of Reason*, London, Tavistock Publications.

Freud, S. (1953), 'Creative Writers and Day-Dreaming', in J. Strachey (ed.), *Standard Edition of the Complete Psychological Works of Sigmund Freud*, vol. 9.

—— (1953), 'The Uncanny', in J. Strachey (ed.), *Standard Edition of the Complete Psychological Works of Sigmund Freud*, vol. 17.

—— (1966), *The Psychopathology of Everyday Life*, trans. A. Tyson, London, Ernest Benn.

—— (1974), *Beyond the Pleasure Principle*, trans. and ed. J. Strachey, London, The Hogarth Press and the Institute of Psychoanalysis.

—— (1977), 'Family Romances', in *On Sexuality*, Harmondsworth, Penguin.

—— (1977), 'Female Sexuality', in *On Sexuality*, Harmondsworth, Penguin.

Gaskell, E. (1914), *The Life of Charlotte Brontë*, London, Smith, Elder and Co.

Gellner, E. (1983), *Nations and Nationalism*, Oxford, Basil Blackwell.

Ghose, B. (1984), *Vidyasagar o Bangalee Samaj*, Calcutta, Orient Longman Ltd.

Gilbert, S. M. and Gubar, S. (1979), *The Madwoman in the Attic: The Woman Writer and the Nineteenth-Century Literary Imagination*, New Haven, Yale University Press.

Goreau, A. (1980), *Reconstructing Aphra: A Social Biography of Aphra Behn*, New York, The Dial Press.

Green, M. (1979), *Dreams of Adventure, Deeds of Empire*, New York, Basic Books.

Grove, P. B. (1961), *The Imaginary Voyage in Prose Fiction: A History of its Criticism and a Guide for its Study, with an annotated checklist of 215 Imaginary Voyages from 1700 to 1800*, London, The Holland Press.

Guha, R. (1982, 1983), *Subaltern Studies: Writings in South Asian History and Society*, vols 1 and 2, New Delhi, Oxford University Press.

Hammami, R. and Reiker, M. (1988), 'Feminist Orientalism and Oriental Marxism', *New Left Review*, no. 170 (July/August), pp. 93–106.

Hill, B. (ed.) (1986), *The First English Feminist: 'Reflections upon Marriage' and Other Writings by Mary Astell*, London, Gover, Maurice Temple Smith.

Hodgen, M. (1964), *Early Anthropology in the Sixteenth and Seventeenth Centuries*, Pennsylvania, University of Pennsylvania Press.

Hulme, P. (1986), *Colonial Encounters: Europe and the Native Caribbean, 1492–1797*, London, Methuen.

Jackson, R. (1981), *Fantasy: The Literature of Subversion*, London, Methuen.

Jacobus, M. (1986), *Reading Woman: Essays in Feminist Criticism*, London, Methuen.

—— (1988), 'The Third Stroke: Reading Woolf with Freud', in S. Sheridan (ed.), *Grafts: Feminist Cultural Criticism*, London, Verso.

Jameson, F. (ed.) (1977), *Aesthetics and Politics*, London, New Left Books.

—— (1984), 'Post-Modernism or the Cultural Logic of Capitalism', *New Left Review*, no. 146 (July/August).

Jones, A. (1986), 'Inscribing Femininity: French Theories of the Feminine', in G. Greene and C. Kahn (eds), *Making a Difference: Feminist Literary Criticism*, London, Methuen.

Kaminsky, A. R. (1968) *George Henry Lewes as Literary Critic*, Syracuse, Syracuse University Press.

Kaplan, C. (1986), *Sea-Changes: Essays on Culture and Feminism*, London, Verso.

Kristeva, J. (1980), *Desire in Language: A Semiotic Approach to Literature and Art*, trans. T. Gora, *et al.*, New York, Columbia University Press.

Lacan, J. (1977), *Ecrits: A Selection in English*, trans. A. Sheridan, London, Tavistock Publications.

Laplanche, J. and Pontalis, J. (1986), 'Fantasy and the Origins of Sexuality', in Burgin *et al.* (eds), *Formations of Fantasy*, London, Methuen.

Lévi-Strauss, C. (1973), *Tristes Tropiques*, trans. J. D. Weightman, London, Jonathan Cape.

Loomba, A. (1989) *Gender, Race, Renaissance Drama*, Manchester, Manchester University Press.

Lovell, T. (1987), *Consuming Fiction*, London, Verso.

Lukács, G. (1977), 'Realism in the Balance' in F. Jameson (ed.), *Aesthetics and Politics*, London, New Left Books.

———— (1978), 'Narrate or Describe?' (1936) in A. Kahn (ed. and trans.), *Georg Lukács, Writer and Critic*, London, Merlin Press.

McCullough, N. V. (1962), *The Negro in English Literature: A Critical Introduction*, Devon, Arthur H. Stockwell.

McKeon, M. (1987), *The Origins of the Novel: 1600–1740*, Baltimore, Johns Hopkins University Press.

Mahmoud, F. M. (ed.) (1972), *William Beckford of Fonthill, 1760–1844, Bicentenary Essays*, New York, Kennikat Press.

Mani, L. (1984), 'The Production of an Official Discourse on *Sati* in Early Nineteenth-Century Bengal', in F. Barker, *et al.* (eds), *Europe and its Others*, Essex, Proceedings of the Conference on the Sociology of Literature.

Marcus, S. (1966), *The Other Victorians: A Study of Sexuality and Pornography in Mid-Nineteenth-Century England*, London, Weidenfeld & Nicolson.

Marks, E. and de Coutrivon, I. (eds) (1981), *New French Feminisms: An Anthology*, Brighton, The Harvester Press.

Marx, K. (1939), *The German Ideology*, ed. Roy Pascal, New York.

———— (1977), *Grundrisse*, Harmondsworth, Penguin.

Marxist–Feminist Literature Collective (1978), 'Women's Writing: *Jane Eyre, Shirley, Villette, Aurora Leigh*', in F. Barker *et al.* (eds), *The Sociology of Literature: 1848*, University of Essex.

Mayhew, H. (1977), *London Labour and the London Poor: A Cyclopaedia of the Condition and Earnings of Those that Will Work, Those that Cannot Work, and Those that Will Not Work*, 4 vols, London, Frank Cass.

Maynard, J. (1984), *Charlotte Brontë and Sexuality*, Cambridge, Cambridge University Press.

Michael, I. (1987), *The Teaching of English: From the Sixteenth Century to 1870*, Cambridge, Cambridge University Press.

Millett, K. (1971), *Sexual Politics* (1969), London, Virago.

Minh-ha, T. T. (1987), 'Difference: A Special Third World Woman's Issue', *Feminist Review*, vol. 25 (March), pp. 5–22.

Mitchell, J. (1984), *Women: The Longest Revolution, Essays on Feminism, Literature and Psychoanalysis*, London, Virago.

Moers, E. (1980), *Literary Women*, London, The Women's Press.

Mohanty, C. T. (Spring/Fall, 1984), 'Under Western Eyes: Feminist Scholarship and Colonial Discourse', *Boundary 2*, vol. 12, pp. 333–58.

Moore-Gilbert, B. (ed.) (1983), *Literature and Imperialism*, Conference Papers of the Roehampton Institute of Higher Education.

Morgan, F. (1987), *A Woman of No Character: An Autobiography of Mrs Manley*, London, Faber & Faber.

Morse, D. (1981), *Perspectives on Romanticism: A Transformational Analysis*, London, Macmillan.

Mullan, J. (1988), *Sentiment and Sociability: The Language of Feeling in the Eighteenth Century*, Oxford, Clarendon Press.

Mulvey, L. (1975), 'Visual Pleasure and Narrative Cinema', *Screen*, vol. 16, no. 13, pp. 6–18.

Myer, V. G. (1987), *Charlotte Brontë: Truculent Spirit*, London, Vision, Barnes & Noble.

Newton, J. L. (1981), *Women, Power and Subversion: Social Strategies in British Fiction, 1778–1860*, Athens, Georgia, University of Georgia Press.

Ngugi Wa Thiongo (1988), *Decolonising the Mind: The Politics of Language in African Literature*, Nairobi, Heinemann.

Olmsted, J. (ed.) (1979), *A Victorian Art of Fiction*, vol. 1, New York, Garland Press.

Parry, B. (1987), 'Problems in Current Theories of Colonial Discourse', *Oxford Literary Review*, no. 9, pp. 27–58.

Pathak, Z., Sengupta S. and Purkayastha, S. (1991), 'The Prisonhouse of Orientalism', *Textual Practice*, vol. 5, no. 2, pp. 194–218.

Perry, R. (1986), *The Celebrated Mary Astell*, Chicago, University of Chicago Press.

Porter, R. (1987), *Mind-Forged Manacles: A History of Madness in England from the Restoration to the Regency*, London, The Athlone Press.

Ratchford, F. (1941), *The Brontës' Web of Childhood*, New York, Columbia University Press.

Rich, A. (1980), *On Lies, Secrets and Silence: Selected Prose, 1966–1978*, London, Virago.

Robert, M. (1980), *Origins of the Novel*, Brighton, The Harvester Press.

Safouan, M. (1983), *Pleasure and Being: Hedonism, from a Psychoanalytic Point of View*, trans. M. Thom, London, Macmillan.

Said, E. (1975), *Beginnings: Intention and Method*, New York, Basic Books.

——— (1978), *Orientalism*, London, Routledge & Kegan Paul.

Sangari, K. and Vaid, S. (1989), *Recasting Women: Essays in Colonial History*, New Delhi, Kali for Women.

Scull, A. (ed.) (1981), *Madhouses, Mad-Doctors and Madmen: The Social History of Psychiatry in the Victorian Era*, London, The Athlone Press.

Segal, L. (1987), *Is the Future Female?*, London, Virago.

Shlovsky, V. (1965), 'Sterne's *Tristam Shandy*: Stylistic Commentary', in L. Lemon, and M. Reis (eds), *Russian Formalist Criticism: Four Essays*, Nebraska, University of Nebraska Press.

Showalter, E. (1977), *A Literature of Their Own: British Women Novelists from Brontë to Lessing*, London, Virago.

———— (1985), *The Female Malady: Women, Madness and English Culture, 1830–1890*, New York, Pantheon.

Skultans, V. (1979), *English Madness: Ideas on Insanity, 1580–1890*, London, Routledge & Kegan Paul.

Smith, O. (1984), *The Politics of Language: 1791–1819*, Oxford, Clarendon Press.

Sombart, W. (1967), *Luxury and Capitalism*, Ann Arbor, University of Michigan Press.

Spencer, J. (1986), *Rise of the Woman Novelist: from Aphra Behn to Jane Austen*, Oxford, Basil Blackwell.

Spender, D. (1986), *Mothers of the Novel: 100 Good Women Writers before Jane Austen*, London, Pandora.

Spivak, G. C. (1984), 'The Rani of Sirmur', in F. Barker (ed.), *Europe and its Others*, University of Essex, Proceedings of the Conference on the Sociology of Literature.

———— (1985), 'Three Women's Texts and a Critique of Imperialism', *Critical Inquiry*, vol. 12, no. 1, pp. 243–61.

———— (1987), *In Other Worlds: Essays in Cultural Politics*, London, Methuen.

Stanley, L. (ed.) (1984), *The Diaries of Hannah Culwick, Victorian Maidservant*, London, Virago.

Sundquist, E. J. (ed.) (1986), *New Essays on 'Uncle Tom's Cabin'*, Cambridge, Cambridge University Press.

Sypher, W. (1969), *Guinea's Captive Kings: British Anti-Slavery Literature of the Eighteenth Century*, New York, Octagon Books.

Taylor, H. (1979a), 'Class and Gender in Charlotte Brontë's *Shirley*', *Feminist Review*, vol. 1, no. 1, pp. 83–94.

———— (1979b), Introduction to K. Chopin, *Portraits*, London, The Women's Press.

Thapar, R. (1966), *A History of India, vol. 1*, Harmondsworth, Penguin.

Todorov, T. (1984), *The Conquest of America: the Question of the Other*, trans. R. Howard, New York, Harper & Row.

Viswanathan, G. (1987), 'The Beginnings of English Literary Study in British India', *Oxford Literary Review*, no. 9.

———— (1990), *Masks Of Conquest: Literary Study and British Rule in India*, London, Faber & Faber.

Watt, I. (1957), *The Rise of the Novel*, London, Peregrine Books.

Whitney, L. (1973), *Primitivism and the Idea of Progress in English Popular Literature of the Eighteenth Century*, New York, Octagon Books.

Willey, B. (1965), *The Eighteenth Century Background: Studies on the Idea of Nature in the Thought of the Period*, London, Chatto & Windus.

Williams, R. (1974), *The English Novel from Dickens to Lawrence*, London, Granada.

———— (1986), 'Novels of the 1840s', in F. Barker, *et al.* (eds), *Literature, Politics and Theory: Papers from the Essex Conference*, London, Methuen.

Wilson, E. (1985), *Adorned in Dreams: Fashion and Modernity*, London, Virago.

Winnicott, D. W. (1971), *Playing and Reality*, London, Tavistock Publications.

Winnifrith, T. (1973), *The Brontës and their Background: Romance and Reality*, London, Macmillan.

Woodcock, G. (1948), *The Incomparable Aphra*, London, T. V. Boardman.

Woolf, V. (1977), *A Room of One's Own*, St Albans, Granada.

———— (1979), *Women and Writing*, ed. M. Barrett, London, The Women's Press.

244

Olmsted, J., *A Victorian Art of Fiction* 98
Onania (1710) 155
Orientalism 5, 8, 13–14, 31–2, 62, 64, 81, 112, 135–6, 142–4, 181, 185–6
Oroonoko 7, 21, 63, 74, 88, 106, 122, 125–6, 128; adventure and Other 36–7; feminist accounts 42–60; noble savage 39–42; novel (origins) 34–6; sexualisation of the land 37–9
Other subject 88, 104, 221–2; in adventure novels 36–8, 40; Black/savage 8, 56–7, 107, 112, 126–8, 133, 138, 142, 145, 154, 161, 173, 178, 186, 211, 217–18; madness 157–8, 160, 178; mirror-image 5, 11–12, 14, 24, 32, 83–4, 140, 175–83; woman (*Jane Eyre*) 101, 107–8, 139, 157, 175–83, 189, 192, 196, 199; woman (*Roxana*) 62–5, 69, 71, 79–84, 86; woman (*Shirley*) 198–202, 204, 206
Oudney, Dr 116
Our Fellow's Play 113

Paine, Tom 14
paintings (in *Jane Eyre*) 191–3, 195
Pamela (Richardson) 61, 93
Parry, Benita 130
Passing Events 142
passion 101, 102, 103, 196
paternalism 106, 129, 201, 209
Pathak, Z. 31–2
patriarchy 129, 131, 171, 196, 197
Pelet, M. (*The Professor*) 165–6
penis envy 69
Percy, Alexander (juvenilia) 132–3, 139–40, 142, 143–4
Percy, Mary Henrietta (juvenilia) 122, 133, 136–9
poetry 137, 187–8, 216, 218
politics of language 19; in *The Professor* 147–71
Ponden House library 115
Pontalis, J. 70
Poole, Grace (*Jane Eyre*) 160, 175

Porter, R. 155
post-colonial subject (of novel) 10–33
postmodernism 20
poststructuralism 20
power relations 59–60, 149, 194, 198, 209–10
Price, Sir Uvedale 51
Prince, Mary 131
Professor, The 8, 172–3, 177, 189, 191, 196, 198–9, 205–6; displace hero 151–4; Englishness 148–51; hysteria/hypochondria 154–6; language and imperialism 163–71; madness/irrationality 156–62; publishing history 147–8
property rights 208
psychiatry 158–9
psychoanalysis 11, 20–1, 23–4, 68–9, 103, 157–8, 183–4
punishment and torture 57–8

Quarterly 93
Quashia Quamina 119, 125–36, 138–9, 143–4, 172

race 5, 9, 182–3; Black protagonists *see Oroonoko*, Quashia Quamina; Black writers 105; class and feminist critic 104–8; in juvenilia 112–36, 138–9, 143–4; Otherness 8, 56–7, 63, 107, 112, 126–8, 133, 138, 142, 145, 154, 161, 173, 178, 186, 211, 217–18
Radcliffe, A. 28
Raleigh, Walter 38, 39–40, 51
Ratchford, Fannie, *The Brontë's Web of Childhood* 110, 115, 120, 137, 144–5
reality 20–2, 24, 26–7, 30, 34, 42, 90, 94–6, 98–9, 102–4, 184–6, 188, 191, 214; *vraisemblance* and 91–3; *see also* social reality
Reed family (*Jane Eyre*) 176–7, 190
religion/religious education 14
Return of Zamorna, The 140, 142